Scribe Publications
WALTZING AT THE DOOMSDAY BALL

JOE BAGEANT frequently appeared on U.S. National Public Radio and the BBC, and wrote for newspapers and magazines internationally. He was a commentator on the politics of class in America, and his book *Deer Hunting with Jesus: dispatches from America's class war* has been adapted for the theatre. He also wrote an online column (www.joebageant.com) that has made him a cult hero among gonzo-journalism junkies and progressives. Joe's second book, *Rainbow Pie: a redneck memoir*, was published in the United States four days after he died in March 2011.

KEN SMITH managed Joe Bageant's website from the time it was launched in 2004, and has promoted Joe's work widely to his dedicated fans and the wider media ever since.

To working people everywhere

WALTZING AT THE DOOMSDAY BALL

THE BEST OF JOE BAGEANT

Edited by Ken Smith

SCRIBE
Melbourne

Scribe Publications Pty Ltd
18–20 Edward St, Brunswick, Victoria, Australia 3056
Email: info@scribepub.com.au

First published by Scribe 2011

Typeset in 11.5/16 pt Janson Text by the publishers
Printed and bound in Australia by Griffin Press

The paper this book is printed on is certified against the Forest
Stewardship Council® Standards. Griffin Press holds FSC
chain of custody certification SGS-COC-005088. FSC promotes
environmentally responsible, socially beneficial and economically
viable management of the world's forests.

National Library of Australia
Cataloguing-in-Publication data

Bageant, Joe.

Waltzing at the Doomsday Ball: the best of Joe Bageant/
essays by Joe Bageant; edited by Ken Smith.

9781921844515 (pbk.)

1. Social classes–United States. 2. Poor whites–United States–Social conditions.
3. United States–Social conditions–1980-.

Other Authors/Contributors: Ken Smith (editor)

305.56097309045

www.scribepublications.com.au

Contents

Introduction

"I'm so damn average that what I write resonates with people", Joe Bageant once told an interviewer in explaining how he had gained a global following for his essays published on the web. In 2004, at the age of 58, Joe sensed that the Internet could give him editorial freedom. Without gatekeepers, he began writing about what he was really thinking, and then submitted his essays to left-of-center websites.

Joe Bageant died in March 2011, having written two books, and 78 essays that were posted on his own website and also on many other sites. The 25 essays reproduced in this book were first published on the web. I've selected them based on many emails from readers, web-traffic counts, and specific suggestions from his online colleagues. They appear here as Joe wrote them, apart from copyediting and light corrections agreed to between me and his book editor, Henry Rosenbloom, Scribe's founder and publisher.

Joe began writing for various publications in his twenties. He once told me how happy and proud he was when he sold his first article to the *Colorado Daily*, unashamedly recalling how he got tears in his eyes as he looked at a check for $5. It was only five dollars, but it was proof that he had become a professional writer. Joe freelanced articles for a dozen years, mostly writing about music, but also writing profiles of people such as Hunter S. Thompson, Timothy Leary, and G. Gordon Liddy. With a family to support, Joe found work as a reporter and columnist for small daily newspapers. Then, for two decades, Joe submerged his rage and natural writing style while working at various hard-labor jobs, before working again as a newspaper reporter, and then as an editor of magazines—one in military history and before that a magazine that promoted agricultural chemicals.

At the age of 17, Joe enlisted in the U.S. Navy, serving on an aircraft carrier. Joe had farmed with horses for several years, tended bar, and considered himself at times to be a "Marxist and a half-assed Buddhist." Always wanting to escape, he embarked on a life-long voyage of discovery that included living in a commune and on an Indian reservation, and, later in life, in Belize and in Mexico.

Joe often said that the Internet allowed him to find his voice. But I would argue that Joe always had his voice, and that what the Internet did for him was to permit him to find a readership. Once his essays started appearing on various websites, Joe soon gained a wide following for his forceful style, his sense of humor, and his willingness to discuss the American white underclass, a taboo topic for the mainstream media. Joe called himself a "redneck socialist," and he initially thought most of his readers would be very much like himself—working class from the southern section of the U.S.A. So he was pleasantly surprised when emails started filling his inbox. There were indeed many letters from men about Joe's age who had also escaped rural poverty. But there were also emails from younger men and women readers, from affluent people who agreed that the political and economic system needed an overhaul, from readers in dozens of countries expressing thanks for an alternative view of American life, from working-class Americans in all parts of the country, and more than a few from elderly women who wrote to Joe to say that they respected and appreciated his writing, but "please don't use so much profanity".

The central subject of Joe's writing was the class system in the United States, and the tens of millions of whites ignored by coastal liberals in New York, Washington, San Francisco, and Los Angeles. In his online essays and books, and also in conversations over beer or bourbon, Joe would rail against the elite class who looked down on his people—poor whites, the underclass, rednecks. Joe was amused that a New York book editor once said to him, "It's as if your people were some sort of exotic and foreign culture, as if you were from Yemen or something."

Joe spent almost as much time answering emails as he did writing essays. Often a response to an email would be rewritten and included in his next essay, and Joe would send thanks to the reader for providing the spark. In the six years that Joe was writing for publication on the web, he answered thousands of emails from readers—sometimes with just one sentence, but often churning out a thousand words or more.

He and I would talk about the response he was getting to his writing. His explanation was that he was the same as his reader friends, ordinary and fearful. "I don't write to them," Joe said in an email to one of his readers. "I don't write for them. And I don't write at them. We merely live on the same planet watching the unnerving events around us, things the majority does not seem to see. So I write about that. And maybe for just a moment, a few friends I've never met do not feel so alone.

Nor do I."

I first met Joe only seven years before he died, but it seems as though I had known him all of my life. I learned later that there were many people who had similarly become friends of Joe, meeting first by email, then by phone, and then often making personal visits to his home in Virginia, or Belize, or Mexico.

In 2004, I was living in Nice, France and had read one of Joe's essays on CounterPunch.com. I sent him an email praising his style and ideas. He replied with a thank-you note, asking if I were wealthy and why I, an American, was living in France. I explained that I lived frugally in a working-class neighborhood of Nice, eating and shopping where the locals did. That started an email exchange and then many phone calls. In one conversation, he said he was bone tired from a daily three-hour commute to a job he didn't really like. I told him that he should take a couple of weeks off and come to France. He did just that.

Joe arrived at the Nice airport with a back-pack and his guitar. We went on daily walking tours of Nice, to my favorite bistros and some historical spots, and I introduced Joe to many of my friends. Joe had been there about a week when he said he wanted to explore the city on his own—my tour-guide services were not needed. I reminded Joe that he didn't speak a word of French and he might get lost, so I gave him a note to show a taxi driver how to get back to my apartment. Joe had said he would be gone about two hours, but it was eight hours later that he returned. He had somehow found a beer bar where French taxi drivers met after work, and had spent the day arguing about politics and the global economy. Joe explained that one of the taxi drivers spoke English and had served as a translator. I like this anecdote because it illustrates how comfortable Joe was with working people, no matter what language they spoke. This ease of meeting and befriending working people was repeated in Mexico, where shopkeepers, gardeners, and taxi drivers would soon treat Joe as a long-lost brother.

It was during this visit to France that I convinced Joe he needed his own website, if for no other reason than to serve as an archive for his essays, which were then scattered all over the web. I told him that I would get it started and teach him how to post to it. But in seven years Joe did not post anything, never once logged onto the server, and kept asking me to do it. He would rarely look at his own website, even when I asked how him he liked changes I had made. It was not that Joe was a Luddite, ignoring the Internet. He spent hours every day reading other websites and answering emails. But when it came to his own site he was humble, almost embarrassed, by the focus on him personally. "I hate this me-me-me stuff," he would say. He was reluctant to have news about himself posted, dragging his feet whenever I suggested that news about his books be posted. He finally agreed that I could write about him and put my name as a tag at the bottom of a post.

I left France five years ago when the dollar/euro exchange rate made it too expensive for me. Eventually, I moved to Mexico. Joe came to visit, and he liked the lifestyle, the Mexican people, and the low cost of living. He stayed in my second bedroom for a couple of months, then got his own place. Joe's wife visited several times a year, and had discussed moving to Mexico when she retired.

While living in Mexico, Joe wrote his second book, *Rainbow Pie: a redneck memoir*, which was released in the U.S. just four days after his death. I wish there were a video of Joe writing this book. He worked on a three-quarter-size notebook, typing fast and furiously with two index fingers, with a burning but unsmoked cigarette in a nearby ashtray.

Between France and Mexico, I had stayed with Joe and his wife, Barbara, in Winchester for a couple of months to help with the editing and proofing of the final manuscript of *Deer Hunting with Jesus*. While in Winchester, I met many of Joe's old friends, some of whom had known him since childhood. This helped me gain an additional understanding of the scorn and condescension of the town's elites toward Joe and his underclass, the poor whites. In addition to his friends, I also met more than a few people who knew Joe but had few kind words to say about him because of his left-wing politics and what they felt was the negative picture he painted of the town. Not only was he rejected by the affluent class, but also by some of the very people he was trying to help—including some people he had grown up with.

The fact that Joe was gaining recognition in other countries did not register with the locals in Winchester. Joe did not consider himself a Christian, so he might object to my citing Jesus's saying that a prophet is not recognized in his own land. While declaring that such a lofty Biblical aphorism would not apply to a redneck, Joe might also have cited the reference in its entirety, chapter and verse.

The sad fact is that Joe was not recognized in his own small home-town of Winchester, Virginia, with its population of 25,000, even though he was certainly the area's most widely published contemporary writer. His hometown newspaper, *The Winchester Star*, never mentioned his name—not even when he was signed by Random House for his first book, *Deer Hunting with Jesus*, nor when the book was getting rave reviews in other countries. Joe would never admit to being bothered by the local newspaper ignoring him and his success, but it was obvious to those who knew him that he would have appreciated some local recognition. He dismissed this slight by explaining that the newspaper's publisher was still angry from decades before when Joe worked briefly as a reporter for the *Star* and tried to organize a union for the editorial staff.

Even though neither Joe's hometown newspaper nor any mainstream U.S. newspaper or news service noticed his death, the Australian Broadcasting Corporation replayed an interview from his book tour a year before. And *La Stampa*, one of the largest and most prestigious newspapers in Italy, published an obituary and another glowing review of the Italian edition of *Deer Hunting with Jesus*.

Looking back now, it is clear that Joe's energy was being sapped in the months before his cancer was diagnosed. Just three days before a massive and inoperable abdominal tumor was discovered, Joe had spent the day riding a horse with Mexican cowboys. But, for a month or two before this, he was finding it increasingly difficult to concentrate sufficiently to finish an essay. I didn't see it at the time. His last essay, 'America: Y Ur Peeps B So Dum', took Joe more than a month to write, in fits and starts. He emailed me a draft of this essay, which was more than 8,000 words—long even for Joe. I cut about 3,000 words from the draft, re-arranged chunks of text, and sent it back to Joe with a note that the draft could potentially be one of his best essays, but that it was a jumble of thoughts and he needed to sweat blood while re-writing it. Rather than coming back with a typically argumentative response, Joe agreed and replied that he would do more work on it. Now I feel guilty about having pushed a sick and dying man to be creative, even though neither Joe nor anybody else knew how ill he really was. But I try not to feel too bad about it, because I think it is indeed one of his best essays.

Things are often more clear in retrospect. One book that Joe often referred to in conversations was *Dark Ages America:*

the final phase of the Empire by Morris Berman. As it happened, Joe and I had both independently been corresponding with Berman, and we learned that Berman was also a sixtyish American expat living in Mexico, just a mountain range to the east of us. Joe and I had been planning to invite ourselves to visit Berman, but it didn't happen. Berman wrote a review of *Rainbow Pie*, and he summed up Joe with a phrase that had never occurred to me, nor probably to Joe either. Berman wrote that the source of Joe's frustration was "extreme isolation", adding that Joe realized the U.S. was the greatest snow job of all time, likening the country to a hologram, "in which everyone in the country was trapped inside, with no knowledge that the world (U.S. included) was not what U.S. government propaganda, or just everyday cultural propaganda, said it was. He watched his kinfolk and neighbors vote repeatedly against their own interests, and there was little he could do about it."

On his last day, with his family gathered around his bed, Joe said: "Dying isn't as bad as I thought it was going be. I'm just going into this blank space where there's nothing."

That's not quite true, Joe. Your books and essays remain with us, and through them you are still alive. Goodbye, good friend.

—*Ken Smith*
Ajijic, Jalisco, Mexico

1

Howling in the Belly of the Confederacy

[March 25, 2004]

"Bluebird, bluebird
Take a letter up north for me
These folks is fixin' to hurt somebody
And it sure 'nuff might be me."
— *From "Bluebird," a traditional Blues song*

How can the region of America that gave us lynching, Jim Crow, Harry Byrd, George Wallace, Taliban Christianity, David Duke, the KKK, Bible hair, Tammy Faye Bakker, congregational snake handling, the poll tax, inbreeding, and chitterlings possibly take another step back down the stairs of human evolution? Beats the hell out of me. But somehow, here in the Shenandoah Valley of Virginia, we have managed it.

Like most modern Southerners who've fled their native states for long periods of time, I have the standard love/hate relationship with my hometown—Winchester, Virginia. On the one hand, it is a backward and mostly irrelevant place where the question of whether Stonewall Jackson had jock itch at the Battle of Chancellorsville still rages right alongside evolution and abortion. To be sure, it is the standard venal Southern place, where poverty and ugliness are thrust into one's face daily, with all the gothic family melodramas of greed and intrigue so often written about in Southern novels. On the other hand, it is the place that made me who I am—a moralizing, preachy, and essentially lazy bastard who likes to drink. I was raised a Pentecostal Baptist, steeped in the gloomy ultra-Protestant assumption that man is a worthless, evil thing from birth and only goes downhill from there. And I still managed to become a raving, socialist heathen. Which proves there's hope for everyone.

But something new and more ominous is afoot down here. Something that scares even a hardened tobacco-stained old toad like me—a clammy, repressive chill. One that not only dampens all political conversation not Pro-Bush, but can even cost you your job in a small town like this one. I'm serious. When I invite like-minded people for cocktails, the atmosphere is distinctly that of a "safe house," as the few local liberals all but whisper their opinions and eye one another, judging just how safe it is to speak one's mind. It's spooky, so spooky that almost none of us is willing to admit it.

I can remember the 1960s, when we still had a left, right, and center in politics, even here in Virginia. Gawd, I feel old. Remembering liberalism here is like being able to remember scrap-paper drives and ration tickets during World War II. It feels so long ago. Anyway, contrary to neo-con revisionist history, neither left, right, nor center was particularly seen as some sort of evil booger. The left may not have been popular, but it wasn't particularly demonized either. My kids do not believe me when I tell them that even during the Vietnam War protests, America was not so dangerously polarized as now, because there was only one issue at hand—the war. Now nearly everything is at issue. Whatever the case, today in the Shenandoah we have only a right and a far right, with some very limp moderates that pass for a left.

Okay, so we do have a few liberals here—mostly transplants and retirees from "up North," old ones whose fires have long since dimmed. They come here for the cheap historic homes and easy retirement in a low-tax state where you can still get domestic "help" four times a month, four hours a crack, to clean your house for less than 180 bucks. Bear in mind, however, that we set a pretty low bar for liberalism around here. If you don't say "nigger" out loud, have ever voted for a Democrat, and can spell "latte", you qualify as a gold-plated liberal. Unfortunately, even the minuscule new generation of Southern "liberals" cannot imagine speaking up on anything, much less taking to the streets in 1960s fashion. Hell, Southern liberals didn't even do it back then. But these younger Virginia liberals see members of their generation who demonstrated at the World Trade Organization talks over in D.C. as dog-strangling homo kooks. For the most part, their generation of Virginians has been reduced to being either brown shirts or light-brown shirts. And when they see a green shirt, well ... you gotta be queer to like green at all.

Ask practically any Winchester native. They'll tell you like it is. And it's like this: "Everyone is America's enemy these days because we Americans have the guts to stand up for what is right." That is the neo-con party line down here, and it is served up with lots of patriot sauce and fear. Even the Europeans are now our enemies. We must become super-militarized because we have the greatest lifestyle in the world and everyone else is jealous of our personal weaponry, our lack of health insurance, and our sheer obesity. Americans love to believe that their gut-level but uninformed opinions are some sort of unvarnished foundational political truths. Nowhere is this more true than here in the Valley, where the "Screw a bunch of pointy headed multi-cultural librul types" is scriptural, and there is a special place in hell for those operating on the reckless assumption that some people are wiser than others and that their opinion just might be worth listening to.

"Europeans are gutless. The U.N. is helpless," goeth the litany. "And it is up to us to run the world." If I've heard this once, I've heard it a dozen times. Five dozen times. The real question here is whether being down-in-the-dirt ignorant makes you a bad person. It's the never-ending conundrum of the South. The jury has been out on that one for 200 years, and longer than that in our town, which even George Washington called one of the most ignorant, mean-spirited, and predatory places in all the colonies. Later, however, Washington rolled out the barrels of rum on Main Street, and the same mean-spirited lot who had been preying on his soldiers elected him to the Virginia House of Burgesses.

Since then, predation has been institutionalized. Down at city hall, rich slumlords, who own 56 percent of Winchester, roam like grazing animals, picking up properties from the elderly widow or the bankrupt redneck who lost his job at the Styrofoam peanut factory for mentioning the word union. We are an anti-union state, therefore we earn only three-quarters of the national average and can be fired tomorrow if we even fart wrong. Local companies maintain a pro-union blacklist. Our city and county governments consist mostly of car dealers who put their homely daughters in TV commercials, and millionaire real estate hotwires and landlords setting up fixes and business connections within the city government. All this while our girthsome, ill-educated polity hoots, cheers, and guffaws at a Fox network made-for-the masses political movie called *America, the Baddest Dog on the Block*, as the power elite pick every pocket in the audience through regressive taxes, stopping only to loot the local treasury on their way out the back door to that money-insulated estate they bought for a song. They are safe from prosecution because their crimes were codified into law down here during and after the reconstruction era. It's the newest "New South" ladies and gentlemen, much like the old one, but with three more layers of lawyers and realtors. Free-market capitalism, Dixie fried.

Now, from your vantage point up north or out west, you might well observe that we are getting exactly the government and society we deserve. But then, if we Southerners long ago got the government we deserve, the rest of America is now getting a dose of the same beefed-up predatory Darwinism. Contrary to all logic, it is the blue-collar NASCAR dads, the ones who get screwed at every turn on the track, who are the staunchest defenders of this feudal system. They are also the most rabid fans of our current national belligerence toward the rest of the world. Said belligerence is particularly manifest in the Virginian's love of personal firearms. Deeply insecure because it seems we can control nothing these days—kids, job security, health care, retirement, the goddam goat-roasting Mexican neighbors. Personal weaponry makes us feel at least a little more potent and able to defend against who knows what. "Long as I got my gun …"

Meanwhile, the very same political/corporate syndicate that screws NASCAR daddy blue is also gouging him bloody for healthcare. Which is a big deal here because we are a very unhealthy people. (Ugly, too, but that doesn't count.) Our huge new regional medical center is by far the largest cause of local bankruptcies. So finally, when the local Styrofoam peanut factory—the one that makes our cancer risk over 100 times the national average—says the hell with it and cuts workers, NASCAR daddy loses his house, and the slumlord is right there at the sale. At least he managed to save the Dale Earnhardt Number 3 commemorative beer cooler and a couple of other family heirlooms.

When a local plant moves kit and kaboodle to Asia, its marginal white male employee, like a tireless but not very smart gun dog, freezes on point and barks, "Asians! The sumnabitches stole our jobs!" But lest even a slow dog catch on to a bad point, the Republican politicos wave him toward Iraq: "Over there! A swarthy bad guy called Saddam done hauled off and killed all them New Yorkers!" Git 'um boys!" HYYYYYEEEEEE! The rebel yell goes down at Bo's Belly Barn—honest to God, it's a real place—and the marginal white males again turn into dogs of war. They didn't do all that paintball practice in the woods for nothing.

Down here, the military is second in reverence only to Christian fundamentalism; war is an honor-bound duty. In fact, the military is hardwired in with the fundamentalist Christian madrassas up and down the Shenandoah Valley cranking out 18-year-old Rambos for Jesus on a production line. These are the ones presently rotating into Iraq, who will return to get their community college certificates in law enforcement (maybe). Those like my nephews, one of whom keeps his .357 Glock in the nightstand—and the Bible on the nightstand with the personal weapons' permit for the Glock inside the Bible. To him, I'm sure there is a fundamental Christian symmetry in this. Just as there is to my other nephew, who just completed, along with his wife, a study of criminology and the Bible at Bob Jones University. Like their parents, they know what has gone wrong in America, who is responsible, and how to correct the situation. Just ask yourself: Who would Jesus kill? Muslims are always hollerin' to meet Allah, and they're more than happy to provide .45 caliber cab fare to heaven. Imagine their Christian faces when they get to heaven and find out the Muslim's next door got all the virgins. Conversely, there are plenty of radical Muslims more than happy to help them enjoy the Rapture. Fundamentalists on both sides are apocalyptic; both pack a lot of heat.

They've got the heat. They've got the meat. They've got the motion. And they are going to, as one radio preacher down here says, "Put God back into the Constitution." All Virginia's neo-cons lack is a truly inspired and brilliant leader. Thankfully, they elected a gibbon to the White House, because there is nearly enough politically in place down here to create a scenario such as we have not seen since 1936 Germany. Like I tell the ole boys down at the Royal Lunch Tavern: "Try not to be too impressed by the purty brown shirts when they hand them out. You ain't seen the price tag yet."

OK then, how to survive all this? Well, it helps to have been born here. So does age. And at my age, having seen many elections and as many wars, I no longer bother to entertain opposing views. Screw Southern politeness, most of which is just avoidance anyway. I rant my commie screed. No problemo. I don't work in this town. Nor do I go to church, at least not frequently enough to be recognized. I have a full bar in my home, and my memory is still good. Good enough to summon up memories of old lovers and sun-struck days of an LSD-besotted hippie youth, when the very earth murmured its love for my sheer existence — for everyone's, really. And I would have you know that the lone brain cell I have been operating on since 1965 is still working just fine, thank you. It's one helluva *big* cell. Doctors tell me it's a double-yolker, weighs about two pounds, and responds primarily these days to red meat, gin, and sex, even the Internet kind. I couldn't be happier with the situation.

Nevertheless, I'm here to tell you this: You goddam Yankee liberals, gays, and other malignant types had better get out and vote. Every last one of you. Otherwise, there's no telling what all this beer, guns, and inbreeding might lead to.

I'm done ranting. You can go now. And while you are up, fetch me my gin.

2

Sleepwalking to Fallujah

[April 28, 2004]

Each workday I commute toward Washington, D.C. along Route 7, where patriotic war slogans are spray painted on the overpasses, and homemade signs jut from the median in support of our "boys in Iraq." Mud-splattered construction trucks rip by with frayed American flags popping in the wind, loaded with burly bearded men and looking very much like the footage of Afghanistan or Angola, minus the 50-caliber gun mounts. Yesterday I saw my first stretch Hummer, painted in desert tan and carrying half-a-dozen soccer-mom types, which rather sums up the point I am trying to make here. There is a distinct martial ethos, the tang of steel and the smell of gun oil in the air around Washington these days, I swear it.

Only a blind microcephalic could fail to notice this systemic militarization of the American culture, and the media's hyper-escalation of warrior worship. Reputedly, our national character is supposed to be improved by all this. But I was in the military for a time—a "young warrior," in Fox Network parlance—and I can confidently say I was not improved one bit by the experience. (Although I did learn to cuss properly, if a bit too much.) That was 35 years ago, back when there was little, if any, mythologizing of Vietnam's warriors, much less patriotic news spasms ejaculated by embedded reporters between the commercials. News was duller then. Certainly not as entertaining as the Jessica Lynch story of a fetching, innocent young blonde wounded while supposedly blazing away at the face of evil itself, only to suffer multiple wounds, before being rescued from some fly-ridden Iraqi hospital (more radio crackling and gunfire, please) by her comrades in arms. After this stirring rescue we were served the titillating dessert of the subsequent doctor's report: She was sodomized by the sweaty, stinking bastards! In the television news business it just does not get any better than this. Pass the corn chips, please.

With television news like that, who needs a rational explanation as to why we are at war? The entertainment value alone is worth it. And therein lies the problem for those of us in that last generation of people who gained most of what they know from reading: We need a tangible explanation for why we are spilling so much blood and bullion in that God-forsaken desert pisshole. Still no answer. Or no new one at least. Oh, there is the standard line that goes, "We are defending democracy and liberating a people from oppression." That old saw was getting mighty dull even back in my day, when it was used to explain Vietnam.

I cannot remember a time when the American public ever asked any important questions of its national leadership. In the American scheme of things, that is the media's job—the media frames the question and the public asks it, after having been appropriately bludgeoned over the head with it. That's our system, by damned, we love it, and it has even been known to work on occasion. Which would be fine, except that Edward R. Murrow has been dead a long time. Since then, the American psyche has been hardwired into a new world communications order, one in which global corporations now pay the freight for national television. Halliburton, Boeing, and Sprint ain't Geritol, and this ain't Ted Mack's Original Amateur Hour. Content with selling us chewing gum or Chesterfields, early television sponsors were not players in the Pentagon defense contract game, and never slept with the government to obtain more bandwidth.

It is tragic that such a promising instrument as television had to grow up at the end of the Age of Enlightenment—just in time to ignite an unholy fission/fusion, a synthesis of mammon and politics amid a culture out of philosophical and spiritual gas. Just when America needed to explain itself to itself, if it were ever to redefine its higher goals and ideas. But television is about emotion, not explanation. It has no patience for ideas (not that we've seen a real idea in 30 years). Ideas? Who gives a fuck? Let's go shopping. The result has been a nation of sleepwalkers, an all-but-expired republic reduced to pure consumption and little else (a fact not unnoticed by the Muslim world.) Hell, even flatworms consume, and sheer quantity is no substitute for a national soul. It took a couple of generations, but here we are now plugged in at the brainstem, just as McLuhan predicted, to television's virtual cathedral of commerce where the devoted receive the sacrament in a straight shot to the cortex—too tired from overwork, or too poor, or too old, or too young, or just too plain lazy to feel anything else—taking in the tribal-war drumbeat called news and the reality shows that pass for experiencing the world beyond work and consumption. McLuhan's electronic hearth casts its shadows on the walls of a withdrawn and slowly rotting republic.

We had warning from poets, writers, and grim futurists, but who would have guessed it would come to this so soon? That we would become so perfectly attuned to capitalist state television, ever trolling for more business, dragging its nets baited with new cars, Disney character-imprinted cell phones, and buckets of fried chicken through a sea of somnambulates. Yet the sleepwalkers all share but one eye, that of the camera, which, as Lewis Lapham put it, "... doesn't make distinctions between treason and fellatio ... between an important senator and an important ape." So images of the grisly specter in Fallujah and Janet Jackson's boob draw the same numb respect. Stop and consider that most Americans get their "knowledge" of the outside world from this medium, then consider that most of the Muslim world gets its notion of America from Baywatch. If that does not throw any thinking person into the grip of a Prozac-proof depression, nothing will. And what about these so-called thinking persons? Where is the voice of their dissent? Well, they are naturally unhappy and making the best noise they can—all two dozen of them.

Despite that brief and fabled moment during the 1960s, the U.S. is not a nation comfortable with dissent. We have never spawned a nationally integrated left-wing opposition in the European sense. A well-behaved people when it comes to public debate, when told by the president on TV that we are at war with terrorism, the overwhelming majority of us line up and salute the flag. More importantly, we do not ask questions. So the question of why a hundred-million-dollar agency dedicates its resources to swabbing the anuses of farting toy dogs never gets asked, just smiled at. And whether we are willing to sustain, say, 25,000 dead American kids in Iraq never comes up, much less gets debated. It is equally unlikely the public will inquire specifically who is best served by the caskets being unloaded daily at Dover, Delaware. By state decree, we are not even allowed to see them. And let us not even begin to ask that greatest of all American spiritual questions: "Who is getting rich from it?" In a society whose business is business, where whoever raises the most money to buy TV time elects the next president, that question is not likely to get answered either. Not by the Bush administration, nor by the media it sponsors through government license handouts, tax breaks, and regulation—or the lack of it.

Hard to believe that not long ago we were asking how we were going to spend the projected $400 billion "peace dividend" that came with the end of the Cold War. That question has now been answered. Thank you and sit down. So who does get rich? As if we didn't know. Of course, there is the Pentagon's coalition of vested interests, which is just about every material and service provider imaginable from Sprint to SpaghettiOs. But in the end it winds up in vastly disproportionate amounts in the hands of the already-rich—those uneasy oligarchs who, since the first Neolithic thug stole all the grain in the village, have lived in fear of losing their advantage.

In this country, the rich have been uneasy from the beginning, and have long thought that perhaps the democratic experiment has gone just about far enough. Their grumbling, political scheming, and sometimes-outright assaults on the common decency of the republic date back to the American Revolution. But now is their hour, thanks to George Bush. George Bush did not invent their fear. He merely rode it into the White House. And as their chosen commander-in-chief, he has certainly handed them, with some preliminary help from his predecessor, Bill Clinton, the promise of ultimate victory in the real war taking place, the ongoing war of which America has ever been in denial—the class war. This time the already-rich are girded for victory, prepared like never before.

As an outer defensive perimeter, they have deployed a far-flung and invincible army. Within the nation has been established a pervasive and relentless Homeland Security Department. All accomplished adroitly at public expense. And with Bush's gift of escape from equitable taxation, they have set about intensifying their real work at hand, protecting themselves with such steep income differences that they will be forever safe—safety to an oligarch being ever rowing the societal boat backward into the past. Thus, if there is any way to return to the uncomplicated world of 1952 Middleburg or Grosse Pointe with enough money to keep their descendants farting through silk for the next 20 generations, these people are going to do it, with the thuggish help of a leering dry drunk and a secretive gang operating from an undisclosed location.

Nobody in their right mind would take them on because American history has taught us one thing, if nothing else: Rich white people with guns will kill everybody in sight if they get spooked. One need only look back at the Ludlow mining massacre, or ask any urban African–American. Better for us to accept the scraps of the roast goat flung to the populi by the government of the feasting rich, and enjoy the meaningless spectacle of the Martha Stewart show trial. Watch the poised and telegenic Condoleezza Rice testify before a stacked 9/11 commission not even allowed to quote the key suspects in its final report; or jeer at the arrogant and thoroughly unlikable Andrew Fastow running laps around Houston before those appointed to administer his very public tar and feathering. Then catch Jay Leno's monologue for deep analysis of both.

So here we are, sleepwalkers in the intellectual and spiritual desert of America, in 2004, at the end of the Enlightenment. We are literally dying for the lack of a new idea to animate our culture, government, and the national mind. If the American mind is an ecosystem, we have fed it toxic waste.

Instead of news we clamor for bread and circuses, gladiators in the Coliseum of the Middle East. Instead of ideas we get data — the jargon of weapons specialists, political-power pundits, and stockbrokers who know the cost of everything and the value of nothing. Every night I listen numbly to the litany of numbers recited by this priestcraft of pundits, all sorts of numbers — jobless numbers, economic indexes, and balance-of-trade figures … and I try to pinpoint the time when the corporate economy, the well-being of faceless monoliths, became our national religion, remembering back to the days when one had to go to the financial pages to find these things out. Now they are inescapable, these somber minute-by-minute reports on the condition and mood of Moloch, whose heart we are told by poets is a cannibal dynamo and whose breath reeks of the stench of war. How many of our jobs did Moloch eat today? How many did Moloch puke back up in Asia? These job numbers, and the number of Americans killed in Iraq, slosh against the beaches of awareness alongside the basketball scores and the number of cockroaches swallowed by a busty blonde on Fear Factor. The American dream of wealth and invincibility has taken on a life of its own, and now dreams us into being. And off on the horizon to the east, the sirens and the wailing never cease, for we have bestowed shock and awe upon Babylon.

-3-

The Covert Kingdom

[May 24, 2004]

Not long ago I pulled my car up alongside a tiny wooden church in the woods, a stark white frame box my family built in 1840. And, as always, an honest-to-God chill went through me, for the ancestral ghosts presumably hovering over the graves there. From the wide-open front door, the Pentecostal preacher's message echoed from within the plain wooden walls: "Thank you Gawd for giving us strawng leaders like President Bush during this crieeesis. Praise you Lord and guide him in this battle with Satan's Muslim armies."

If I had chosen to go back down the road a mile or so to the sprawling new Bible Baptist church—complete with school facilities, professional sound system, and in-house television production—I could have heard approximately the same exhortation. Usually offered at the end of a prayer for sons and daughters of members in the congregation serving in Iraq, it can be heard in any of the thousands upon thousands of praise temples across our republic.

After a lifetime of identity conflict, I have come to accept that, blood-wise, if not politically or spiritually, these are my people. And as a leftist it is very clear to me these days why urban liberals not only fail to understand these people, but do not even know they exist, other than as some general lump of ignorant, intolerant voters called "the religious right," or the "Christian Right," or "neo-con Christians." But until progressives come to understand what these people read, hear, are told, and deeply believe, we cannot understand American politics, much less be effective. Given fundamentalist Christianity's inherent cultural isolation, it is nearly impossible for most enlightened Americans to imagine, in honest human terms, what fundamentalist Americans believe, let alone understand why we should all care about them.

For liberals to examine the current fundamentalist phenomenon in America is to accept some hard truths. For starters, we libs are even more embattled than most of us choose to believe. Any significant liberal and progressive support is limited to a few urban pockets on each coast and along the upper edge of the Midwestern tier states. Most of the rest of the nation, the much-vaunted heartland, is the dominion of the conservative and charismatic Christian. Turf-wise, it's pretty much their country, which is to say it presently belongs to George W. Bush for some valid reasons. Remember: He did not have to steal the entire election, just a little piece of it in Florida. Evangelical born-again Christians of one stripe or another were then, and are now, 40 percent of the electorate, and they support Bush 3–1. And as long as their clergy and their worst instincts tell them to, they will keep on voting for him, or someone like him, regardless of what we view as his arrogant folly and sub-intelligence. Forget about changing their minds. These Christians do not read the same books we do, they do not get their information from anything remotely resembling reasonably balanced sources, and in fact, consider even CBS and NBC super-liberal networks of porn and the Devil's lies. Given how fundamentalists see the modern world, they may as well be living in Iraq or Syria, with whom they share approximately the same Bronze Age religious tenets. They believe in God, Rumsfeld's Holy War, and their absolute duty as God's chosen nation to kick Muslim ass up one side and down the other. In other words, just because millions of Christians appear to be dangerously nuts does not mean they are marginal.

Having been born into a Southern Pentecostal/Baptist family of many generations, and living in this fundamentalist social landscape, means that I gaze into the maw of neo-con Christianity daily. Hell, sometimes hourly. My brother is a fundamentalist preacher, as are a couple of my nephews, as were many of my ancestors going back to God-knows-when. My entire family is born-again; their lives are completely focused inside their own religious community, and on the time when Jesus returns to earth—Armageddon and The Rapture.

Only another liberal born into a fundamentalist clan can understand what a strange, sometimes downright hellish family circumstance it is—how such a family can love you deeply, yet despise everything you believe in, see you as a humanist instrument of Satan, and still be right there for you when your back goes out or a divorce shatters your life. As a socialist and a half-assed lefty activist, obviously I do not find much conversational fat to chew around the Thanksgiving table. Politically and spiritually, we may be said to be dire enemies. Love and loathing coexist side by side. There is talk, but no communication. In fact, there are times when it all has science fiction overtones—times when it seems we are speaking to one another through an unearthly veil, wherein each party knows it is speaking to an alien. There is a sort of high, eerie mental whine in the air. This is the sound of mutually incomprehensible worlds hurtling toward destiny, passing with great psychological friction, obvious to all, yet acknowledged by none.

Between such times, I wait rather anxiously and strive for change, for relief from what feels like an increased stifling of personal liberty, beauty, art, and self-realization in America. They wait in spooky calmness for Jesus. They believe that, until Jesus does arrive, our "satanic humanist state and federal legal systems" should be replaced with pure "Biblical Law." This belief is called Christian Reconstructionism. Though it has always been around in some form, it began expanding rapidly about 1973, with the publication of R.J. Rushdoony's, *The Institutes of Biblical Law*.

Time out, please. In a nod toward fairness and tolerance — begging the question of whether liberals are required to tolerate the intolerant — I will say this: Fundamentalists are "good people." In daily life, they are warm-hearted and generous to a fault. They live with feet on the ground (albeit with eyes cast heavenward), and with genuine love and concern for their neighbors. After spending 30 years in progressive western cities such as Boulder, Colorado, and Eugene, Oregon, I would have to say that conservative Christians actually do what liberals usually only talk about. They visit the sick and the elderly, give generously of their time and money to help those in need, and put unimaginable amounts of love and energy into their families, even as Pat Robertson and Rush Limbaugh blare in the background. Their good works extend internationally — were it not for American Christians, there would be little health care on the African continent and other similar places. OK, that's the best I can do in showing due respect for the extreme Christian Right. Now to get back to the Christian Reconstructionists.

Christian Reconstruction is blunt stuff, hard and unforgiving as a gravestone. Capital punishment, central to the Reconstructionist ideal, calls for the death penalty in a wide range of crimes, including abandonment of the faith, blasphemy, heresy, witchcraft, astrology, adultery, sodomy, homosexuality, striking a parent, and "unchastity before marriage" (but for women only.) Biblically correct methods of execution include stoning, the sword, hanging, and burning. Stoning is preferred, according to Gary North, the self-styled Reconstructionist economist, because stones are plentiful and cheap. Biblical Law would also eliminate labor unions, civil rights laws, and public schools. Leading Reconstruction theologian David Chilton declares, "The Christian goal for the world is the universal development of Biblical theocratic republics." Incidentally, the said Republic of Jesus would not only be a legal hell, but an ecological one as well—Reconstructionist doctrine calls for the scrapping of environmental protection of all kinds, because there will be no need for this planet earth once The Rapture occurs. You may not have heard of Rushdoony or Chilton or North, but, taken either separately or together, they have directly and indirectly influenced many more contemporary American minds than Noam Chomsky, Gore Vidal, and Howard Zinn combined.

A moreover covert movement, although slightly more public of late, Christian Reconstructionism and Dominionism have for decades exerted one hell of an influence through their scores of books, publications, and classes taught in colleges and universities. Over the past 30 years their doctrine has permeated not only the religious right, but mainstream churches as well, via the charismatic movement. The radical Christian right's impact on politics and religion in this nation has been massive, with many mainstream churches pushed rightward by its pervasiveness without even knowing it. Clearly the Methodist church down the street from my house does not understand what it has become. Other mainstream churches with a more progressive leadership simply flinch and bow to the radicals at every turn. They have to, if they want to retain members these days. Further complicating matters is that leading Recoconstruction thinkers, along with their fellow travelers, the Dominionists, are all but invisible to non-fundamentalist America. (I will spare you the agony of the endless doctrinal hair-splitting that comes with making fundamentalist distinctions of any sort—I would not do that to a dog. But if you are disposed toward self-punishment, you can take it upon yourself to learn the differences between Dominionism, Pretribulationism, Midtribulationism and Posttribulationism, Premillennialism, and Millennialism. I recommend the writings of the British author and scholar George Monbiot, who has put the entire maddening scheme of it all together—its corporate implications, governmental and psychological meaning—in a couple of excellent books.)

Fundamentalists such as my family have no idea how thoroughly they have been orchestrated by agenda-driven Christian media and other innovations of the past few decades. They probably would not care now, even if they knew. Like most of their tribe (dare we say "class", in a nation that so vehemently denies it has a class system?), they want to embrace some simple foundational truth that will rationalize all the conflict and confusion of a postmodern world—some handbook that will neatly explain everything, make all their difficult decisions for them. And among these classic American citizens, prone toward religious zealotry since the Great Awakening of the 18th century, what rock could appear more dependable upon which to cling than the infallible Holy Bible? From there it was a short step for Christian Dominionist leaders to conclude that such magnificent infallibility should be enforced upon all other people, in the same spirit as the Catholic Spanish conquistadors or the Arab Muslim Moors before them. It's an old, old story, a brutal one that mankind cannot seem to shake.

Christian Reconstruction and Dominionist strategists make clear in their writings that homeschooling and Christian academies have been and continue to create the Rightist Christian cadres of the future, enabling them to place ever-increasing numbers of believers in positions of governmental influence. The training of Christian cadres is far more sophisticated than the average liberal realizes. There now stretches a network of dozens of campuses across the nation, each with its strange cultish atmosphere of smiling Christian pod people, most of them clones of Jerry Falwell's Liberty University in Lynchburg, Virginia. But how many outsiders know the depth and specificity of political indoctrination in these schools? For example, Patrick Henry College in Purcellville, Virginia—a college exclusively for Christian homeschoolers—offers programs in strategic government intelligence, legal training, and foreign policy, all with a strict, Bible-based "Christian worldview." Patrick Henry is so heavily funded by the Christian right it can offer classes below cost. In the Bush administration, 7 percent of all internships are handed out to Patrick Henry students, along with many others distributed among similar religious rightist colleges. The Bush administration also recruits from the faculties of these schools—for example, in the appointment of right-wing Christian activist Kay Coles James, former dean of the Pat Robertson School of Government at Regent University, as director of the U.S. Office of Personnel Management. What better position than the personnel office from which to recruit more fundamentalists? Scratch any of these supposed academics and you will find a Christian zealot. I know, because I have made the mistake of inviting a few of these folks to cocktail parties. One university department head told me he is moving to rural Mississippi, where he can better recreate the lifestyle of the antebellum South and its "Confederate Christian values." It gets real strange real quick.

Lest these Christians be underestimated, remember that it was their strategists whose "stealth ideology" managed the takeover of the Republican Party in the early 1990s. That takeover now looks mild in light of today's neo-con Christian implantations in the White House, the Pentagon, the Supreme Court, and other federal entities. As much as liberals screech in protest, few understand the depth and breadth of the rightist Christian takeover underway. They catch the scent but never behold the beast itself. Yesterday I heard a liberal Washington-based political pundit on NPR say that the radical Christian right's local and regional political-action peak was a past fixture of the Reagan era. I laughed out loud (it was a bitter laugh) and wondered if he had ever driven 20 miles eastward on U.S. Route 50 into the suburbs of Maryland, Virginia, or West Virginia. The fellow on NPR was a perfect example of the need for liberal pundits to get their heads out of their asses, get outside the city, quit cruising the Internet, and meet some Americans who do not mirror their own humanist educations and backgrounds. If they did, they would grasp the importance The Rapture has taken on in American national and international politics. Despite the media's shallow interpretation of The Rapture's significance, it is a hell of a lot more than just a couple of hundred million "Left Behind" books sold. The most significant thing about the "Left Behind" series is that, although they are classified as "fiction," most fundamentalist readers I know accept them as an absolute reality soon coming to a godless planet near you. It helps to understand that everything is literal in the Fundamentalist voter universe.

Yes, when The Rapture comes, Christians with the right credentials will fly away. But you and I, dear reader, will probably be among those who suffer a thousand-year plague of boils. So stock up on antibiotics because, according to the "Rapture Index," it is damned near here. See for yourself at http://www.raptureready.com. Part gimmick, part fanatical obsession, the index is a compilation of such things as floods, interest rates, oil prices, and global turmoil. As I write this, the index stands at 144, just one point below critical mass, when people like us will be smitten under a sky filled with deliriously happy naked flying Christians.

But to blow The Rapture off as an amusing-if-scary fantasy is not being honest on my part. Cheap glibness has always been my vice, so I must say this: Personally, I've lived with The Rapture as the psychologically imprinted backdrop of my entire life. In fact, my own father believed in it until the day he died, and the last time I saw him alive we talked about The Rapture. And when he asked me, "Will you be saved? Will you be there with me on Canaan's shore after The Rapture?" I was forced to feign belief in it to give a dying man inner solace. But that was the spiritual stuff of families, and living and dying, religion in its rightful place, the way it is supposed to be, personal and intimate—not political. Thus, until the advent of the new radical Christian influence, I'd certainly never heard The Rapture spoken about in the context of a Texan being selected by God to prepare its way.

Now, however, this apocalyptic belief—yearning, really—drives an American Christian polity in the service of a grave and unnerving agenda. The pseudo-scriptural has become an apocalyptic game plan for earthly political action: To wit, the Messiah can only return to earth after an apocalypse in Israel called Armageddon, which the fundamentalists are promoting with all their power so that The Rapture can take place. The first requirement was the establishment of the state of Israel. Done. The next is Israel's occupation of the Middle East as a return of its "Biblical lands," which, in the radical Christian scheme of things, means more wars. These Christian conservatives believe peace cannot ever lead to The Rapture, and indeed impedes the 1,000-year Reign of Christ. So anyone promoting peace is an enemy, a tool of Satan—hence the fundamentalist support for any and all wars Middle Eastern, in which their own kids die a death often viewed by Christian parents as a holy martyrdom of its own kind. "He (or she) died protecting this country's Christian values." One hears it over and over from parents of those killed.

The final scenario of The Rapture has the "saved" Christians settling onto a cloud after the long float upward, from whence they watch a Rambo Jesus wipe out the remnants of the human race. Then, in a mop-up operation by God, the Jews are also annihilated, excepting a few who convert to Christianity. The Messiah returns to earth. End of story. Incidentally, the Muslim version, I was surprised to learn recently, is almost exactly the same, but with Muslims doing the cloud-sitting.

If we are lucky as a nation, this period in American history will be remembered as just another very dark time that we managed to get through. Otherwise, one shudders to think of the logical outcome. No wonder the left is depressed. Meanwhile, our best thinkers on the left ask us to consider our perpetual U.S. imperial war as a fascist, military/corporate war, and indeed it is that, too. But tens of millions of hardworking, earnest American

Christians see it as far more than that. They see a war against all that is un-Biblical, the goal of which is complete world conquest, or put in Christian terminology, "dominion." They will have no less than the "inevitable victory God has promised his new chosen people," according to the Recon masters of the covert kingdom. Screw the Jews, they blew their chance. If perpetual war is what it will take, let it be perpetual. After all, perpetual war is exactly what the Bible promised. Like it or not, this is the reality (or prevailing unreality) with which we are faced. The 2004 elections, regardless of outcome, will not change that. Nor will it necessarily bring ever-tolerant liberals to openly acknowledge what is truly happening in this country, the thing that has been building for a long, long time—a holy war, a covert Christian jihad for control of America and the entire world. Millions of Americans are under the spell of an extraordinarily dangerous mass psychosis.

Pardon me, but religious tolerance be damned. Somebody had to say it.

-4-

Staring Down the Jackals

[May 30, 2004]

Somewhere in hell tonight, the Devil's wife is setting out an extra dinner plate for America, where presumably we will be toasted by history's other war criminals. Let's face it. When we backed a maniac killer like Saddam Hussein, funded the Taliban, and slept with the treacherous Saudi princes as the price of our national narcotic — oil — we'd pretty much bought a place at the dinner table. But when we embraced that murderous old sack of guts, Ariel Sharon, as international brother and accomplice in all things Middle Eastern, we were not merely displaying a sick taste in friends; we acceded to becoming war criminals. The entire world sees that, and has seen it for years.

Every liberal man and woman of good will I know predicted that our latest Iraq crusade was just that — folly. But it has exceeded our worst nightmare, devolving from the cowboy fantasies of a dry drunk from Texas, into a hideous torture flick. Complete with hoods, leather straps, cross-dressing, sexual humiliation, and trophy-corpse display. All it took was a couple of digital cameras in the paws of the ruddy-nutted sons and dominatrix daughters of this nation's patriotic trailer courts—a few grisly candid photos to send home to the family over the Internet. Click-click-click-click-click! And the entire sorry lie of the cowboy liberation of Iraq melted in a puddle of international revulsion.

About the best the war's apologists and paid pundits can come up with is that "Abu Ghraib is by no means My Lai" and that "Iraq is not Vietnam." Well, no, not yet. But it is already looking a lot spookier and more perverted than Nam ever was. As a journalist 30 years ago I documented returning Vietnam veterans' stories of U.S. atrocities in that war. I still have a few photos of smiling young Americans poking cigarettes into the mouths of severed Viet Cong heads, and I can tell you the grins of the young Americans in Abu Ghraib are not one bit different. They still look like high school kids at some ghastly kegger.

Those Iraq War apologists make some strange, logic-defying leaps to dismiss parallels with Vietnam, only to fall flat on their asses, as each week brings more undeniable similarities. The American public seems not to notice their ass falling or the similarities. We continue to kill droves of innocent civilians, innocents who in turn kill us until, finally, the innocents we are supposed to be liberating become our targets. Thousands of American kids are snuffed out, or mutilated for life. Many more thousands of Iraqis suffer the same. Billions are poured into firepower to blast dust and human beings into the dry mush that nourishes that specter called war. Iraq may be a dryer venue than Southeast Asia, but if this is not another Vietnam, it is a rip-snorting good imitation.

Assuming Iraq does not become a protracted Vietnam-style battleground—though all those brand spanking-new permanent bases there make one a bit suspicious—we, nevertheless, as that old Iran-Contra scammer Colin Powell pointed out, have to pay for and own what we have broken. Personally speaking, I never wanted Iraq as the 52nd state (Israel being the 51st to the tune of countless billions), and I doubt you did either. But if we are, as the neo-conservatives claim, destined by historical circumstance to make such annexations, we certainly could have picked two less troublesome pieces of real estate than Israel and Iraq. Now that we've got them, we are in deep shit, darlin'.

Before all of us who saw it coming get too smug here, permit me to drop a turd into the punchbowl. Bush and his neo-con thug cronies did not accomplish this all by their lonesomes. Every American owns some piece of the blame for the sorry decline of our "republic." (Aren't we all getting tired of this term "republic" being thrown around by every writer in the country these days?) And part of that blame belongs to liberals—even we far-lefties so fond of pointing out that any nation built on the twin pillars of Negro slavery and the ethnic cleansing of the Red Indian sprang from corrupt seed to begin with. But now that we have become another nasty example proving that absolute power corrupts absolutely, well, that's as bad as it gets. And from that condition, no nation has ever returned but by a terrible road.

If anything can stop this imperial court of jackals, the jackals we allowed to steal an election (without breaking out in open street rebellion, as we probably should have done), the ones currently looting the national treasury, the ones spoiling for Armageddon and wiping their asses on the Constitution, it is you, me, and about 100 million other Americans who may or may not decide to vote in November. Even if we cannot drive the jackals away from the carcass of our Constitution, we can redeem ourselves as individuals. Let me share with you these lines by Vachel Lindsay. I know Lindsay is uncool among the literary gaggle these days, but let me do it anyway:

I am unjust, but I can strive for justice.
My life's unkind, but I can vote for kindness.
I, the unloving, say life should be lovely.
I, that am blind, cry out against my blindness.

Come, let us vote against our human nature,
Crying to God in all the polling places
To heal our everlasting sinfulness
And make us sages with transfigured faces.

—from "Why I Voted the Socialist Ticket," by Vachel Lindsay

Yes, we can still vote, still affect the outcome of an election, despite the ominous Diebold–Bush voting-machine mob syndicate now shaving the dice in the back room. And let's admit it: Most of us are not that thrilled about the horse-faced, clearly insincere John Kerry, even if he did speak out against atrocity as a much younger man. Incidentally, some would see that as a basic moral obligation—others would see it as opportunism during a distinctly anti-war era. Whatever the case, we have been handed Kerry as the stage-prop alternative to George Bush in a long-running quadrennial drama, produced and directed by capitalist ideologues.

If you will remember, we did have other options. In our hearts we all know that Nader, Kucinich, and Sharpton were the only candidates speaking the whole truth. Whether they would have acted on their own words may be another matter. We will never know because liberals, being too worried about picking the right actor in the televised popularity contest that we call elections, never seriously considered them anyway. Speaking the truth does not count for much these days. Instead, we let a corrupt system and our own lack of moral gumption sucker us into allowing yet another multi-multi-millionaire vie for the part of (try not to laugh, please) "leader of the free world." I spent years interviewing some of the fabulously rich, and almost every one of them lived in delusion. So we'll vote for Kerry's delusion. Later we will learn that he is the answer to nothing. Yet he gets a shot at sitting behind the most powerful mahogany desk on the planet because of fabulous wealth and ambition. Just as George Bush did.

In fairness to the Democratic Party, however, it must be said that not all of them are part of the current liberal séance trying to get in touch with their principles. Thank God for people like House Democratic leader Nancy Pelosi. If that woman ever wants to run away with a has-been redneck leftist writer, I'll be scratching gravel toward the West Coast.

In his 1957 classic, *The Undiscovered Self*, Carl Jung examined in detail Nazi Germany's mass psychosis and the dangers of learning "to submit absolutely to a collective belief." Here is what he observed:

> The truth is that we don't know for certain whether something similar might happen elsewhere. It would not be surprising if it did and if another nation succumbed to the infection of a uniform and one-sided idea. America seems to be immune because of the outspoken counter-position she has adopted, but in point of fact she is perhaps even more vulnerable than Europe, since her educational system is the most influenced by the scientific *Weltanschauung* with its statistical truths; her mixed population finds it difficult to strike roots in a soil that is practically without history. The absence of a historical and humanistic education so sorely needed in such a circumstance leads, on the contrary, to a Cinderella existence.

Today, we watch the "infection of a uniform and one-sided

idea" spread out across the globe again, behind a flying wedge of our own storm troopers. And this time those uniforms are enough to give Joseph Goebbels wet dreams, with their spooky high-tech variations on the hideous get-ups so preferred by despots. We seem to prefer big dark-lensed, insectoid chem/ bio facemasks and desert greys, instead of Nazi black gabardine and silver skull jewelry, or the dripping gold braid of the Latin dictator.

And as to you, Carl Jung, well, I regret to tell you that we are staring submissively straight into the face of the jackal again. That "outspoken counter-position" you pointed to is faint stuff now, lo these 47 years later. The kind of thoughtful liberals who contemplated you and your meditations under your pear tree are a timid bunch these days. Tell me this, Carl. From your vantage point out there in the void, does it appear to be too late? What do we need to break this awful spell upon us?

No reply? Well, that's OK, my old friend. Sleep the sleep of the ages. Go back to your cosmic dreaming, because I think I already know what we need.

I think we need some cast-iron, double-bottomed sons-of-a-bitches in the liberal leadership and in the rank and file. Real fire-breathers who know why Emma Goldman and Joe Hill and Eugene Debs (and, yes, you too Carl) were important. People who will sit their children and grandchildren down and teach what the school system will never teach in its never-ending process of churning out overweight little consumers. Teach them that Adam Smith's unseen hand is unseen because it never existed. Teach them that it was our unquestioning collective belief in this fable that had, when hitched to our "chosen people" Protestant religious complex, long ago set us spinning toward the psychotic endgame now in play.

So how did we come to be such a nation? How did we come

to elect the jackals in the first place? I am reminded of a story an acquaintance once told me. During World War II he made friends with a German prisoner, and once asked the prisoner how Nazi Germany could possibly have come into being, how ordinary Germans could be so compliant. "Imagine what would happen," replied the prisoner, "if John Dillinger were elected president of your country."

Lest I sound too self-righteous, I admit that during the '90s I behaved just like the rest of the flaccid American middle class, and was far more a part of the problem than the solution. I was throwing money around like a Texas wildcatter in a Lubbock brothel. Some years I barely knew where the local election polls were, but knew exactly what floor at Harrods's in London you could find the last silver cigarette cases. That was pure mindless consumption, untethered to the geo-political reality that created my affluence. In doing so, I helped this American Empire — which writer Jeffrey St. Clair aptly dubbed the "Empire of the Locusts" — run through the greatest natural bounty ever bestowed on any civilization in a scant 225 years, then move on to turn the rest of the world into a sweatshop. I regret my hubris. As for those 225 years, they are small potatoes as empires go. More ancient nations know that the ground beneath them has seen many, many previous empires pass over with the tread of their armies and the same hubris in their citizenry. So it will be with ours. We will collapse at some point, in all likelihood taking the ecology of the planet with us.

But until then, there are still some of us old bastards around who have seen enough in our lifetimes to call things what they really are. And we are not about to end up as more liberal roadkill alongside this historical crossroad. We are ready to lend our bad backs and grumpy attitudes to the fight for the soul of this nation with which we are stuck. Like the country songs says, "My head hurts, my feet stink, and I don't love Jesus." So get out of my way and, Katy, bar the door! I for one am taking to the streets, joining every damned faggot commie tree-hugging protest march that comes rattling the pike. I don't care if these are the last days of the empire of the locusts. I don't care if the entire jackal nation is at our very throats. Let whatever history remains record that some of us went down with a fight, and that perhaps a few of us indeed became "sages with transfigured faces."

5

Drink, Pray, Fight, Fuck

[January 26, 2005]

You may not meet them among your circle of friends, but there are millions of Americans who fiercely believe we should nuke North Korea and Iran, seize the Middle East's oil, and replace the U.S. Constitution with the Christian Bible. They believe the United States will conquer the entire world and convert it to our notions of democracy and fundamentalist Christian religion. And that will happen, says my Christian neo-conservative friend Dave Henderson, "when we elect a man with the balls to use our nukes." You may not believe me, and if you don't I cannot blame you for never having been exposed to such folks. Only an idiot or a masochistic observer of the American scene would subject himself or herself to these Americans. I like to think I am the latter, but the jury is still out.

In understanding how such ominous political ideations manifested themselves in this country, it helps to look back 450 years to a group of Celtic cattle thieves killing one another in the mud along Hadrian's Wall—the Borderers. Fanatically religious and war loving, these Scottish Protestants made their way first to Ireland as the "Ulster Scots," then to American shores during the early 18th century. Known to most Americans as the Scots–Irish or Scotch Irish, the Borderers brought cultural values that govern (some would say screw up) the political emotions of millions of Americans to this day.

Nearly a third of Americans have Borderer ancestors, though they know little about them, if they know anything at all. Even informed people generally know zilch about the influence this culture continues to exert on America, although that may be about to change somewhat with the current spate of hagiographic Scots–Irish books. One is James Webb's *Born Fighting*, wherein all that is good in America is attributed to Scots–Irish willingness to make war. This is quite in tandem with our self-justifying national storyline. Americans have always described themselves in Borderer terms and values, such as "fierce, liberty loving," "individualistic," "freely religious," and "fighting to defend our way of life." With the neo-conservative takeover of American politics, this has intensified, and we see a supercharging of these themes in the forms of fanatical religiosity, hatred of government, bellicose piety, and, in a new twist, the technological fist of Jesus smiting the swarthy godless heathen in the name of a crude-oil-stained flag.

The homeland of the original Borderers was a squalid place. Denuded of forests and incapable of growing enough food to support its inhabitants, much less to produce enough to sell within the traditional English culture of commerce, the natives survived by and gloried in "reiving" (cattle rustling.) It was a land of alternating famine and overpopulation, the only constant being warfare between England and Scotland along the fluctuating border. Rooted in centuries of national fighting—and in those rare times of peace, inter-clan warfare among themselves—they maintained their fierce ways, clan loyalties, and holdings. The right to hold any turf they occupied was determined by their ability to defend it. Holding such miserable land was a worthwhile effort mainly in as far as it created clan proximity so it could be held. It was a vicious, near pointless circle. Given the unceasing looting, burning, and moving, the Borderers built impermanent earth-and-log dwellings called "cabbins". Within their smoky cabins they lived a quick-tempered, hard-drinking, volatile lifestyle, one that anthropologists say can still be seen in American trailer courts today. So the next time you see one of us drunkenly kicking in a neighbor's car door in some trailer court parking lot at 1.00 a.m., try to remember: That's not a brawl you're witnessing, it's cultural diversity.

More importantly, however, in the off-time between fights, the Borderers embraced the most fanatical form of Calvinism—embraced it so thoroughly they almost hugged it to death. In justifiable reaction to the corrupt Catholic Church of their times, the Johns, Knox and Calvin, established the democratic from-the-bottom-up Kirk organization of the Presbyterian Church, with Jesus Christ himself as the church's only primate. After failing in efforts to make Scotland's government a theocracy, Presbyterian Scots settled for the next-worst thing—putting Christ as the arbiter of all civil government. Ever haters of earthly authority, they deemed that any civil government was only as legitimate as the degree to which it was Biblical, and reserved the right to resist it on those grounds. (By now you must be smelling a theme here, for chrissake! I'm trying. Work with me, people!)

As theological ideas go, John Calvin had slammed one out of the park. Halfway around the world and across four centuries, he is the undisputed father of American Christian fundamentalism, which still clings to those same conclusions about government. His American Borderer descendants are busily dismantling the mainspring of their hated government, the U.S. Constitution, and for the last 30 years "Dominionist" fundamentalists have worked politically to replace it with Biblical law according to their own interpretation. Calvin would jump out of that grave and demand a high five if he knew what his movement has accomplished in the world's most powerful empire.

Looking back, it is hard to believe such a motley swarm of border Celts as arrived in America could accomplish all that. They certainly appeared unlikely candidates when they began migrating here during the first 75 years of the 18th century. So unsavory were their habits that even fellow Calvinists, the New England Puritans, did not much accept them. The East Anglican followers of Cotton Mather's brand of Calvinism were less than enamored with the Borderer practice of drinking in church, and their low hygienic standards. Eventually the Borderers found themselves once more (where else?) on another border. This time it was the border of civilization, the frontiers of British North American holdings in Pennsylvania. True to form, they were exactly where they were not supposed to be—tilling soil and killing Indians west of the Allegheny Mountains against King George II's prohibition.

In the long run, however, these unwashed, hard-fighting fanatics turned out to be useful to the aristocracy in developing their vast land grants in the colonies. For example, from the 1730s onward, the Virginian elite sought to populate the Blue Ridge Mountains as a barrier between the Indians and their lowland slave plantations, and to make fortunes selling the Blue Ridge and the Shenandoah Valley to those willing to settle there. Thus, elites such as Thomas Lord Fairfax, and the Byrd and the Beverly families, brought in Borderers, along with sturdy Pennsylvania Germans. The Borderers were more than willing to keep the Indians, and later the French, killed back to some appropriate line along the Alleghenies, and Virginia's leading families indeed made fortunes that stand today from the land sales, particularly from the Germans. The Borderers often squatted on almost as much as they purchased or shot at rent collectors. But so long as Borderers could pour powder and buy rum, their villages and cabinsteads were considered a reasonable success. Sort of.

The young officer George Washington, while building Winchester's French and Indian War frontier defenses at Fort Loudoun, called our town one of the most ignorant, mean-spirited, and predatory places in all the colonies, a tradition we have thus far managed to maintain. That did not keep Washington from marching said uncouth souls—my ancestors among them—into the Alleghenies to "take a pull," as an early account puts it, at the menacing French and the murderous feathered heathen. Not too many years later, when the elitist, land-speculating Washington entered politics, he had barrels of rum rolled out on our main street, and the same mean-spirited Winchesterians elected him to his first public office, the Virginia House of Burgesses. Which goes to show that no political idea or personage is so unpalatable to us that it cannot be washed down with a drink, or otherwise made acceptable through God rhetoric or patriotic, bloody shirt-waving. It still works. Repeated showings of Twin Towers' footage and beheadings via Internet streaming are the kind of bloody shirt that an America steeped in Borderer culture can grasp. To hell with explanations about oil and global resentment of U.S. imperialism.

Ever hateful of authority and government, we working-class products of Borderer values have remained useful to the rich and the politically ambitious—including many of the same elite families, the Byrds, Lees, Carters, Glasses, etc.—in the ensuing 260 years. During the Civil War, although too poor to piss straight, we nevertheless died to protect slavery on behalf of the elite (40 percent of all wealth in the South was in the form of slaves held by the elite). Later, during the Jim Crow era, we Virginia Borderers were indispensable to the Harry Flood Byrd political machine in helping "keep the niggers down," as they used to say. We shut down the state's public schools and sent our kids to school in the church basements during Byrd's "massive resistance" campaign. And to this day we can be counted upon for bellicose objection to such government oppression as health care for the poor, equitable taxation on the rich, fair labor practices, seatbelts, environmental laws, and stopping state-line gun sales to out-of-state urban criminals.

But a good blood-rousing war is where we truly shine, and where God, glory, and mayhem really come together. I currently receive emails from Iraq, compliments of a born-again co-worker, which I in turn forward to progressive friends in liberal sites—who promptly write them off as the screed of religious nutjobs. Which they are. But that doesn't take into account that there are millions of said nutjobs who exercise their right to vote. Here is one from a U.S. government-sponsored "imbedded reporter," writing for the church newsletter of an Arlington Virginia Assembly of God congregation. He is a smalltime bakery shop owner deemed a news reporter by the administration, one of many rabid evangelists sent to Iraq along with legitimate journalists:

Blessings from the land of Babylon!
　　I just want to praise GOD for when I am weak HE is strong. LORD I know not what to do but my eyes are on YOU, JESUS.

So much to talk about and I do not know where to start ... It makes me so angry that these quiet warriors receive no appreciation from the media and a lot of other people in our nation for the sacrifices they make. They are truly 'a genuine blessing to this nation as every other soldier before them has been.' ... It is criminal of those parrots of the media back home who stand with their lie for political gain and who profit from the blood and pain of our fallen soldiers. This nation need unite. The media is a pack of lying, deceiving whores who will go to any length to defeat George Bush and the righteousness of this cause to set these helpless people free from antichrist spirit through Saddam and his wicked sons, Uday and Usay ... All of those who had recently lost their comrades said "We have a job to do and that is a risk of the job. These people need us here and we can not leave until the job is done." ... I am fighting back tears as I think of them right now. Oops I lost the fight, I need to wipe my eyes. It is criminal the pressure that the media puts on these soldiers and their families to try to defeat George Bush and get their wicked agenda through. There are two lords, we follow one or the other. There is JESUS or there is the devil. The media follows the devil and perpetrates his wicked lies upon this nation to the destruction and endless pain of so many. Stand up against the aimless babbling of those whose father is the father of lies, Satan. Call those liberal lying rags like the Washington Post, L.A. Times, N.Y.Times, CBS and the CNN [communist news network] and voice your disapproval of their lying. ... I say stand and deliver in the name of JESUS ... Decide today where you stand for the LORD is coming soon and we will all be held accountable for "who we been hangin with". The LORD said "be away from me for I never knew you." As the song goes "do you know JESUS and does HE know you."

And they say we do not engage in holy wars.

The American Borderer take on the world is that it was always a tough place, and is getting tougher. Which is damned hard to argue with, and few of us would. But after that, the American penchant for emotionalism and simplistic solutions kicks in. I myself nearly succumb to it at times, the most recent being this morning after viewing the videotaped beheading of Eugene Armstrong in Iraq. It was done slowly, over minutes, in sawing motions. Belief in a universal humanist socialism is the only thing that gets me through days such as this, and then but barely at times. Then I remember that the beheading was a political media event calculated to serve all sides in the struggle for the world's worst emotions. It serves one side as proof of the power to avenge American imperialist policy and invasion. It serves the other as proof of Muslim savagery, providing another bloody shirt for the American public. But ultimately it serves to elevate raw emotionalism above thoughtfulness, which is always a good thing for extremists, whether they are radical jihadists or a militant U.S. capitalist junta.

By the end of the day I am usually back to the realization that global starvation killed far more people this day than the de jour bombing or fighting in the Middle East. Starvation just doesn't pull the kind of audience ratings a beheading does, and does not sell as much advertising for news shows. It does not satisfy an unspoken global energy policy, and it does not fulfill a national religious mass psychosis regarding good and evil. Most of all, mercy is not profitable. If it were, we would be seeing more close-ups of children with sunken, fly-covered eyes. But the fundamentalist working man in the taverns and the churches, the in-the-dirt ignorant one steeped in the American Borderer ethos, cares about none of the above. (The reader may call me arrogant for saying what I know is true. But I've been there and still live there ... so ask me if I give a damn.) For him, it comes down to this: Drink, pray, fight, and fuck. Kill the bad guys. Life ain't really that complicated. Get over it, folks.

So here we are, the Borderer people who "shaped America," as the history books like to say. Today we can be found everywhere in America. Although most of the early Borderer immigration took place in Pennsylvania, from there they spread north and south, and later west, and assimilated into the cultures they found. Those that went south identified with the South during the Civil War. Those that went north identified with the North, and so on, as they spread their strain throughout the entire nation. And what a strain! Every damned one of them part wampus cat, "part Cherokee," meaner than a wad of snakes on a griddle, ever malleable by the swells, and more than happy to give any deserving Muslim a .45 caliber ticket to paradise. Ready to ship out for the next holy war on any shore that flies a heathen flag. To our minds, what could possibly be wrong with making the world heel to an empire piloted by Calvin's ghost and anointed by God? Love us or hate us, we are nevertheless the same touching, pathos-ridden, stubborn, God-obsessed folks who gave you Johnny Cash, Andrew Jackson, Ma Barker, Ronald Reagan, Mark Twain, country music, NASCAR, Edgar Allen Poe, John Hancock, and Bill Clinton.

As I write, I am monitoring a local online discussion between two old friends. One is a news vendor and the other is a factory worker. It runs like this:

> Let's take a couple of camel jockeys and crucify them on TV down on the Mall in D.C.
>
> Hell, yes! If the Muslims can behead our guys, then we Christians can crucify theirs!
>
> ALLLLLL RIGHT!

This may be a digital age, and that conversation may be in cyberspace, but if I close my eyes I can almost smell the peat fires and hear the rasp of claymores slipping their sheathes at Bannockburn.

I gotta tell you one last Scots–Irish anecdote because, well hell, I don't know how to get out of this thing. Hereabouts in the Blue Ridge we still have plenty of full-strength Scots–Irish, what the sociologists and historians call "vestigial cultures." Meaning tough-assed little inbreds of the old mold. So anyway, out on the loading dock at the local Rubbermaid plant, forklift driver Jodie Macauley, a skinny, twitchy middle-aged redneck, failed to show up for a couple of days. When he returned to work, he explained to the dock foreman that he'd been in jail. "Whatta hell for?" asked the foreman. "Waall, these two tractor-trailer trucks hemmed me in on the road. So I pulled my pistol and shot out the radiator of the truck behind me. But, please don't tell nobody here, sir, because these days there is some people who think doing that kinda thang is weird."

Yeah. Right.

6

It Ain't Easy Being White

[March 11, 2005]

"As nightfall does not come all at once, neither does oppression. In both instances, there is a twilight when everything remains seemingly unchanged."

—*William O. Douglas, associate justice of the Supreme Court*

"Would the sonofabitch who super-glued my hair to the bar when I passed out please come take your goddamned beating like a man!"

—*Pooty Jenkins, welder*

"Pooty, don't you ever wash them booger hooks of yours?" That's Carol the bartender watching Poot pick up his Royal Burger with two blackened hairy paws that look like they just finished welding a greasy transmission housing back together—which is exactly what they did. "Carol, darlin'," Poot replies, "*fuck you.*"

Nobody ever claimed that dining at a working-man's joint

like Burt's Tavern was a polished experience. Or even sanitary.

Whatever the case, some of us will be buying Poot rounds tonight because (a) he tends to get drunk and forget to pay his tab, and (b) he just lost his job at the metal-fabrication plant to some sweatshop in Bangkok. Pooty has been here an hour already, long enough to get warmed up for the evening. "I'm gonna follow my job to Indyneezya! Um-hum! Then I'm gonna strangle the livin' piss out of the little motherfuckin' gooks." Never mind that Bangkok is in Thailand, not Indonesia. It has little bearing on this evening, which I suspect will be a long one.

"Shuddap, ya goddam ape!" yells someone in the back. Poot is a goddamned ape. Even his own wife says so. She once stood up in the tavern and called Poot "nothin but a goddamned ape!" which has become sort of the Pooty meme around here. The punch-line. Whenever he gets to be too much, someone will say, "Aw, Poot, yer nuthin but a goddam ape," and everybody will laugh and Poot will let up on whatever offensive or tedious jag he happens to be on at the moment—usually Redskins football or deer-hunting laws.

He's a fun ape, though. Pooty is the guy who once bolted one end of a 60-foot chain to the rear bumper of a police car, and the other to the Confederate statue in front of the court house, then raced right down Main Street by the police station at 1.00 a.m. The result was moreover predictable with regard to both the police-car bumper and officer Danny Fogle's sphincter. We were 17 then, full of piss 'n vinegar, and not above such pranks as greasing the railroad tracks through town with lard. If a kid pulled that stunt today he'd get 10 years, assuming he escaped being gunned down in the street—"greased" by the cops, as it were.

Meanwhile, back in Bangkok.

Your job doesn't have to get shipped to bumfuck Asia to get hosed in the workplace by foreigners here in Winchester. We've got 4,000 Mexicans in this town of 29,000. Nearly every one of them is illegal, but the authorities pretend not to see them because they provide the cheap labor for the local elite's plants and businesses, and wipe the brie off the liberal college faculty's countertops after the cocktail parties.

So it is understandable that one of the things which fries local working folks' asses about liberals is their denial of the problem of illegal immigration—the crushing effects on wages for working-class whites. It is also one of those things liberals will just never get. Liberals are so scared of being labeled racists that they simply refuse to acknowledge the issue. And besides, it's not educated liberals' jobs being taken by the Mexicans. But ya know what? If I stood up on a box in any beer joint or veterans' hall in the country and said, "Clean up illegal immigration, no more wetback wages for anybody," I'd get cheers and free rounds on the house. It ain't racist, it's plain dollars and cents.

Nevertheless, the Bush administration and business of all type likes cheap, terrified illegal workers, and is not one bit moved by all those little brown carcasses in the Sonora Desert. By avoiding the issue or advocating services for the illegals already here, liberals give working-class folks the impression they approve of slave-wage labor and non-citizens receiving public funds—which they don't, of course. But most Americans think they do. Most of working white America does not like it and would be more than happy to see an 18-foot border wall with machine-gun emplacements and a minefield between the two countries. We have a disconnect here, folks. Anyway, it's not a good idea to get on a soapbox at Burt's about medical care for illegals. The guy you are talking to probably doesn't have health insurance. When we get universal health care, the illegal Mexicans can have free medical services. Maybe.

HELLO, YOU TWO-BIT LIBERAL MAMMY JAMMERS!!!! THIS IS THE SCREAMING MAN, THE BOOZE-DRIVEN, SMACK-LUBRICATED CORPSE OF THE ALTER-EGO OF JOE BAGEANT — A SAVAGE REMNANT OF WHEN HE WAS A BETTER MAN. NOWADAYS THAT PUKE KEEPS SCREAMING MAN SUPPRESSED DOWN BEHIND HIS GONADS WITH MASSIVE DOSES OF HOG TRANQUILIZERS AND A PAIR OF VICE-GRIPS ON HIS ASSHOLE ... IT IS A NATIONAL TRAGEDY THAT SCREAMING MAN, WHO HAS ENOUGH HAIR IN HIS ASS TO WEAVE AN INJUN BLANKET, IS TRAPPED INSIDE A GODDAM POTBELLIED GIN-SOAKED, GIBBON-LIKE JOE BAGEANT — A DESPICABLE OLD PUD-POUNDER WHO LETS WHORING HIMSELF ACROSS THE INTERNET PASS FOR A LIFE. RIP THE FAT BASTARD'S THYROID OUT WITH A SALAD FORK ... FREE THE SCREAMING MAN!

Ahem. Meanwhile, Lucian Bandister, the only regular black patron at Burt's, is telling Carol that, "It takes a white man to really kill. It takes a Ted Bundy or a Jeffrey Dahmer. While blacks and Hispanics are out there hustling dope and boosting cars, you've got your dynamic white males slipping around raping, killing, and like eating 25 goddamned people before they get caught!"

Given enough beer, Lucian—like everyone else at Burt's—is a social commentator, historian, and expert. They can expound on anything. But these days at Burt's you won't hear a word about one thing—terrorism. Not unless you bring it up. Despite all the blood-in-the-face patriotic rage supposedly felt by working people over 9/11, I am going to commit heresy and say not one shit-faced patron here tonight believes that the world changed on 9/11. What happened in New York City was just another televised event here among the NASCAR and Jimmy Johnson smoked-country-ham crowd. It was never real to them. Not to people who have never been to New York, and to whom New York is just an imaginary place on television where idealized liberal nether-worlds and nightly murders are electronically served up. And the Twin Towers? It is safe to say that none of these stump jumpers in downtown Deliverance ever even heard of them until they went down in a cloud of asbestos dust and smoke on their TV screens. Yet coastal intellectuals such as Norman Mailer are writing about how 9/11 psychologically affected working-class America's sense of virility, security, confidence, national mythology, etc. Not really. Now if the Styrofoam peanut plant across town closes down, eliminating 500 local jobs, *that* is world changing around here. You have a hard time believing it, don't you? Yes, I can imagine.

HELL, YES, I CAN BELIEVE IT! THESE PEOPLE SHOULD NEVER HAVE BEEN ALLOWED TO BREED! BIG MISTAKE! NOW THEY ROAM THE STREETS, THESE "UNDEAD" VIRGINIANS, ROTTING THROWBACKS FROM AN EARLIER AGE WHEN THEIR ANCESTORS ALWAYS RESERVED FRIDAY NIGHTS AS "LYNCHIN' NIGHT." HELL, YES, I CAN BELIEVE IT!

Of course, two years ago everybody was absorbed in that Mobius tape loop of the planes crashing. It was an emotional topic for a while. But so is a football game. For a while. And it still provides the bloodiest shirt Americans will ever wave, an excuse to avenge something, strut around patriotically and root for our side. Just like a big football game, but with explosives and torture. And for us Southerners it provided a fresh opportunity to kill dark-skinned people, always a blessing in the slave states.

But if you stop and think about it, all the scare noise was and still is coming out of the media and the feds, not the people. Same goes for the war in Iraq. On the whole, Americans haven't given a flying fuck about wars, other than for entertainment value, since Vietnam went sour on them. "Iraq War? Pick up a couple of magnetic yellow ribbons at the Seven Eleven, will ya?" And that is it. Of course, if you pour enough beer and rag on the subject long enough, you'll get some heated arguments going about the war or the treatment of Taliban and al-Qaeda prisoners held in Guantanamo.

MISTREATMENT OF TALIBAN AND AL-QAEDA FIGHTERS IN CUBA? OH MAMA THUMPING SON OF CHRIST! THESE DESERT APES WERE LIVING IN A CAVE, SHITTING IN A HOLE IN THE GROUND, AND WIPING THEIR ASSES WITH THEIR FINGERS AFTER EATING BURNT GOAT MEAT OFF A STICK. THEN THEY WERE CAPTURED, SEDATED WITH HIGH-QUALITY NARCOTICS, AND FLOWN TO GITMO, WHERE THEY GET THREE SQUARES A DAY, HOT BATHS, AND ONLY GET UP TO BEAT OFF. THAT'S A LIFESTYLE SCREAMING MAN CAN UNDERSTAND AND APPRECIATE — ASSUMING THE DRUGS ARE STRONG ENOUGH. THESE FUGGIN' CAMEL-JAMMERS FIGURE THEY DIED AND WOKE UP IN THE GODDAM LAP OF ALLAH!

Back to the subject, I think working-class Americans have always been like that. Insulated. A little time in the National Archives listening to taped interviews reveals that most Americans were not much moved by Pearl Harbor at the time either, because, aha! Hawaii was simply not real to them. Especially before television. At the time of the attack most Americans didn't much give a rip, even though the newspaper headlines screamed "NIPS HIT PEARL HARBOR!" And everybody asked themselves, where inna hell is Pearl Harbor?" Half the country, particularly the South and the Midwest, wouldn't have even known World War II was going on if it were not for the shortages. American life was isolated and insulated by distances then. You'd never know that from the propaganda and hoopla generated since.

Now we are insulated by ignorance, body fat, cheap spectacle, and electronics. Hang around the working-class places very long and you'll see that they almost never talk about current events. They never mention politics except in an election year. They never mention any issues larger than sports, movies, and where to get good ribs and seafood, and why GM just can't seem to build a decent engine. They put up flags and patriotic symbols because it seems like the right thing to do because everybody else does. But no conscious analysis takes place. Most working whites, blue-collar, technical, service, or whatever, are nonpolitical. And to the extent that they hold beliefs, they hold the beliefs they think they are expected to hold. Just like they hold little flags and ribbons for the troops. That's to tell you who they believe they are, Americans and Americans only. Plain Americans, cut from the rest of the world by a self-isolating belief that it's better to be American than anything else, even if they really can't prove why. Ignorance is bliss and, somehow, America is where everyone supposedly dreams to be. No depth of thought and consciousness involved or required. There is the American on top, and the rest of the world that is envious and plotting to steal their freedom.

In the end, maybe we cannot count on white Americans to change. An African–American friend writes me that:

> As long as Americans have that belief, Bush is safe and the world is in trouble. For all I know, the liberals and the suburbanites, even the progressives and leftists, are a bunch of know-it-alls with the same supremacist tendencies in sheep clothing. They just can't shed this hubris of the curse of being better than the rest of the world for no good reason. There is something pathetic about this worldview. So I'll just work with people of color because they don't seem to have this illusion

and actually like other cultures and the world. They are the future and they need to be in power because they will change the status quo. I don't believe that white people in general want to change anything at all.

One thing for sure. Traditionally, we can count on working white Americans to go off in a homicidal swarm to "defend our way of life," whenever our leaders periodically declare it to be threatened. Whenever they nail the cowhide to the barn. Right now we have a full-blown case of the cowhide syndrome. Anyone who grew up on a farm knows what happens if you butcher a cow and then nail the hide up high on the barn. The rest of the cows go absolutely freaking berserk until it is removed. Now George Bush and the neos have nailed the hide on the barn, and they have no damned intention of taking it down. For the moment, however, it is not election season, so things have calmed down a bit, and it is mostly the neo-con leadership and the liberal herd that is agitated and bellowing out there. Everybody else is at Wal-Mart.

Most people here in Burt's Tavern never get exposed to anything liberal —which is to say, universal, generous, and just—unless it comes from within their own families or their church. This being the South, they never expect an ounce of mercy from the workplace or any kind of government. Especially government. If they did, many could be made to understand the virtues of liberalism the same as the rest of the world does. Not all of course, but many. I've convinced quite a few of them myself. It's about education. We all need educating.

So when I suggested last month in a column that there should be an organized effort to inform and educate lower-income working people, I got emails that said: "That is the most ridiculous, inane thing you've ever written," and "Our problem with you guys is you fat, stupid, sweaty, mouth breathing, redneck, dolphin killing numb-nuts reelected George Bush."

Still another reader did not share my optimism about educating the working classes:

> White trash suffer from what psychiatrists call "no insight." They will never agree with anyone from outside their zone of consumer culture ignorance because their desperate pride includes the right to be dreadfully wrong about everything and telling people more educated than themselves to "fuck off!" That's what makes them feel good. The only thing that gets a redneck's attention, besides the next six-pack, is a good swipe upside the head with a two-by-four. And when the self-awareness dawns, it's too late, because he's bankrupt, homeless, and in jail.

Finally, we have proof of liberal rage.

Allow me to address the skepticism of many lefties: Do you think red-state working folks are too damned dumb to recognize the truth if and when it is ever presented in relevant terms? OK, don't answer that. But buried under the cholesterol, fear, and consumer state-indoctrination, it is there. And lest you get too proud, remember: You voted for Kerry. We all be dumb sometimes, brutha. Most of the time, really. So educating working-class folks is worth a try if for no other reason than that the alternative is just too awful to contemplate—Dale Earnhardt on the ten-dollar bill. I can't help but believe that if informed folks, like those on websites such as this, helped people focus on their mutual class-enemies, then the Bush bandits would have plenty to worry about.

And besides, the fundamental difference between true liberalism and conservatism in America today comes down to a simple question: Are we or are we not our brother's keeper? Well?

Can white people be trusted at all?

As someone who grew up poor, rural, and white, but moved to the city and took advantage of the educational opportunities we once had in this country, I probably represent an imperfect synthesis of snot-assed liberal and redneck Southern dirt-eater. More of the latter, because the taste of dirt has real staying power. Which is why I moved back here to Winchester, Virginia, five years ago to be around the only people with whom I ever felt completely comfortable (which is not the same thing as shared values, or I'd have swallowed a can of lye the first week back). Despite attempts to be hip, cultured, and urbane, I know I am a seed of that tribe of ignorant white dickheads who drive the trucks, fight the wars, and vote for people like George Bush. Smalltown working folks. And I can tell you this: It sucks out here in the heartland.

Many people who idealize rural or small-town America either never grew up there or haven't been back in 30 years. The place has gone to hell. Rural America is now a cold, heartless place that is very difficult to escape from, where the rules of hard work and honesty no longer apply. The only people making any dough in rural and small-town America these days are bankers, lawyers, doctors, and a few with government jobs. Thanks to the new global economy, it is hard and desperate terrain for working people. Mean, too.

OH, FER CRYING OUT LOUD! THIS PUTRID GENETIC CESSPOOL CALLED THE HEARTLAND HAS GOT TO BE PURGED WITH FIRE AND FEAR! BURN OUT EVERY CRACKER FROM HERE TO KANSAS. THIS IS WHERE THE GODDAM ICED-TEA SLURPING, PIE-GOBBLING BASTARDS BREED! FRY ALL THE PORK-FACED PUD-PUMPERS. KICK ALL THEIR CARS OFF THE BLOCKS AND BULLDOZE THEIR VERMIN-INFESTED

TRAILER HOMES. IT'S ONLY A MATTER OF TIME UNTIL SOMEBODY'S
DOG GETS EATEN, SOMEBODY'S CHIA PET GETS SCALPED! WHERE
THE HELL IS THAT GODDAM GENOCIDAL NAZI JEW SHARON WHEN
YOU NEED HIM?

There is really no nice way to say it. Even allowing for the
way the system manipulates and exploits them, working white
Americans, all things considered, are becoming a mean people.
Being forced to eat shit and ask for seconds just to have any kind
of a job makes you mean. So they hang on to being white. They
believe in the tacitly acknowledged white privilege, though they
get damned little if any of it. Working whites share the same
European culture of material accumulation and consumption
with the corporate elite who own their lives. They believe in
private property, they do not distinguish between their trailer
and the boss's monster mansion. They believe in defending it
with weapons. They believe in consumption. They believe in
the myth of the entrepreneur and the self-made man. It's all
bullshit, but they believe it because they are part of the three-
quarters of Americans who have no more than a high school
education—just enough to absorb political propaganda and
marketing messages. And they are going to stay that way as
long as we let corporations and crony capitalism continue to
reduce our working brothers to a mere resource.

Challenging prevailing political and economic systems is
something that educated people do. So to change their fate (and
the fate of the ecosystem, the nation, and a lot of other things),
working-class America will have to become more educated.
Regardless of the way it appears, red-state working-class
Americans can be reached. But we have to humble ourselves.
Admit that they have been screwed by the system more than
most of us (and admit that we are at least partly to blame for
their situation—we had more power than them and we let the

system go bad). Elsewise we are all screwed. And if we are all screwed anyway, and it sure as hell looks like that from the end stool at Burt's, it is because the richest nation on earth broke John Locke's social contract by not providing quality universal higher education. Just like it refuses to guarantee health care.

Reaching out is asking intellectuals to abandon the intellect as a bridge-building device and to move over into intuition and compassion to create the understanding needed. Compassion necessarily requires some degree of selflessness—not a common attribute to folks accustomed to the "me-first" high-self-esteem world of American liberalism. It's a hearts-and-minds kind of thang.

One last kick at the liberal dog.

Just like the Republican junta's biggest potential enemy is their own hubris, this is ours. Let's be honest. The liberal elite is not entirely a Republican myth. This generation of white liberals is not involved in class issues—it's become more concerned with trendiness. To average working Americans, television series such as *Friends* and *Sex and the City* are the face of modern liberal culture. Those average Americans are not wrong. The very fact that most elite celebrities call themselves "liberal" and don't receive any heat tells you something is very wrong. A real class warrior would spit on the materialistic, narcissistic celebrities.

American liberals define themselves and the issues that concern them within the same consumer-culture machinery as the conservative elites do. This *is* the main difference between educated liberals and less-educated working folks. Neither are citizens of the United States or anything else. The United States no longer has citizens. It has consumers. So middle-class liberals delude themselves into thinking they are so different from people like Pooty, Dink, and the others who break wind and pool sticks down here at Burt's Tavern. Most liberals are not in a much higher income bracket, but their consumer choices—paid for on credit—allow them to mimic the ruling class: Starbucks vs. Sanka … Mother Jones vs. George Jones … Mark Twain vs. Shania Twain. There is little hope for us until we realize that these ultimately meaningless consumer choices are not representative of any competing or compelling values, but are merely distractions that stimulate and keep alive class divisions and hatreds.

For the time being, at least, American liberalism has George Bush to blame for everything. And much the same as a zoo ape enjoys even negative attention, George Bush, peeling his lips back and mocking the crowd, is having the time of his life. But one of these days we will have to deal with the real reason that middle-class white American liberals hate Bush. Liberals hate Bush because he is a traitor to the white classes. Bush revealed the true face of American power and exposed it as the corrupt hoax it really is. He is a "cowboy" imperialist as opposed to the more acceptable kind—the Kennedy, Carter, Clinton type who conducted their dark little murders at the edge of the empire in secrecy while Americans wasted most of the world's resources. The Anybody But Bush crowd would have approved the use of force against Iraq if it had been presented by a senator from a blue state with a bullshit UN resolution, as opposed to a simple 'Yeeee-ha' from a retarded frat-boy from Texas and overwhelming international revulsion. Either way, the ruling political and corporate elites still maintain their privileges and status. The ABB movement was not about stripping anyone of those; it was simply about keeping up self-serving appearances to preserve our Jabba the Hutt worldview and lifestyle.

It is 2.00 a.m., and Pooty is in top form now and still determined to follow his job to Indyneezya and "make gook sauce out of the little fuckers." But he won't. Instead, he will take a job with no benefits at Skink's Welding, a locally owned non-union sweatshop, and he will lay down welding beads on refrigeration units for about half what he made before.

And SCREAMING MAN is raging against his imprisonment, lo, these many years, "AAARRRGGGHHH! MY HYPODERMIC PLEASE! (MMMMMMM ... TOO MUCH DOG WORMER IN THAT LAST DOSE OF ACID.) GIN ... MORE GIN! AND RAW MEAT! ... I MUST HAVE RAW MEAT!"

And all heads in Burt's are turned toward the front window where, outside, police car lights are flashing as the cops search a teenager for dope in front of the train station. The young blonde cops act like characters they've seen in crime dramas. In the distance is the approaching light and horn of a C&X train, BLOOOOOOOOOOOOOOOOOOOONK BLOOOOOOOOOOOOOOOOOONK! The police car lights bounce off the storefront windows, and there is the smell of beer and the past and a sure-enough approaching apocalypse. And the whole damned sad hologram of America rises up, arching over the scene.

Nothing to do but go home, break out the Old Grandad, and drink it straight up from a rusty canteen cup. The voice of a ghost breaks in on the reverie.

AND DON'T EVEN BOTHER TO WASH THE MOTHERFUCKER!

Right, Hunter.

7

What the "Left Behind" Series Really Means

[December 19, 2005]

"Jesus merely raised one hand a few inches and a yawning chasm opened in the earth, stretching far and wide enough to swallow all of them. They tumbled in, howling and screeching, but their wailing was soon quashed and all was silent when the earth closed itself again."
—*from* Glorious Appearing: the end of days, *by Tim LaHaye and Jerry B. Jenkins*

"The best thing about the Left Behind books is the way the non-Christians get their guts pulled out by God."
—*15-year-old fundamentalist fan of the series*

That is the sophisticated language and appeal of America's all-time best-selling adult novels celebrating the ethnic cleansing of non-Christians at the hands of Christ. If a Muslim were to write an Islamic version of the last book in the "Left Behind" series, *Glorious Appearing*, and publish it across the Middle East, Americans would go berserk. Yet tens of millions of Christians eagerly await and celebrate an End Time when everyone who disagrees with them will be murdered in ways that make Islamic beheading look like a bridal shower. Jesus—who apparently has a much nastier streak than we have been led to believe—merely speaks, and "the bodies of the enemy are ripped wide open down the middle." In the book, Christians have to drive carefully to avoid "hitting splayed and filleted corpses of men and women and horses." Even as the riders' tongues are melting in their mouths and they are being wide-open gutted by God's own hand, the poor damned horses are getting the same treatment. Sort of a divinely inspired version of ,"Fuck you and the horse you rode in on."

This may be some of the bloodiest hate-fiction ever published, but it is also what tens of millions of Americans believe is God's will. It is approximately what everyone in the congregation sitting around me last Sunday at my brother's church believes. Or some version of it. How can anyone acquire and hold such notions? Answer: The same way you got yours and I got mine. Conditioning. From family and school and society, but from within a different American caste than the one in which you were raised. And from things stamped deep in childhood—such as coming home terrified to an empty house.

One September day when I was in the third grade, I got off the school bus and walked up the red dust-powdered lane to my house, only to find no one there. The smudgy white front door of the old frame house stood open. My footsteps on the unpainted gray porch creaked in the fall stillness. With increasing panic, I went through every room, and then ran around the outside crying and sobbing in the grip of the most horrific loneliness and terror. I believed with all my heart that The Rapture had come and that all my family had been taken up to heaven, leaving me alone on earth to face God's terrible wrath. As it turned out, they were at the neighbor's house scarcely 300 yards down the road, and returned in a few minutes. But it took me hours to calm down. I dreamed about it for years afterward.

Since then, I have spoken to others raised in fundamentalist families who had the same childhood experience of coming home and thinking everyone had been "raptured up." The Rapture—the time when God takes up all saved Christians before he lets loose slaughter, pestilence, and torture upon the earth—is very real to people in whom its glorious and grisly promise was instilled and cultivated from birth. Even those who escape fundamentalism agree that its marks are permanent. We may no longer believe in being raptured up, but the grim fundamentalist architecture of the soul stands in the background of our days. There is an apocalyptic starkness that remains somewhere inside us, one that tinges all of our feelings and thoughts of higher matters. Especially about death, oh beautiful and terrible death, for naked eternity is more real to us than to you secular humanists. I get mail from hundreds of folks like me, the different ones who fled and became lawyers and teachers and therapists and car mechanics, dope dealers and stockbrokers and waitresses. And every one of them has felt that thing we understand between us—that skulls-piled-clear-to-heaven redemption through absolute self-worthlessness, and you ain't shit in the eyes of God, so go bleed to death in some dark corner—which stabs us in the heart at those very moments when we should have been most proud of ourselves. Self-hate. That thing that makes us sabotage our own inner happiness when we are most free and operating as self-realizing individuals. This kind of Christianity is a black thing. It is a blood religion that willingly gives up sons to America's campaigns in the Holy Land, hoping they will bring on the much-anticipated war between good and evil in the Middle East that will hasten the End Times. Bring Jesus back to Earth.

Whatever the case, tens of millions of American fundamentalists, despite their claims otherwise, read and absorb the all-time best-selling "Left Behind" book series as prophesy and fact. How could they possibly not, after being conditioned all their lives to accept the End Times as the ultimate reality? We are talking about a group of Americans, 20 percent of whose children graduate from high school identifying H_2O as a cable channel. Children who, like their parents and grandparents, come from that roughly half of all Americans who can approximately read, but are dysfunctionally literate to the extent they cannot grasp any textual abstraction or overall thematic content.

Most of my family and their church friends (mainly the women) have read at least some of the "Left Behind" series, and if pressed they will claim they understand that it is fiction. But anyone who has heard fundies around the kitchen table discussing the books knows the claim is pure bullshit. "Well, they do get an awful lot of stuff exactly right," they admit. Beyond that, most fundamentalists delight in seeing their beliefs as "persecuted Christians" become best sellers "under the guise of fiction," as the Pentecostal assistant who used to work with me put it. "They show the triumph of the righteous over those who persecute us for our faith in God." Fer cryin' out loud, Christianity is scarcely a persecuted belief-system in this country, or in need of a guise to protect itself. Year after year, some 60 percent of Americans surveyed say they believe the Book of Revelations will come true, and about 40 percent believe it will come true in their lifetimes. This, from the 50 percent of Americans who, according to statistics, seldom if ever buy a book.

Fetishizing of the End Times as a spectacular gore-fest visited upon the unbelievers is nothing new. But the sheer number of people gleefully enjoying the spectacle of their own blackest magical thinking made manifest by mass media is new. Or at least the media aspect is new. It reinforces the major appeal of these beliefs, the appeal being (to restate the obvious) that they get to pass judgment on everyone who disagrees with them, and then watch God kick the living snot out of them. It doesn't get any better than that.

All my life I have seen these people, and there are no more or less of them proportionately than before. It is simply that (a) they have built their own massive media, and (b) educated middle-class folks are noticing them now because they vote, and a major political party is willing to violate the church-state boundary to get their votes. They have always been out here and, as I say, always in about the same percentages. Think about that. It took me a while to accept it, too. But George W. Bush learned the significance of this while campaigning for his daddy back when he was supposed to be at his National Guard meetings. Part of his job was to bring in the fundie Christian vote for Poppy. Come George's turn to play poker for the presidency in that quadrennial rich man's game we call elections, Sparky knew what cards to play. The effete John Kerry had not a clue. Still doesn't. Neither did you. Right? Don't feel bad. I even knew that the great unwashed tribes of the faithful were out here, wrote spooky and panicked articles about it before the elections, and still underestimated the capability of the death-obsessed Christian right.

Lookie here. If you think I'm overcounting, think one more

time about those "Left Behind" books that have sold over 65 million copies at this writing. Sold to people who do not even like or buy books. Gore Vidal and Susan Sontag never wrote anything that sold 65 million copies. That lead-footed prose and numbing predictability that Jerry Jenkins and Tim LaHaye grind out in the "Left Behind" series might not even be called writing. But whatever it is, at least 65 million folks that our nation failed to educate find deep meaning and solace in it. LaHaye has also sold 120 million non-fiction books, which makes him the most successful Christian writer since the Bible.

Sales figures aside, it is entirely possible that the "Left Behind" series is as important in our time and cultural context as was, say, Harriet Beecher's Stowe's *Uncle Tom's Cabin* in its time, wherein Lincoln called it "the little book that started the big war." The truth is that LaHaye is among the most influential religious writers America ever produced and is the most powerful fundamentalist in America today. He is the founder and first president of the eerily secretive Council for National Policy, which brings together leading evangelicals and other conservatives with right-wing billionaires willing to pay for a conservative religious revolution. He is far more influential than Billy Graham or Pat Robertson, and was the man who inspired Jerry Falwell to launch the Moral Majority. He gave millions of dollars to Falwell's Liberty University. He's the man without whom Ronald Reagan would never have become governor of California, and the man who grilled George W. Bush, then wiped the cocaine off George's nose and gave him the official Christian fundie stamp of approval. He created the American Coalition for Traditional Values that has mobilized evangelical voters, putting neo-conservative wackjobs into political offices across the nation. In short, he is the Godfather of Soul, fundie style. When the man lays it down, his peeps doo dey duty.

Scratch LaHaye and you'll find an honest-to-God surviving John Bircher. In the 1960s, when LaHaye was a young up-and-coming Baptist preacher fresh out of Bob Jones University, he lectured on behalf of Republican Robert Welch's John Birch Society. We are talking about a man who believed that Dwight Eisenhower was an agent of the Communist Party taking orders from his brother, Milt Eisenhower. Along the way, LaHaye extended his paranoid list of villains to include secular humanists who "are Satan's agents hiding behind the Constitution." And the only way to destroy them is to destroy their cover.

I have asked preachers about the "Left Behind" books. They all claim to have reservations about them. Fundie preachers are snarky about any beliefs that do not precisely mirror their own, and no two ever agree completely. They publicly find fault with the apocalyptic "Left Behind" books, even as they privately enjoy the books' popularity. Most say the series overestimates the number of people going to heaven. Which figures, given that their stock and trade is the divine exclusivity of a club called "The Saved." No sense in ruining the brand by franchising it too cheaply.

Same goes for television as for the Christian pop-lit. Fundamentalists delighted in the NBC series *Revelations*. Admittedly, it was a bullshit job from network people who had not the slightest understanding of the subject, but could smell more money the closer they got to it. They were right. Christian fundies sucked it up. Coolly as if butter wouldn't melt in their mouths, the fundies I know denied they enjoyed *Revelations* at all because the producers "got some things wrong" (as if it were possible to be wrong regarding dire predictions made centuries ago by superstitious mystic fanatics about something that never came to pass). They say the main thing wrong was having

Christ return as a little child. Most hardcore fundies preferred their vision of a Rambo Jesus arriving to beat the fuck out of everybody who ever disagreed with Him or them—sinners' eyeballs turning to putrid jelly, blood flowing everywhere, etc. (In *Revelations*, Jesus arrives on horseback wearing a blood-soaked robe.)

These media products are more than harmless American Christian kitsch culture or just more American religious swill. Swill it may be, but it is also dangerous propaganda, and the writers know damned-well that propaganda value. Just as the propaganda value of associating Jewish people with rats in Nazi Germany helped the German populace accept persecution of the Jews, the "Left Behind" books foster a morality that excuses horrors done to "non-believers." Forget about sanity and reason. Christian fundamentalist media promotes a hermetic worldview cut off from reason. From the standpoint of those who consume such media messages, it is not so much propaganda as it is an abundant offering so complete as to be a parallel bizzaro world of its own. It gives answers to questions not even asked.

It is a world in which the secretary-general of the United Nations is the anti-Christ (Left Behind), and the "Clinton Crime Family" deals in cocaine and is linked to the Gambino family (Joshua Project, and other sources.) It is one in which abortion doctors are microwaving and eating fetuses, according to testimony given by anti-abortionists before a Kansas House subcommittee (WorldNetDaily, of course), and where crowds of good folks get teary-eyed as the Reverand Pat Evans, of the NASCAR "Racing for Jesus Ministries' rumbles onto the track. Evangelical NASCAR? Yup. What ABC called America's "unapologetically evangelical sport." I can see you, dear reader, running and holding your head and screaming at the thought.

Yet it's true. At Bristol and Talladega, the earth is shaking for Jaaaayzus! Now that we have Evangelical NASCAR, what, I ask you, can ever go wrong?

"To be saved is to fall into the ludicrous and satanic flippancy of false piety, kitsch."
— *Trappist monk Thomas Merton*

Forty years later, Merton is still right. Like most American liberals, not to mention all of Europe and the rest of the world, I learned through education to write off the U.S. born-again literature as kitsch religion, merely bad theology in an unholy marriage with bad writing. Another product of the American Jesus industry. If we liberals can name it, assign it to some appropriately vulgar and sentimental corner of our degraded culture, and then remain tolerant of it, we feel have dealt with the damned thing. After all, it is the comparative worldview of the teeming red-state masses. But there is a certain arrogance in such pop-cultural erudition and thin worldliness, isn't there? In itself, our attitude is too flip.

It took coming home to a born-again red state for me to realize how cultural documents such as "Left Behind" or the movies *Revelations* and *The Passion of the Christ* do great harm, and at a critical time when we are facing economic upheaval, fighting illegal wars, and suffering deep religious antipathies across the planet. "Aw," my liberal New York and West Coast friends tell me, "That is overstating the case. The Democrats will eventually be back in power." We cannot afford to wait a few more years and see. No matter if the Dems actually can be elected back into powerlessness, they will have needed at least some of these people's votes to get there. Next election we will find out if it is possible to be elected without the fundamentalist Christians. So far, the Democrat political elite, who only take their thumb out of their ass to change thumbs, has not been able to stop the religious right's relentless push. And I think it is because, at least from where I sit right now, the Democrat establishment has not offered, much less delivered, and is incapable of delivering, what my people really need—decent educations, so they will not be prey to 3,000-year-old superstitions. The left has yet to demand for all Americans a genuine absolutely free education, an opportunity to enjoy a life of the mind, or to even know that such a thing exists. Hell, you got yours and I got mine, right? So screw'em. We progressives have failed. We were always and still are our brother's keeper, and now the throw-away Americans—the ugly little dickhead at the car wash, and the truck driver, and the guy who delivers the bottled water to our offices—are coming to get our assess, even though they aren't quite sure why. My Random House editor told me not to get on a soapbox about this, but I cannot help it. (Sorry, Rachel.)

I am not trying to be smart-assed, but to indicate the fear of what is unfolding around me as a person living in the belly of the beast. The reality gap between fundamentalist and urban liberals is unfathomable. Liberal observers watching from a safe distance in New York or San Francisco conclude it is pure stupidity that caused millions of Americans to continue support of the Bush junta in the face of overwhelming evidence of lies, deceit, and contempt for the Constitution, even as the fat cats raided their retirements and picked their pockets at every turn. Others think it is just plain meanness that attracted them to Bush. And so do I sometimes, because stupidity (the Jesus stockcar entries should be proof enough) and meanness are surely part of the attraction to a certain type of conservative—that poisonous toad Karl Rove being their chief deity of meanness for meanness's sake.

There remains one nagging problem. Despite their masochistic voting patterns, fundamentalists are very ordinary and normal Americans—people who, often as not, go out of their way to help others and endorse most American values. So how do we reconcile the warmth and good nature of these hardworking citizens with the repressive politics, intolerance, nationalism, and war-making they support? Why do such ordinary people do such awful things? The Germans have been wrestling with that one for 60 years, and 60 more years from now they still will have not solved the riddle in any meaningful way for the rest of the world. Barring ecological and cultural collapse, historians will say that America suffered under the same sort of extraordinary delusion, a national hallucination of God and empire and exceptionalism. The thing about a hallucination—and take it from a person who has enjoyed many fine ones on various chemicals and herbs—is that it is a convincing reality in its time. Try talking to a fundamentalist about politics and God for an hour. You will see the spell that holds sway. Let us be thankful for pro sports, or we would have nothing whatsoever to talk about on those rare occasions when a fundamentalist and a liberal ever bother to speak to one another.

Allow me to get down to the nub of this and say what urban liberals cannot allow themselves to say out loud: "Christian majority or not, the readers of such apocalyptic books as the "Left Behind" series are some pretty damned dumb motherfuckers caught up in their own black, vindictive fantasy." There. I said it for you. Let us proceed.

Beyond that, there is a more mundane aspect of the success of the "Left Behind" books. It is fair to say that "Left Behind" readers are happy to discover a pop-lit phenomenon that they can participate in at all—popular literature that doesn't conflict with their insulated and armor plated worldview. At last they have something else to read besides *Guideposts* and *Reader's Digest*, both of which pass as highbrow lit in most fundamentalist households. Aw, come on. You know it is the truth, the same as I do. If you go into the homes of most fundamentalists, you will not find many books at all, much less books that contain real ideas. Now they have the "Left Behind" series, the huge sales of which, as they see it, validate their beliefs. I know I am painting with a mighty wide brush, but so what? It's by-and-large true. Considering that by no means do all fundamentalists believe in The Rapture, and that the whole Rapture thing is a cult within a larger cult, the popularity of the "Left Behind" series says something about the sheer scale of apocalyptic Christianity in the American heartland today. Do the readers believe the books? Again, I would say most do. Here are a couple of typical reader testimonials for the books:

> This series of books is the best I have ever read. I have looked long and hard to find a resource that put scripture into easy to read, and understand format. Many people I know get frustrated when they try to read scripture because they have trouble understanding the language. ... Now after reading these books I have a better understanding of where I stand at this moment.

> I started reading the Left Behind series in 2000 with the first book in paperback. ... I read it and was impressed with how well written it was and have read or own every book. In impact, it has gotten me closer to God than where I was before. ... I grew up in church, but was always afraid of what

was supposed to happen at the end times. I was afraid of the Book of Revelation, because the thought of all of the evil that had to be fought terrified me. While reading the Left Behind series, I followed along with my Bible, and I am so excited that I am understanding and learning more than I ever have. I am no longer afraid of the fight against evil, because I know that I am on the side of the greatest and most powerful force. Thank you for getting me started on this path of learning.

These people may not be your neighbors or friends, but they are ordinary and typical Americans. If you, the reader, are a college-educated middle-class person, then folks like those above outnumber you roughly three to one in this country. If that is not reason enough to drink, then I don't know what is. No matter what happens in the next election, we are going to be dealing for a long time to come with millions of voters who think that "Left Behind" is great literature, spiritual guidance, and a political primer all in one. Do we really think that cartload of bloated hacks called the Democratic Party knows what to do about this? Do you really think Howard Dean has a clue about how to deal with this entire class of Americans? And besides, as I've said, even if the Dems can get elected again and restored to the impotency they have come to represent, they will have needed these people's votes to get there. Or they simply will not get there. So let's not expect the Democratic political elite to save us from watching the fundie takeover attempts escalate in the future. (In which case, assuming my book makes some real dough, I will be watching from abroad, thank you.) Essentially, it comes down to the fact that a very large portion of Americans are crazier than shithouse rats and are being led by a gang of pathological misfits, most of whom are preachers and politicians. We are not talking about simple religious faith here. There is a world of difference between having religious faith and being a born-again zealot who believes in his heart that he is thumping Darwinian demons out of classrooms, and that Ted Kennedy is the anti-Christ. Trading down to the Democratic Party of the pussies really will not save us. It will just buy a little time. But we have whipped the hell out of this dead horse before, haven't we? Forgive me.

Meanwhile, we are left to contemplate communication with these folks, people whose leaders deliver unfathomable pronouncements such as the following one regarding family finances and the national economy from a Christian radio broadcast:

The mystery of the harlot of Jerusalem is solved, people! Praise the Lord! Deuteronomy 15:6 says plain as the nose on your face that "For the LORD thy God blesseth thee, as he promised thee: and thou shalt lend unto many nations, but thou shalt not borrow; and thou shalt reign over many nations, but they shall not reign over thee. Therefore, the harlot is NOT the gentile nations! The harlot controls and rules over the gentile nations, sitting on them." Rev 17:1. And there came one of the seven angels which had the seven vials, and talked with me, saying unto me, Come hither; I will shew unto thee the judgment of the great whore that sitteth upon many waters: Rev 17:15. And he saith unto me, The waters which thou sawest, where the whore sitteth, are peoples, and multitudes, and nations, and tongues. *Now is that not proof enough?*

Get that?
Me neither.
But what the hell. It makes sense to millions of voting

Americans. So do I hear a great big Amen out there?

Amen!

I get reminders of fundamentalism's dark magical thinking every day. And it is always the little unexpected ones that slap me hardest with the reality that these people are in the grip of their mass delusion 24 hours a day. A couple of weeks ago, I loaned my brother my old truck until he could get his engine rebuilt. A week later, he retuned it with much sincere thanks and a smile. On the vent window of my truck is a 4-inch decal, a silhouette of two square dancers. (My father-in-law, who gave me the truck, was a square dancer.) When I climbed into it the next day, I noticed that the square dancers were covered over both inside and outside the glass with two layers of duct tape. After all, we cannot be riding around in trucks with demonic emblems blasting out invisible rays of Satan's "Power of the air," can we?

8

Revenge of the Mutt People

[January 12, 2006]

"There are some things so disgusting that only a white man would be willing to do them."

—*Walter Wildshoe*, Coeur d'Alene Indian

Many years ago I worked at an industrial hog-farm owned by the Coeur d'Alene Indian tribe in northern Idaho. The place stank of the dead and rotting brood sows we chopped out of farrowing crates—bred to death in the drive for pork production. And it stank of the massive ponds that held millions of gallons of hog feces and rotting baby pigs, and every square inch was poisoned by the pesticides used to kill insects that hogs attract and the antibiotics fed to hogs from hundred-pound sacks. The Indians refused to suffer those kinds of conditions; they wouldn't even manage the place. They contracted it out. As my friend Walter Wildshoe said, "Only a white man would work there."

The hog farm, however, offered one company benefit. The white manager gave employees any young pigs that developed large tumors—those with tumors smaller than golf balls went to market with the rest of the hogs—or were born with deformities such as heads scrunched sideways with both eyes on the same side, or a leg that stuck out of the top of their body instead of the bottom. We employees would butcher and eat them. Among hog farm employees, all of whom were tough descendants of the Scots–Irish mutt people, free pork of any kind was prized, deformed with tumors or otherwise. You never saw a Swede eat the stuff.

So I took these pigs home and, using a huge old butcher's knife, slashed their throats in the woods, right in front of my two kids—aged two and four at the time—without flinching, even as the pigs screamed almost like humans and thrashed around, splashing thick dark glops of blood everywhere. It bothered me not one bit, just like it never bothered my daddy or granddaddy. Nor did it seem to bother my children as they watched, just like it didn't bother me as a child when my uncle handed me sacks of barn kittens to drown in the crick. And Walter would shake his head and say, "Only a white man would wrestle a hog with a butcher knife. An Indian would shoot the motherfucker with a gun."

My point here is that, by an early age, we rural and small-town mutt people seem to have a special capacity for cruelty—compared say, to damned-near every other imaginable group of Americans. For instance, as a child, did you ever put a firecracker up a toad's ass and light it? George Bush and I have that in common. Anyway, as all non-whites the round world understand, white people can be mean. Especially if they feel threatened—and they feel threatened about everything these days. But when you provide certain species of white mutt people with the right incentives, such as free pork or approval from God and government, you get things like lynchings, Fallujah, the Birmingham bombers, and Abu Ghraib.

Even as this is being written, we may safely assume that some of my tribe of mutt people are stifling the screams of captives in America's secret "black site" prisons across the planet. Or, on a more mundane scale of cruelty (according to CBS footage), kicking hundreds of chickens to death every day at the Pilgrim's Pride plant in Wardensville, West Virginia, just up the road from where I am writing this. Or consider the image of Matthew Shepard's body twisted on that Wyoming fence. All these are our handiwork. We, the mutt-faced sons and daughters of the republic. Born to kick your chicken breast-meat to death for you in the darkest, most dismal corners of our great land, born to kill and be killed in stock-car races, drunken domestic rows, and, of course, in the dusty back streets at the edges of the empire. Middle-class urban liberals may never claim us as brothers, much less as willing servants; but, as they say in prison, we are your meat. We do your bidding. Your refusal to admit that we do your dirty work for you, not to mention the international smackdowns and muggings for the republic—from which you benefit more materially than we ever will—makes it no less true.

Literally from birth, we get plenty of conditioning to kill those gooks and sand monkeys and whoever else needs killing at any particular moment in history, according to our leadership. Like most cracker kids in my generation, from the time I could walk I played games in which I pretended to be (practiced for) killing—Japs, Indians, Germans, Koreans, African Zulus (as seen in the movies *Zulu* and *Uhuru!*) variously playing the role of U.S. cavalry, Vikings a la Kirk Douglas, World War II GIs, colonial soldiers, and, of course, Confederate soldiers. As little white cracklets, we played with plastic army men that we tortured by flame, firecrackers, burning rivulets of gasoline, kerosene, or lighter fluid. And if atomic bombing was called for, M-80s and ash cans. We went to sleep dreaming of the screams of the evil brutes we had smitten that day, all those slant-eyed and swastikated enemies of democracy and our way of life. Later, as post-cracklets in high school, we rode around in cars looking to fight anyone who was different, the "other," be they black, brown, or simply from another school or county. As young men, we brawled at dances and parties, or simply while staring at one another bored and drunk. We bashed each other over women, less-than weight bags of dope, money owed, and alleged insults to honor, wife, mother, or model of car—Ford versus Chevy. In other words, all of white trash culture's noblest causes. With the "fighting tradition" of the Scots–Irish behind us, we smashed upon each other ceaselessly in trailer court and tavern, night and day in rain and summer heat until finally, we reached our mid-50s and lost our enthusiasm (not to mention stamina) for that most venerated of Borderer sports.

Said meanness is polished to a high-gloss murderous piety most useful to the military establishment. Thus, by the time we are of military age (which is about 12), we are capable of doing a Lynndie England on any type of human being unfamiliar to us from our culturally ignorant viewpoint—doing it to the "other." Sent to Iraq or Afghanistan, most of us, given the nod, can torture the other as mindlessly as a cat plays with a mouse. That we can do it so readily and without remorse is one of the darkest secrets underlying the "heroes" mythology that the culture machine is so fervently ginning up about the ongoing series of wars now just unfolding. And when one of us is killed by a rooftop sniper in Baghdad, we weep and sweat in our fear, band closer together as Border brothers in the ancient oath of ultimate fealty and courage. And we meant it and we do it.

About half of the Americans killed in Iraq come from communities like Winchester, Virginia; or Romney, West Virginia; or Fisher, Illinois; or Kilgore, Texas; or ... About 45 percent of the American dead in Iraq come from communities of less than 40,000, even though these towns make up only 25 percent of our population. These so-called volunteers are part of this nation's de facto draft—economic conscription—the carrot being politically preferable to the whip. The carrot does not have to be very big out here, where delivering frozen food wholesale to restaurants out of your own car entirely on commission is considered a good self-employment opportunity. I'm serious. One of my sons did it for a couple of months.

Once you grasp the implications of such an environment regarding the so-called American Dream, the U.S. Army at 13 hundred bucks a month, a signing bonus, and free room and board begin to look pretty good. Even a nice, long ass-kicking tour of the tropics killing brown guys becomes attractive. Especially compared to competing with other little brown guys at home, humping "big-roll sod" across ever-expanding MacMansionland. In the process, we mutt people learn worldly lessons that the post-graduate set raving about the jobless economy cannot know. For instance, we know firsthand that there is no way to beat little brown sod-balling guys willing to sleep in their cars and live on canned beans and store-brand soda. Better to go "volunteer" for the Army.

Along with the military come those big bucks for college later—up to $65,000, which, according to current wisdom, is more than enough to buy your way out of the beans-and-soda pop car camp at the edge of the new Toll Brothers development. Maybe some poor kids do go to college on their military benefits. But, personally speaking, I can count the number on one hand I know who ever did. Most of them were black. The rest seem to go to the local truck-driving school (rip-offs designed to collect government money) or the ITT "vocational career training," again designed to hoover up federal dough. Let's be honest here: graduating from the average American cracker high school here in the suburban heartland is not exactly the path to Harvard Yard. Your best educational option is probably the one you are looking at on the matchbook cover.

Now that education has been reduced to just another industry, a series of stratified job-training mills, ranging from the truck-driving schools to the state universities, our nation is no longer capable of creating a truly educated citizenry. Education is not supposed to be an industry. Its proper use is not to serve industries, either by cranking out feckless little mid-management robots or through industry-purchased research chasing after a better hard-on drug. Its proper use is to enable citizens to live responsible lives that create and enhance their democratic culture. This cannot be merely by generating and accumulating mountains of information or facts without cultural, artistic, philosophical, and human context or priority.

"No one should be forced to dive into an ocean of debt to learn how the world works, much less escape minimum wage hell. It should be enough just to want to know. Then too, look at our educational institutions. Academia, at least from this outsider's perspective, is an almost impenetrable veneer of elitist flatulence and toxic competition. Jesus, no wonder this country is in such sorry shape."
　—*Arvin Hill, Texas philosopher*

How in the hell did knowledge become so commoditized in America? Dumb question. After all, what do we expect from a nation of pickle vendors who will charge you for the air you breathe, and then make you beg for your change? At first blush, higher education and the working-class Scots–Irish mutt people seem to be oil and water. Maybe so. But the majority of them also have a snowball's chance in Florida of getting a higher education. Especially when it comes to the institutions of learning that constitute our elite springboard into careers in law and politics, business and science — the Yales and the Harvards and the Princetons.

For example, according to the *Wall Street Journal*, Asians constitute about 2 percent of the population, but make up over 20 percent of Harvard graduates. About one-third of Harvard graduates identify themselves as Jewish. Together, Jews and Asians make up about half of Harvard graduates. Subtract these, plus the 15 percent minority quota, and that leaves maybe 40 percent of openings for the 75 or 80 percent of white Americans who are not Jewish, Asian, Latino, or black, or whatever. Now throw in the skew of northeastern WASPs at elite universities, and we are left with maybe 20 percent of openings for 60 percent of white Americans. It presents a sorry damned picture of liberal East Coast WASPs and Jews and minorities getting all the prime educational gravy. The neo-con leadership is right when they tell working white Americans that the system has been stacked against them by an unseen hand, though they never mention that their own kids are among the silver spooners rowing around in the Ivy League gravy boat.

I know I'll get clobbered by Jewish and black critics for pointing this out. But liberal refusal to see white people as also being diverse, and seeing that some of them indeed need their own sort of affirmative action, is exactly the kind of thing that helped the neo-cons lead these working white people by the nose. Education is everything. You know it and I know it. And what the white working classes don't know because lack of education has hurt you and me and them.

So why in the hell don't we help this group of people into college and into the institutions that are elite springboards to careers in law and politics? Why not have affirmative action for Appalachian kids from the Ohio Basin or from the deep south, or anyplace else where tens of millions of kids grow up in houses containing not a single book, except possibly the Bible? Why don't we do these things? Part of the reason is that this stubborn, proud people does not whine, beg, or threaten its way to gain access to education, employment, or anything else. And part of it is because we unquestioningly accept a system that calls greed and self-interest drive, thus letting the prosperous professional and business classes pretend there is no disparity around them for which they might just be partially responsible, even as they pay the maid and the gardener who lack health insurance a pittance—or see that their mechanic's bill reads, "repare of fuul injection, $105." And because liberals have driven secularism into the ground and broken it off, and need to actually adhere to some religious values—real ones—even if we don't feel particularly inclined toward religion. (Psst! Everybody else in America *does* feel inclined toward it.)

So we will either see that Americans, religious or not, get educated equally so they won't be suckered by political and religious hucksters, or, if not, we must accept that uneducated people interpret politics in an uninformed and emotional manner, and accept the consequences. America can no longer withstand the political naiveté of this ignored white class.

Middle-class American liberals cannot have it both ways. It has come down to the simplest and most profound element of democracy: Fairness. Someday middle-class American liberals will have to cop to fraternity and justice and the fact that we are our brother's keeper, whether we like it or not. They're going to have to sit down and actually speak to these people they consider ugly, overweight, ill educated, and in poor taste. At some point down the road, all the Montessori schools and Ivy League degrees in the world are not going to save your children and grandchildren from what our intellectual peasantry, whether born of neglect or purposefully maintained, is capable of supporting politically. We've all seen the gritty black-and-white newsreels from the 1930s.

As a member of this peasantry, I quit school at the age of sixteen in the eleventh grade to join the U.S. Navy. I hated school, hated the class differences in a small town that make life so miserable during adolescence, when one's community and social status is being nailed down permanently for anyone planning on staying here. As a former young white cracklet, I can say with all confidence that when you live with a rusty coal stove in the middle of the living room for heat, your old man smells of gasoline and motor oil no matter how much he bathes, and your mom suffers from strange, unpredictable behavior due to untreated depression, you do not much feel like inviting the doctor's daughter home. Or anyone's daughter for that matter. Doctor's son—college, career, golf, nice car, and a bimbo. Redneck laborer's son—well, if you stay out of trouble, there's always room for one more broad-shouldered chinless pinhead stamping out bright-yellow plastic mop buckets on the injection molds at Rubbermaid.

Thus, at 16 and choosing options, I decided that launching fighter jets from the deck of an aircraft carrier to kill gooks, and the notion of pussy and booze on some exotic foreign shore, looked damned good. When I think about what happened to my boyhood friends who stayed home and put in 30 years at Rubbermaid, my choice doesn't sound that bad, even today. They all became redneck ultra-conservatives, mostly out of some sort of fear and bitterness that I can never seem to put my finger on. But I knew these people in a younger and more hopeful time. I know they were capable of—not to mention deserved—more than they got out of life. Maybe their bitterness stems from that.

Meanwhile, their kids do the same as they did. Go uneducated. Sometimes I walk the street on which I grew up. And when I look around, I see the same kinds of kids as ever. They are all fatter, but they are the same cigarette-smoking, know-nothing white punks that I was, the tough sons and daughters of the unwashed. In my old neighborhood, where over one-quarter of adults do not have a high school diploma, there are lots of yellow ribbons in the windows, Marine Corps and Army parents' icons on the porches and scrubby lawns—evidence enough that you do not need an education to contribute something of value to the far-flung perimeter of our expanding empire of blood and commerce. Pure meanness is highly valued in Caesar's legions. Lots of Americans don't seem to mind having a pack of young American pit bulls savage some flyblown desert nation, or running loose in the White House, for that matter, as long as they are our pit bulls protecting Wall Street and the 401(k)s of the upper middle class.

The problem is this: Pit bulls always escalate the fight, and keep at it until the last dog is dead, leaving the gentler breeds to clean up the blood spilled. We mutt people, the pit bulls, have always been your own, whether you claim us or not. And until you accept that you are your brother's keeper, and help deliver us from ignorance, you will continue to have on your hands some of every drop of blood spilled—from the sands of Iraq to the streets of East L.A. All the socially responsible stock portfolios, little hybrid cars, and post-modernist deconstruction in the world will not wash it off.

-9-

Madmen and Sedatives

[September 11, 2006]

Nobody talks about it out loud, but a few million Americans are seriously doubting their sanity these days. Or having their sanity doubted. Or both. They seldom speak their minds because what is going on in there is a vision of society that conjures grave doubt, if not outright horror. It is the kind of stuff that will get your ass kicked off the island in a heartbeat. Nobody wants to hear it.

Yesterday I was gridlocked with my wife in traffic near the new mall, surrounded by cars full of monsters. Every redneck face and bloated or coifed middle-class head in every vehicle was a grotesque, awful thing. In them you could see the meanest kind of white-man ignorance or smug middle-class obliviousness, the kind that could care less if all the babies in Iraq were fried on spits in the Green Zone of Baghdad, so long as their nails get done on Saturdays. (Ah, you've seen the monsters too, haven't you!) There was that fleshy, overweight killer ugliness America seems to produce these day, the faces of a happy motoring people whose armies hold the world at gunpoint so they can stuff down pizza and check out this town's newest mall. Underneath the ugliness, there's a festering mean streak caused by the frustration of knowing deep-down that government and commerce are corrupt—everybody knows this, but tolerates it for fear of losing their bling. The choice was ever thus (de Tocqueville noted its beginnings), but now it has become a waking nightmare. One that brings up rage for some of us—rage that, if expressed in the wrong places and too often, will get me thrown into the psych ward if I tarry too much longer here in the land of the free.

"Looky there," I told my wife, who was driving, "A fucking car wash, right over the spot where Nancy Hanks Lincoln's mother was born! I remember when it was in a cornfield. And all these zombies who don't give a crap about the bloody sand and sweatshops they create, just so they can buy a cheap skirt, and drive cars worth 10 years of wages in most of the world through a goddamned car wash! If every American died tomorrow, it is unarguable that the planet would be way more sustainable for not having to feed their greed!" On the inside I was bawling and screaming at the same time. I go off on these tirades increasingly these days. It is not good.

I could see by my wife's face that she was wondering if "getting Joe some help" was in order. Oh yes, getting some help—which, in America, means calling the authorities, in this case the psychiatric medical ones. Advanced technology and the skills of the medical cadre of the super-state offer its citizens wondrous ways to reach out to those in need of help. But it always comes down to prescribing drugs or possibly of even being locked up "for your own good," until your ideations are more "normal."

And so it is that many of us keep the rage inside as best we can, unwilling to destroy a job or a marriage. And there are many of us, judging from the emails I receive from readers—men and women alike, mostly over 40 with lots at stake—who fear being judged unstable by the well-intentioned folks around us who never in their wildest thoughts would consider themselves good Germans. At any rate, who wants to be seen as unbalanced at the very moment in our lives when we unexpectedly find ourselves seeing Americans and America as they really are (and may have always been) for the first time? Not that it required insight. The sheer scale and pervasiveness of our national condition, plus decades of exposure, made it so damned obvious we could no longer escape it.

Regardless, inside me it gives rise to an alter ego I call THE SCREAMING MAN, who, luckily for me, only screams inside my head. I've come to learn lately that plenty of other Americans have their own SCREAMING MAN, and even see the same monsters I see in the traffic. (A big thank you to the *L.A. Times* reporter who was the first to tell me he saw the same creatures). The thought that so much of my readership is composed of such folks is worrisome at times.

Once the monsters in the traffic reveal themselves, life can never be the same. We are left to go about doing all the ordinary things we always did, but with building, inexpressible moral outrage, living out our lives as rote actors in a theater of iron. Inside the iron theatre—a place surrounded by high walls of normalcy, where to discover a window to the outside is considered madness—the majority have apparently learned their scripts too well. So we are left sitting in traffic jams to fester on our evil situation.

The great evils, both past and present—the American genocide against the red Indian, My Lai, and the uncounted others like it; Chairman Mao's purges; the Israeli war crimes against the Palestinians; the Muslim slaughter in Darfur,

Bosnia; and, most notably, the Holocaust—were not carried out by sociopaths, but by ordinary people who believed in their states, their leaders, and their gods. The machinist who made instruments for Nazi Germany felt no guilt. Nor does the anonymous mailroom employee in the Department of Homeland Security. I make a living by editing military-history magazines, thereby providing "pompous reaffirmations of a great past amid present mediocrity and immediate disorder," as Marguerite Yourcenar put it. And right next door to my workplace, Pakistani and Croatian programmers design death-dealing aircraft circuitry for Curtis Wright, yet inside our florescent lit, air-conditioned reality, there is not an ounce of guilt, much less a sense of accountability. Our work feels unquestionably ordinary, just as does the work of the traffic monsters, most of who work in Washington, D.C., or the beltway around it.

Sheesh!

How did we become so numb to the greatest moral issues of our time? Our time? Probably in human history, considering the irrevocable destruction of our ecosystem. Especially considering that 40 years ago they seemed to dominate the national arena ... the Vietnam War, civil rights ... A hell of a lot of wrong choices built the 200-year-long road to where we now find ourselves, and I must admit that my generation did its share of the paving, laying down much of the roadbed during the Sixties. Despite much talk since then about the Sixties' fight for moral justice—talk still easily launched by the pop of a chardonnay cork or the appearance of The Grateful Dead at the local arena—my generation, nearly to a man or woman, regardless of affluence, has traded principles for simple materialism. Assuming of course, that they had any identifiable principles, which most didn't.

Perhaps it was only part of this country's ongoing struggle to accept successive waves of immigration, but the Sixties saw a push toward openness, toward diverse viewpoints and values. There has always been great pressure on our social and public institutions to be capable of accepting the diversity thronging at its doors, a pressure yielded to only when it looks like things are about to blow sky high: "OK, niggers, you can ride in the front of the bus. Pssst! Jeeter, get out the fire hoses and turn the dogs loose." No institution is more pressed than the educational system—"Aw, now the Mexicans want bilingual education!"—which has been handed the responsibility of building character by parents, and charged by the state with creating obedient, functional citizens who can multiply at least to the sixth power, are willing to file income-tax forms, and at least pretend they don't smoke pot. We are talking about bare-minimum standards here, although lately the multiplication standard has been dropped in favor of a willingness to be subjected to surveillance and mass body-cavity searches at football games. In a nation where real education remains under suspicion by both the devoutly religious right and the all-but-antireligious left, it was natural that school administrators and four million-or-so college-graduate state teachers—themselves products of the mediocrity characterizing our common-denominator approach to democracy and education—would arrive at the "morality is all a matter of opinion" solution. It was the only way out. And, besides, from their standpoint, it looked true.

(Hissss ... crackle ... can this truly be a signal through my fillings?)

AW, SHUT THE FUCK UP, BAGEANT! NO MORAL ISSUE EVER GOT "EXPLORED" IN THIS COUNTRY. NEVER! THEY JUST GET EXPRESSED IN LOATHESOME SHORTHAND AT DISGUSTING LENGTH BETWEEN

G.O.P. CRETINS WHO, IN THEIR HALF-WITTED SELF-DELUSIONS BELIEVE THAT RONALD REAGAN SHOOK HIS FIST AT THE BERLIN WALL AND ENDED THE COLD WAR ... AND FAGGOT DEMOCRATS, A MISERABLE LOT NOW FORCED TO PRETEND THEIR VOTES WILL EVER BE COUNTED AGAIN!

Godammit, I was trying to establish rational discourse here. Now where was I? Oh, yes. The erosion of moral principles ...

So now we find principles treated as mere opinion by most young people and their parents—call it diversity tolerance-overshoot—and any answers posed to the great questions of our age neatly written off. Global warming? Just some scientists' opinion. The unjustness of our wars? More opinion. Inequity in society? In whose opinion? Wastefulness of our lifestyle? A matter of opinion.

Over the course of two generations of this, a predictable thing happened. Because the first generation avoided the questions, the second one never learned that they could be asked. The atmosphere could not be riper for pure, triumphant consumer capitalism and its inherent militarism. (Somebody has to clear the way for Wal-Mart democracy.) If there are no overarching public moral or intellectual questions, then the only remaining questions are material ones: Which is best? The iPod or the RCA Lycra Micro Jukebox? Headphones, cell phones, and polyphonic ring tones, everyone is plugged into the white noise of pure commerce. It's the new "Turn on, tune in, and drop out." I liked the old version better. Used appropriately, LSD posed the great questions. And sometimes highlighted a few answers, too.

But it doesn't take a psychedelic experience to pursue the kind of truth inherent to fleshly human existence, the kind that seeks justice from within our bones. In fact, it takes effort to avoid it. I've never seen a culture or human being that did not have an inherent sense of justice, an innate desire for balance. Most consider this to be the spiritual side of man, if they consider it at all. Many do not. A huge portion of the world is commodity addicted, while another portion is simply looking for a warm, dry spot in which to shit or lay down and die. There is not much room for contemplation of the finer points of existence in either instance. Whatever the case, the American lack of even minimal spiritual observance inducted us into the Empire's cast of featureless players inside the Iron Theater. Nobody needs answers to meaningful questions that are never asked, or dare not be asked.

Some days, however, change does seem to be afoot, as it certainly must be, given that change is the world's only constant. A majority of Americans now disapprove of the war in Iraq. Just three years ago, when I started writing from this town's taverns and churches, working people therein absolutely loved George Bush. Now they have returned to their normal state of political apathy, seldom speaking of Bush, but with one difference—they no longer approve of his war, and express disapproval generally in the form of grumbling. They grumble because television has given them permission to do so, through its constant touting of polling results expressing "dissatisfaction" with the war. Being "dissatisfied" with something, a war in this case, is more in accordance with their programming as consumers, not citizens. They will never get permission to be really pissed off, much less pissed off enough to burn anything down.

Television polls never specifically count the outraged and the heartbroken, thus reducing our deepest emotions, once more, to mere opinion in another opinion poll. Outrage is impermissible, except for the pretend outrage of talking heads in televised panel debates, which has entertainment value, thus profitability. Which is why the majority of Americans know little about Cindy Sheehan. Sorry to say that here, in lefty blogdom, but it's true. Cindy Sheehan has never been on Oprah.

When and if Sheehan ever is on Oprah, we will know we have won regarding the war in Iraq. We will have won if your standard for victory is acknowledgment by the high priestess of emotional vapidity, and Barnes and Noble sales, talked to by a woman who uses her child rape as a credential. In her particular celebrity delusion, she considers herself the emotional caretaker of the nation, the Martha Stewart of the soul. Lusting for proximity of your cause to celebrity may be a gratifying short-term antidote, but lusting for universal justice is the ultimate cure.

But even assuming that getting within four feet of Oprah Winfrey constitutes victory, we will have won far too late for the already-dead on both sides. Vietnam proved that the Empire's wars are easier to stop than the overall trajectory of national hubris and folly. Winning is stopping wars before they start, or creating a society wherein war is the last resort, not a casual preemptive option. As for the growing rejection of the war, copping to the obvious in the face of defeat and then claiming the moral high ground after we have scorched it and everyone on it—well, that's no victory at all.

Which leaves me here to fester on celebrity and moral victory under the looming possibility of forced medication by the state. Hmmmm …

Where the hell are you, Aldous Huxley?

So are they gonna medicate me and you, or what? Surely I must have some time left before that happens. And if they don't, then I'll have to do it myself anyway. You cannot win in the Iron Theater. What its producers and directors want to happen is destined to happen. They are always in control.

And when it comes to control, you can't beat the good ole U.S. pharmaceutical industry, which has clearly met the challenge of adult rage and despair, and is now doping down the kids before they even hit puberty. Over the past six years, mental-health drugs prescribed to children have jumped 550 percent. Recently, the NFC (New Freedom Commission on Mental Health) recommended mandatory mental-health screening for 100 percent of America's school children, and drug treatment for all children "judged to be in need of drugs." Hell, every kid in the whole damned country needs drugs, if only to face their future in the global gulag being constructed for them.

Godammit, Huxley, you saw it coming, didn't you? But I don't think it will be nearly as much fun as your grim vision. You held out the possibility of science perfecting bread and circuses—Soma. Now *that* was an idea, bud! Three brands of pharmacological reality: Technicolor Soma, a pleasant hallucinogen; Soma medium, a Valium-like tranquilizer; and El Crusho black gold, the heavy sleeping pill. And for the rugged, freedom-loving individualist, you offered those tropical islands offshore. There was really nothing coercive about it all. If the corpocracy had listened to you, Hux, about how to do oppression the right way, I'd be curled up in the lap of Halliburton right now, gurgling happily. I have nothing against state-controlled euphoria if they don't skimp on the euphies. By the way, Hux, can I do the Technicolor on the Island? Or will I be kicked off that one, too?

Anyway, we seem to be truly dicked now. Man the machine-making monkey is so proud of the machines he has created that he now pushes toward the machining of human nature itself. Why not? It was always so damned unpredictable. So, yes, dammit, let's do'er! Let the scientific and economic machinery we have created remake us in its own likeness. Let there be technology without wisdom, and efficiency without human benefit. Let there be one blissful nation of highly medicated sleepwalkers in a scientific hell that, if you get doped up enough, feels like paradise.

So what about that rage, huh? My own personal experiences tell me that, being part of human nature, it's also unpredictable stuff. Tonight I went to a dinner party given by a freedom-hearted couple, the female half of which is probably the most intellectually courageous woman in town. I can't know that with certainty, because even the most liberal people in this Southern burgh would never dare to invite me to dinner. Word has gotten around.

Two hours into the dinner party, I did a bad thing. I called a nice-enough but gutless, apolitical guest "one more ignorant, motherfucking American wanting respect for his self-imposed blindness," adding that, "Everything is not just an opinion, you know." My good wife stood horrified. (Yes, there was alcohol involved.) Now, I know I am not the judge of that man's days, and that he has the right to his opinion or non-opinion. But some days I cannot summon up even the dinner-party pretense of respect for American denial, and this was one of those days.

By way of rationalization, I tell myself that if Diogenes of Sinope could live under a tub and take shots at the entire Greek world, then I am entitled to a snootful and an occasional outburst, despite the disparity between my talents and the long dead old Greek's. It's either that, or the deer rifle and water tower solution. Or the cheap online polemics you are now suffering. All of which is more bullshit, but it is the best I can do at the moment to rationalize bad behavior.

It is 11.00 p.m., after the dinner party, and I sit in this muggy summer darkness on a bench in front of the Stonewall Jackson Headquarters Museum, located right behind my house.

Stonewall Jackson sat on his horse and sucked on lemons while he calmly managed the slaughter of thousands. I should probably take up lemons instead of gin. But at least I am guilty of mere stupidity, not slaughter. Tomorrow I will repent. Maybe. Depends upon whether anyone with legal authority finally decides I need help. Meanwhile, any kind of resistance, even the stupidest sort waged against fools, gives relief on a hot night inside the Iron Theater.

This anger will all come out in the morning as prose. Most likely, bad prose. (It did, and you are reading it now.) But at least it will be out. Hell, there is only the world at stake.

This essay is for Al Aronowitz, "The Blacklisted Journalist" (1928– 2005), a friend and mentor in art.

-10-

Somewhere a Banker Smiles

[December 6, 2006]

It's hard as hell to keep conspiracy theories out of one's mind these days. And I'm not talking about "Who really brought down the Twin Towers? or the "Are Zionists behind the Iraq War?" kind of stuff. The booger stalking my ragged old mind these days puts both of those in the shade. And it runs like this:

Is the consumerist totalization of this country and the world really a conscious plot by a handful of powerful corporate and financial masters? If we answer "yes," we find ourselves trundled off toward the babbling ranks of the paranoid. Still, though, it's easy enough to name those who would piss themselves with joy over the prospect of a One World corporate state, with billions of people begging to work for their 1,500 calories a day and an xBox chip in their necks. It's too bad our news media quit hunting with live ammo decades ago, leaving us with no one to track the activities and progress of what sure-as-hell seem to be global elites, judging from the financial spoor we find along every pathway of modern life.

In our saner moments, we can also see that it does not take dark super-centralized plotting to pull off what appears to have been accomplished. Even without working in overt concert, a few thousand dedicated individual corporate and financial interests can constitute a unified pathogenic whole, much the same as individual cells create a viable dominant colony of malignant organisms—malignant simply by their anti-human, anti-societal nature. We don't see GM, Halliburton, Burger King, and CitiBank lobbying the state for universal health or clean rivers, do we? But mention unions or living wages, and the financial colony within our national Petri dish shape-shifts into a Gila monster, squirts venom on the idea, and shits money all over Capitol Hill. I looked at all this as coincidence for years until the proposition finally strained credulity so much that I threw in the towel and said, "Fuck it. There is only so much coincidence to go around in this world."

Put another way, the global decision-makers, international planners, financial institutions, political parties, media conglomerates, corporations, and banks form a hegemonic, accumulative bloc working in concert to coordinate the extraction of wealth from first and third world alike. A series of privately held international institutions to which and from which money can be moved to leverage nations and populations according to their needs is probably gonna do just that because they can. National territory doesn't mean shit to such people, and those who govern said territory mean even less, except to the extent they can obstruct or incite resistance. People like Castro and Chavez. But even they are just the thorn in the lion's paw.

Consider this: The war in Iraq has been immensely profitable for the people who make weapons and for the contractors who supposedly rebuild what the weapons destroy. They profit in either case. And the longer the war goes on, the more they will make.

Meanwhile, the money for both is obtained through extraction practiced upon the world's laboring poor. But the big money, the "juice," as street people used to say, comes from squeezing the orange of American society for more work, more production, and more tax money. Some of us older oranges are feeling pretty wrung out these days, and are getting hard as hell to get along with. Yet the squeeze doesn't seem to bother most Americans at all. The pressure has been so great and so constant that no one any longer feels it. It has become so pervasive as to be incomprehensible to ordinary people. For example, seventy cents of every income-tax dollar goes to pay for past, present, and future wars. Education gets two cents. As Michael Parenti has pointed out, the cost of military-aircraft parts and ammunition kept in storage by the Pentagon is greater than the combined federal spending on pollution control, conservation, community development, housing, occupational safety, and mass transportation. And the U.S. Navy spends more money on its never-ending development of a submarine rescue vehicle than is spent for public libraries, occupational safety, and daycare centers combined.

Collectively, these financial super-elites, who either do or do not exist, must be at least somewhat aware that they are managing the world. Otherwise, why would we have Davos conferences and such—global financial conferences where the likes of Bill Clinton and Al Gore and John Kerry are merely the entertainment, mere proof of the attendants' prestige? Can it be true that the world's real players practically yawned at Alan Greenspan's cryptic little speeches while waiting for the backstage action with the real movers and shakers from Goldman, Citibank, and others, none of whom we have ever heard of but nevertheless are said to account for the drop in gas prices in the U.S. just prior to the 2006 mid-term elections? Word has it that they changed the index last July so oil-futures holders would be forced to dump in October and November, creating a mild glut during the elections. If that is true, we can probably thank them for the Dow reaching 12,000 last month, too.

Meanwhile, back in Camp Davos, the lustful, pathologically approval-seeking, bright, student teddy bear from Hope, Arkansas entertains the new global elites. And everyone has Beluga caviar and chopped hardboiled quail eggs afterward, even as more than one billion people live on less than one dollar a day. "And have you tried the unborn calf veal poached in Peruvian sheep's milk at the Swiss bank suite? It's to die for!" Nobody is remotely worried about blowback from that billion people eating moldy cassava or rat-urine polluted rice, because poverty, well, poverty is not threat, is it? Just a source of cheaper labor. "Now, about the oil crude taps and NYMEX ..."

Personally, I've decided they are real and that they constitute an unseen class, and that they are mid-stage in becoming the most powerful class the earth has ever seen. One that American politicians not only refuse to publicly acknowledge, but, when pressed, flatly swear does not exist. Show me the Republican or Democratic leader who says, "Politics is economics by other means, and our own Federal Reserve Bank is a privately held institution, not a governmental one, and is an interlocking part of the global financial network which owes allegiance to no country or ordinary citizens, regardless of nationality." Or, "My corporate campaign contributions come from people whose every action is directed at extracting two things from you, my dear voter: Your money and the cheapest possible labor you can be driven to provide. The absolute cheapest possible payment to you for the hours of your life consumed by work, which, depending upon the degree of your delusion, is called either a job or an exciting career."

No American politician is going to admit that. You must go to Venezuela or the smoldering dumps of Manila or the fields of Chiapas to hear that sort of truth.

Admittedly, there is at least some reason for fear among these elites. The U.S. economy, the real, material economy, is dreadfully weak, having been so gutted by parasitic speculation. The only source of strength left here is the military, which is currently at play in an effort to gain control over the world's energy-supply, and make damned-sure no one gets any funny ideas about using anything but dollars in trading oil. But the real players say, "Well, then, let the Americans keep it if they can! If the U.S. loses, someone else wins. No matter. We can leverage our position from any emerging market point on the globe. And doesn't China look like a real comer, old boy! History is long. The Chinese understand that." Thus we find the Chinese creating joint American holding companies to buy up commercial U.S. real estate at bottom dollar after the crash. At some future point, it could neatly offset their current loans to the U.S. for more consumption of Chinese goods. And if the Americans get too pissy, the Chinese can always turn off the money spigot.

On the other hand, this monstrous class of parasites has not yet won over the entire world. America seems to be their only complete victory, and that one will hold only as long as superheated consumption can be sustained. They have only been at it for maybe 40 years, and are still pouring the foundation for the global gulag, setting the rules as they go.

And they are hitting at least a few speed bumps: "Why is Castro still stinking up the joint, fer godzsake? And now we've got that friggin Mexi-nigger dwarf, Evo Morales, in his goddamned stinky little dime-store sweater, strutting around like he was president or something. And why inna hell hasn't somebody smoked these bastards? Doesn't the CIA do anything for their paychecks anymore?"

Probably not. Last we heard, the CIA was sidelined, sent to the benches until they come up with those goddamned weapons of mass destruction.

Meanwhile, a Chinese economist calculates the U.S. trade deficit, a Swiss bank exec orders another bottle of wine, and a Shia youth receives instruction in how to blow up an oil pipeline.

Only the Chinaman and the bank exec are smiling.

11

Escape from America

[February 12, 2007]

Hopkins Village, Belize

It is near midnight, and Rex and Pluto, the dogs sleeping in the sand under my cabana, emit happy, gurgling growls, as if chasing imaginary rabbits in their dreams. I lie in bed just breathing in and breathing out, and feeling so free that I've laughed out loud a couple of times tonight—something I have never done in my life. At least not while simply looking at the ceiling. Tomorrow I will not worry about losing my ass in the declining real-estate market. I will not commute three nerve-grinding hours a day, or nervously engorge myself in front of my laptop for hours on end. Nor will I wake up with the crimes of the Empire running like adding-machine tape in my head, annotated with all the ways I contributed to those crimes by participating in the American lifestyle. After more than two years of effort, I'm outta the gilded gulag, by damned, and tell myself that I have at last quit being part of the problem—or at least as much as much as anyone can without living stark naked in a Himalayan cave and toasting insects over a dung fire.

When I arrived in Belize a few weeks ago, I vowed never to write about this country, mainly because the Americans I write to are more interested in American politics, religion, class issues, and the Iraq war. How the hell could anybody with more than an inch of forehead not be anxious over those things? But the contrast here is so stark it seems unavoidable to write about the view of America from Belize and Hopkins Village this one time. I must say that from down here the Empire does not look much different. No worse, no better. But the stress and stench of the Empire is less in this Caribbean breeze, and the mark of the beast is sharper from a distance.

The effect of moving was immediate. As one expat told me years ago about what would happen, whole days go by when I do not think of America at all, much less rage against it—something I would previously have considered impossible. But when you do, you do so more calmly and lose no sleep over the criminals presently running the enterprise up there. Occasionally, the thought occurs that a peaceful mind could kill my pitiful little career as a pissed-off lefty writer. Then I look around Hopkins Village at these eminently sane, if poor, Garibano (or Garifuna, a mixture of Carib Indian and African) people and think, "So what? Everything is a goddamned identity in America, writing included." Identity is a racket in a nation of media-controlled clones. And besides, who wants to be a one-trick pony in the consumer zombie parade? In the end, though, leaving was absolutely a matter of saving my sanity. It came down to either becoming one of those bugfuck crazies ranting on the faaaaar left end of the Internet, or busting out of America to find something resembling balance near the end of a life marked by anxious imbalance and contradiction. The personal freedom to do that clearly lay elsewhere and, after some scouting, I decided on Hopkins Village, Belize. It simply felt more free. More real.

In places like Hopkins Village you can still send your kid to the store to bring back cigarettes. Now the politically correct set up there in the States may be blowing soy milk out their noses at the thought, but it represents a degree of freedom from government control. And besides, it is not America's business how the black Garinago people of Belize run their lives. In Belize it is not against the law to drink and drive, and there are no speed limits. Here in Hopkins you can build your house without a permit or inspections, sell real estate without a license, drink liquor openly while you happily burn trash in your front yard. You can peddle homemade darasa—grated, spiced banana wrapped and cooked in banana-leaf wrappers—or barbeque pork to the neighbors from your front porch with no interference from health inspectors.

Most of this non-interference is simply because it is not in the national character. And part of this non-interference is due to a lack of expensive regulatory infrastructure. Faced with choosing between running schools for children down in the wilds of the Toledo district, or busting Aunt Lula for peddling pig's tails stewed in red beans on the street corner, the government gives Aunt Lula a pass. It's a loose place, a libertarian's wet dream.

In a hardscrabble, make-do country where everything is scarce, especially motor vehicles, looseness is a good thing. Hitchhiking ("riding thumb") is considered a respectable way to get around the country, and most folks will stop for you. Most people do not own cars, but there are taxis in the larger communities, and buses to and from about anywhere. Otherwise, it's you and your trusty bicycle. If you've never brought home a load of eight-by-four foot sheet-metal roofing in a taxi, or a ten-foot two-by-four on a bicycle, you haven't lived. In our village of 1,300 there are only about ten motor vehicles. There are days when I wish we had a tad more transportation infrastructure around here.

Yet, thanks to the dearth of material infrastructure, I fulfilled some ecological goals almost by accident. I use only three or four gallons of water per day, plus another five gallons on washday for a total of about 26 to 30 gallons a week. The average American household must use hundreds of gallons per person, when you figure in laundry, lawns, car washes, etc. But this is possible for me because the sanitary maintenance of daily life is so much simpler. Two sets of shorts, one pair of khakis, and a white shirt—which passes for dressed-up around here—four T-shirts and my old fishing vest do not require much wash water. The cold-water showers here (bear in mind that the water temperature is in the mid-70s most of the year; in the mid-90s if you have a water tank standing in the sun) run very lightly and use only a gallon or two on those occasions when we do not bathe in the sea after sunset. When it comes to petroleum, I'd guess that my transportation needs, a 37-mile bus ride to Dangriga every week or so, do not even add up to a gallon, judging from the U.S.$2.50 bus fare in a country where petrol runs over six U.S. dollars a gallon. Of course, no one would advocate that Americans adopt Third World methods, but there is such a thing as too much transportation infrastructure—especially if it is unsustainable, high maintenance, and mainly dedicated to buying fried chicken and bad tacos.

In the States, I long ago quit watching television "news." But down here in my scruffy little corner of the free world, I watch Al Jazeera every night after the evening toke and cup of the local bitters. I am here to tell you, dear hearts, that Al Jazeera is what PBS ought to be. Especially its new documentary channel. Al Jazeera, or AJ as they say, presents the world and the primary issues of class, the high and the powerful, and the haves and the have-nots, straight up, pretty much leaving you to form your own opinions. At the same time, when it comes to documentaries, AJ warns viewers that they will be seeing documentaries made with a point of view, documentaries that are not afraid of showing passion or compassion. I just about fell off the barstool when it ran a documentary about how the low-salt diet scam plays into the hands of Big Pharma as a symbiotic rip-off, and why no other country in the world falls for it except the U.S. and its lapdog, the U.K. It's been so much fun I found myself craving a bag of Doritos and wishing I could order a pizza.

Last night I watched a homemade Argentine documentary on the Canary Island boat-people. But rather than presenting the misery porn so common in American documentaries ("Ain't them starving little black children pitiful, Henry? They got no legs. Something about landmines or whatever."), the amateur producer delved into the boat-people's families back in Mali and the destruction of their small-scale sugar industry by global corporatism. AJ's documentaries may vary in quality, but you've got to love a channel where producer Danny Schecter is a star and Howard Zinn is considered a wise elder. Tonight he is taking calls, most of them deeply intelligent, from all over the planet regarding America's current condition. He looks very worn and tired, and speaks the truth in full context. And I won't even go into the, uh, attributes, of the Al Jazeera's weather babe. PBS was never like this.

There are rumors that Al Jazeera may yet come to American television. Hard to imagine, but let's hope so. It may not even be possible to hold the jack rabbit attention spans of most

Americans with full-context news, or full-context anything, for that matter. Yet I'd be willing to bet that if more Americans were exposed to AJ's world coverage, especially the second and third worlds, people would respond. Not a majority of Americans, mind you, because most of us are too poorly read and uneducated to care. Even so, we're not completely heartless—just kept blind and ignorant through the media's relentless strip-mining of our culture.

When you are among the Garibano, a people whose culture is relatively intact, the American marketplace's stripping of culture and its commoditization of human experience is glaring. Even more so for the fact that it goes unnoticed by our citizens. Try to rally Americans against corporations and all you get is a blank, flat response. Their entire lives have been spent watching smiley-face media presentations of giant corporations. They constitute our entire cultural landscape, and average Americans cannot imagine the corporations that provide them with goods, services, and jobs as being bad in any way. With particular thanks to television and the capitalist state's ethos, corporations are now seamlessly interwoven into our deepest identities, both personal and national. Consequently, while I was watching Howard Zinn, back in the States the National Geographic Channel was running television specials on the Harley Davidson factory and the Peterbilt truck plant, narrated in patriotic tones very much resembling the old Soviet Russian domestic propaganda and Chinese "people's films." In the U.S. television industry, these shows are categorized as "educational," though their purpose is the same as the Reich's 1930s productions—to attach the people's identity to the "ingenuity and raw power" of the American fatherland, to create pride in the accomplishments of the corporate state and, ultimately, to perceive consumption as triumphal.

Having been down here several times over the decades, I've learned that, after a while, no matter how fond you are of Belize and its people, you get the occasional urge to get smashed with one of your own American kind. And though I am naturally attracted to political refugees like myself, there really aren't that many here for political reasons. In fact, there aren't as many American expats in Belize as one would think, given the state of things up there. When you meet a "white fella," it's likely to be a Pentecostal or Jehovah's Witness sporting a long-sleeved shirt and bad necktie, and sweating like a pig in rut. The largest concentration of expats—mostly grumble-and-fart know-it-all retirees and wry old drunks looking for the cheapest place to drink up their pensions, God bless them—seems to be up north in Corozal, where they can easily get to the Wal-Mart store just across the Mexican border.

But those expats you do meet in the less-traveled parts of Belize, both from America and elsewhere are, often as not, humdingers. You get a retired California pot grower; old libertarian Alaskan "pipeliners"; IRS fugitives; German anarchist–lesbian couples running jungle B&Bs; child-support skippers; and senior citizens completely worn out from their tour of duty in the U.S. labor camp and no longer willing to fuck with the bureaucracy that was supposed to take care of them. In short, just about everybody America no longer wants these days.

Some got wise long ago, like Warren, a rawboned and grizzled ex-hippie who runs a small sawmill in the community of Silk Grass Village. He settled here in the early Seventies, married a Mayan/Hispanic lady, and began to build his mill. Before coming here to the Stann Creek district of Belize, he walked the entire coast of India. It took him years. What was walking the Indian coast like? "Weird," he answers. This morning, after delivering a load of lumber, Warren sat on the car seat that passes for lawn furniture in our yard and, with the sun glistening on his unshaven jaw, told me about his plans to move deeper inland, back to his farmstead in the Maya Mountains, where he tends a few acres of orange trees on weekends. His eyes grew distant, then he said, "Time was when you could get a good start here on pure grit, settle in with a machete, an axe, a rifle, a tent, some garden seed, and build a family and a life. A business even." I have no doubt he's done that, just as some Indians in the deep jungle southward still do. Warren continued, "The kids are grown and they run the sawmill. I just want to take my horses and go up where it's quiet. No bustle." Bustle? If Silk Grass has 500 dwellers beneath its thatched and tin rooftops out there in the savannah, I'd be damned surprised. Anyway, it somehow seems doubtful America could produce such an iconic figure of self-sufficiency these days.

Then there is Cosmo. Coz is a black Belizean-born American citizen, a Creole raised in Oakland, California, with dual citizenship. A former Xerox repairman, he moved back to Belize in 2000 at the age of 42, following the crooked election of George Bush. Now, Coz is not an especially political animal. He's pretty much just an animal. But he has a golden gut and instinct: "Bush has a mean streak, ya know, and when you put guys like that in charge of the plantation, the first thing they do is whup on some niggers to limber up. Then they lock the door and go after everybody else. After the election I said to myself, 'That's enough! Black people seen this movie before.' And I split. Besides, there are other things in life than motherfucking toner cartridges and a 401(k)."

One of those other things is reefer, and Cosmo burns down his share, evidently not having inherited the overall Belizean habit of moderation, when it comes to the herb. But weed is cheap enough in Belize, and he manages to live on about $700 a month in a tiny, unpainted beach cabana much like my own. Coz may stay stoned, but he has nevertheless managed to make a major contribution to imbibing culture down here—the Hopkins Tin Cup Martini. There are certain things necessary to any attempt at civilized life in a tropical clime, and the martini is one of them:

Hopkins Tin-Cup Martini

Using a large mouth-wash bottle cap which holds one liquid ounce, pour three shots each of Travelers Vodka and Mayfair Dandy Dry Gin (Belizean brands) into an ice filled fruit jar.

Add one-third teaspoon of bitters (a local herbal drink extracted from the contribo vine by soaking it in 200 proof rum). Stir lightly.

Pour into a porcelain-coated tin cup (the metal cups leave a bad aftertaste), preferably a cup that has been kept in the freezer of your four cubic foot Korean-made plastic refrigerator.

Skewer two olives from your jealously guarded supply onto a six-inch straw plucked from a broom, and drop into cup.

Serves two generously.

Oh, would that Belize were all Tin Cup Martinis and Toucans. It is easy to let things like jaguars, Mayan pyramids, and lyrical Creole chatter under moonlit palms fool you into thinking you have escaped America. First of all, you are probably making your money from some American source (in my case, writing), so you will have to return periodically, whether you want to or not. At some point, though, unless you are a trust-fund maggot chewing your way through daddy's wad, one of America's elite coercive syndicates will bring you to your knees, drag you back and, once again, wring every dollar out of you it can before it takes out the pliers for your gold teeth as you run screaming toward the border. For expats, it is usually America's medical-extortion syndicate. Big Med gets everybody in the end, except the rich who have escaped with their booty to places like nearby Placencia or San Pedro out there on Belize's coral reefs, where they suck down rum punch and tear up the reefs with their twin Chrysler engine boats.

A 60-year-old American who's been in Belize for 20 years, Shirley is one of those likable fuddy-duddies, the sort of Magoo figure America turns into bag ladies. After working and paying taxes for two decades in the U.S., she saw the writing on the wall. She now runs a tribal arts-and-crafts shop, which in a place like Hopkins Village is equivalent to share cropping in the Gobi Desert. But if you are frugal, as in Carmelite-nun frugal, you can subsist on what's left after you pay your U.S. income taxes in a funky, approximate bliss. Until Big Med steps in. When a Belizean doctor suspected Shirley might have a subcutaneous lymphoma on her back and recommended that she see a cancer specialist, Shirley panicked, as most people do. After getting a second opinion, which came up with the same, "Maybe it's cancer, maybe it's not. You need a specialist" diagnosis, she packed her duds and flew to Houston, where many American expats go for major health treatment, particularly surgery.

Shirley stepped off the plane in Houston and straight into the remorseless maw of medicine American-style. They CAT-scanned her every which way to hell, ran every conceivable test and a few inconceivable ones. (Since when is there a link between "The Big C" and Lyme's Disease?) Then came the parade of quick-buck consulting doctors that American hospitals foist upon patients to extract as much money out of insurance companies as possible. "Patient D-7228, Marvel,

Shirley D., negative for subcutaneous lymphoma," pronounced Big Med. Shirley was at the hospital for six hours. The bill was $12,000. Problem was, she didn't have insurance. And she certainly did not have twelve thousand bucks in some coffee can buried in the sand back in Belize. So she was left to beg, borrow, and scrape her way along an even more penurious path than before—one she still walks today.

Because of reflex and acculturation (even though she could have been treated for free in Cuba by some of the best doctors in the world, the only good doctors are in America, right?), for most Americans there is no complete escape from America short of death—and even then it's bound to be expensive, unless you, like the Garibano villagers, refuse to make a fetish of the act of dying. By their lights, when it's your time, it's your time. You let the docs have a reasonable shot at it, then move on. If you die, there will be a wake, then nine days later a big all-night party known as Beluvia thrown in your honor—after which, if you are a practitioner of the local African Dugu religion, your spirit will be consulted as a respected advisor for the ages to come. For your advice from the afterworld, relatives and community pay you in the form of ritual dancing, drumming, and food offerings.

The point is that if you plan an escape to a Third World society (and, let's face it, all those Americans who plan to run to immigrant-proof New Zealand have not checked the facts), it's probably better to adopt Third World philosophy and ways, rather than trying to hang onto soulless and illusory first-world security in a Caribbean culture where even chickens, despite the fact that they are heartily eaten, are considered to have souls.

Speaking of chickens, Cosmo tells me that "the rich Americans have outlawed roosters down in Placencia," a small Garibano village to the south. That is the word passing from person to person up through the Belizean coastal villages of Barranco, Punta Gorda, and Seine Bight, and here to Hopkins Village. Seems the roosters crowed too early for the Americans who've built the expensive seaside homes, or those staying in the swank new hotel there. "No more chiken on da plate fa Placencia," he adds in mock dialect—meaning that without fertilized eggs, the villagers, or what's left of them in Placencia, anyway, cannot breed future chickens for meat and eggs. Now they will have to buy Belizean Mennonite-raised chicken at the same expensive grocery store as the whites—where, like everywhere in Belize, most food prices are about the same as in the States because nearly everything is imported from the States. And to do that they will have to work for the Americans for a paltry $1.50-an-hour Belizean minimum wage, or perhaps $2.00 if they hold their tongues and play the good, shuffling Caribbean darkie.

The Americans feel quite benevolent about it all. "It creates jobs for Belizeans," they crow. Maybe so. But I can remember Placencia 30 years ago, before the hotels and the white people came, when having a fulltime job was not the end-all of life down there. In fact, almost no one in the village had a real job, except the fishermen and the handful of Brit soldiers who once frequented Her Majesty's tiny army R&R compound in Placencia (as an alternative to the British-built and -sanctioned whorehouse in Belize City, still legally operating as Raul's Rose Room). There was not a single vehicle in the village, and no true passable road through the mangrove to the mainland. The Garifuna had to travel in and out by small boat or on the ferry and, sure, nobody had a flush toilet. There were even a few pigs that ran loose. But Placencia's Garifuna got by well enough without wiping the white Americans' toilet bowls and carrying out their liquor bottles. It's pretty much the same as in the

States, where the big dogs have moved to the seventeenth floor and are pissing down on the rest of us. The white man has been convinced that it is only raining, but the truth is that we are all Garifuna now.

The founder of Belizean democracy was a not particularly inspired but nevertheless astute man named George Price, who was extremely wary of tourism and wanted to keep it out. His successors have not been so fortunate, being caught in the vise of global capitalism. Little Third World countries don't get such choices. They have to suck it in and live in the spotlight in front of their constituencies on failed promises made by great powers, and invariably get kicked out of office in the yeasty Belizean political environment. Generally, they grab up some of the public dough while they are juggling promises they can never fulfill. A helluva lot of what strikes us as tin-pot theft in Third World governments stems from desperation. Unlike in the U.S., where congressmen and senators come out of office set for life with connections, consulting jobs, and fat pensions, when a mid-level Belizean politician fails to get reelected, he or she often returns to the scant livelihood of his village or the "bak a town" in Belize City or Dangriga. In other words, political graft and thievery in the U.S. Congress are institutionalized, and in Belize it is socialized. In the U.S., the dough is in the financial establishment. In Belize, it is in tourism. In any case, if there is a scam to be run or a buck to be stolen, you'll need to buy a politician or two to do your bidding—someone in the legislature who can make it legal. It doesn't matter which party, either in Belize or America.

Tiny Belize is run by two parties—the liberal PUP and the conservative UDP—which together constitute the same kind of elite political class we have in the U.S. Everyone is in bed together, but in a much smaller bed with shorter sheets.

Belizeans in general are not fooled by either party, or the politicians' "sweet mouths," and regularly throw out entire parties at election time. But, like Americans, they have no real choices in the two-party shell game. The difference between this little country and America is that ordinary working Belizeans understand that the choice is an illusion. Right now, the UDP is busy looting the nation's treasury, outraging everyone except the conservative business class and the American, Taiwanese, and British interests with which they are aligned. Meanwhile, the liberal PUP builds up a head of steam for a takeover in the next elections, with no real plan—just a ride on public outrage at the lawlessness of the conservative reign. Sound familiar? As in the U.S., the pendulum swings, but not very far from the financial interests of the elites. To be fair, though, the PUP, like the Democrats in America, does a little more for the people when it is in power. As little as it can get by with. Or, again like the Democrats, manage to pump up the impression that they do.

The political elites come and go from office—though, mostly, they just swap seats, the same as in America. But for folks in Hopkins Village, life remains about the usual things, mostly about waiting: waiting along dusty roads for the buses, waiting for the water or electricity to come back on, waiting for the rains to stop, waiting for the rains to start, waiting for the next opportunity in life that might never appear. Frustrating as it can be, people understand and accept that they cannot push time or most of the events in their lives. Waiting gives much time for reflection and contemplation. For instance, you can actually feel a Sunday in Hopkins. Most daily activities come to a complete stop, and it is considered a time for conversation and quiet thought—the scarcest things of all for Americans, for whom such mental space is crammed with cookie-cutter diversions neatly packaged and sold to them by the corporate state. Any chance for reflection and, consequently, inner growth is filled with cheap media spectacles or synthetic recreational activities.

In fact, as I write this, a handful of Americanized locals, and American and Canadian advance men for U.S. resort developers, are over at the beachside Internet cafe/bar right now, gathered on this particular Sunday to watch America's biggest cheap-media spectacle of all—the Super Bowl. A big screen projector has been set up under the open-air thatched roof cafe for the occasion. At first I was tempted to join them because, much as I hate football, the company of fellow Americans can be pleasing. Then a big, red-faced white guy came reeling drunkenly toward me and shook my hand in the best Dale Carnegie fashion. "Hello, I'm Ryan," he boomed, and started rattling off something about nearby beachfront acreage. I thought about how developers have illegally bulldozed and seized half of the Hopkins Village Cemetery with complete impunity. Like Cosmo says, "When you put guys like that in charge of the plantation, the first thing they're gonna do is whup on some niggers to limber up." Apparently, even dead ones will do. So it was a "no thanks" to Ryan Red Face, and I walked the beach homeward toward my cabana.

There really is no place to escape from America, and more than likely it will have been already established at your destination before you even arrive. For the most part, temporary mediating respite is about all you can expect. But in the big picture, given peak oil, ecological collapse, and an empire hell-bent on wreaking its own destruction, even temporary respite looks pretty damned good from the high front porch of this jack-leg cobbled-together Garifuna shack in the first light of tonight's moon. Down below, the neighbors have washed the dinner dishes; the kids, fresh from their baths, sit on their parents' laps, smelling of soap, listening to the elders talk as they sip their bitters beneath the spreading blue mango tree, whose leaves now appear purple in this balmy semi-darkness. I've had it worse. We all have.

Stay strong.

12

In the Reign of the One-nutted King

[March 5, 2007]

Not long ago, protesting Danish construction workers won a historic victory against workplace tyranny—they retained their company-sponsored on-the-job beer breaks. Heartless employers being what they are, they had asked workers to pay half the cost of the beer. Oppression is ever boundless. About that same time last fall, a couple of hundred American protesters gathered in a Washington, D.C., parking lot. Chronic liberal malcontents, they had the gall to ask why our government was slaughtering hundreds of thousands of abysmally ordinary folks in Iraq, people moreover like themselves who, even under Saddam Hussein, whose reign was so infamously marked by his penchant for black-velvet paintings and the most sordid kinds of torture, nevertheless managed to do what most common folks in the world do—they sent the kids off to school every morning, cursed Baghdad's traffic, and perhaps fudged a little on their taxes. So why are they being wiped out at great public expense, and for no apparent reason?

This being a free republic, the American protesters stood in the parking lot, packed buttock to belly button inside one of our fatherland's designated Free Speech Zones (a bad case of branding if ever there was one), and though they are no longer called that, the function is still the same. Jabbing their signs upward, the protesters tried to wedge their message into the wavering thicket of signage above their heads. Between rather strangely meterless chants, such as "One, two, three, four, end the war!" the evil librul protestors were left to contemplate just what the Plexiglas-faced squadrons of police ninjas might do should one of the dissidents make a cautious move toward the Porto Johns, which were placed slightly over the yellow painted line that assumedly marked the outer boundary of free speech in America. Was it better to ease over into the Porto John, or to hold it until the "designated hour of disassemblage"? However ineffective state-supervised dissidence may be here, protesting is hard going in America. No Dane's beer-wrecked bladder could survive it.

Pity the poor American left, who would be considered right-wing moderates in most of the world; in America, being against any war makes you a far leftist. Any time American leftists start pointing at the root causes of our national disease, they are neatly handed a fresh bloody war to oppose. Each new generation of the left gets its energies sapped, gets locked into the position of continually opposing one war, then another and another. Ever since World War I they've been standing on the street corners or in the parks—or, more recently, inside the Free Speech Zones, way the hell out at the edge of town. At any rate, they can never come close to naming the dark and profitable tumor at the heart of America, the economic system under which we all live. To survive and grow, the American system needs war, making war inevitable. To keep up the pretense of freedom, it needs harmless dissent.

America has a long record of stifling dissent exactly when dissent is most needed. Democracy American-style means we get free speech for trivial matters but not for life-and-death issues. When an election is stolen, the very party from whom it was stolen refuses to protest the theft because, well, "Nobody likes sour grapes, do they?" thereby assuring future electoral thefts. When America supplies Israel with cluster bombs to kill Palestinian children and grandmothers, you don't see rallies against Israel or American arms cartels. You see yet another exercise of free speech on behalf of those things that the politicians and corporations could care less about, and thus grant us permission to "dissent" upon. Issues such as gender and identity, or just about anything related to sexual freedom: "Go ahead, parade and rant about your own penises and vulvas. Just don't challenge the banks, the war machine, or the fraudulent democratic process by which we manage the people. Remember, fucking with these things is called terrorism. So stick to your own narrow 'issues' like sexual freedom, and nobody will get hurt. Got it, punk?"

Good ole sexual freedom, one of the American left's favorite golden oldies. It's not as if sexual freedom has not been a fact of life in this country ever since the puritans lost that fight in the Sixties and Seventies. Sure, there is a small but very damned-loud contingency of bitter-enders making a last stand at imposing restrictions that the public has already rejected. But we did win the sexual revolution, my friends. Look around at the movies, gay- and lesbian-focused TV shows, and pre-marital and extra-marital sex as the main fare in magazines, popular novels, and TV shows. Hell, we've even created a couple of new sexes I still haven't figured out—all those "crosses" and "trans" whatevers. We may not have become the Amsterdam of the New World (which, as near as I can tell, is Rio de Janeiro), but we nevertheless won.

Better yet, people stand up for what they have won, too. Bill Clinton is living proof. The fact is that Clinton, despite cigars, blowjobs, impeachment, and $40 million spent by the Republicans to rub his face in a cum-stained dress on television for years on end, remains massively popular. Every year we find him waving to the world from near the top of the list of the world's most admired men. As a martyr symbol for sexual freedom, all his supposed sins—not to mention his genuine crimes against humanity—were washed away. Much is attributed to his charm, his Oxford encyclopedic mind, and his fried-chicken grin. But he is no more charming than Ronald Reagan was, even if Clinton could spot that senile old saint of the Republican Party a hundred IQ points and still whip him on *Jeopardy*. Yet charm and smarts will only get you so far, not to mention into a lot of trouble if you happen to have Clinton's libido. Clinton's charm was only by comparison to the mostly second-string power-hungry puds who preceded and succeeded him in that bugged Oval Office chair.

The truth is that Clinton, like Reagan, fucked over millions of the poor, sentenced uncounted children to death by embargo, and shipped millions of American jobs wholesale to the slums of Mysore and Mexico City. He was as close to being a Republican as you can be without getting the mandatory lobotomy and a wet kiss from Ted Haggard. Still, though, millions of Americans refuse to repudiate him because his right to sexual privacy represented their own, still represents their own, and all the Bible-haired gasbags on the Christian Broadcasting Network and all the sexually frustrated Holy Rollers in the country are not going to turn things around. We won that one.

But we have never won against a war until it is too damned late, and the Pentagon and the Halliburtons of this country have wrung every blood-stained buck from it and moved on toward setting up the next one. Yet the left, perhaps sensing the futility of protesting the latest war from inside their free-speech cages—which seem only to be reserved for war dissenters—dissipates its energies further by charging at the sly Republican matador's array of fluttering capes, one of which is labeled sexual privacy. No cage required. You can usually parade that one right down the street, further proof that the fatherland is a free land, and that the powers that be could care less about that issue.

While we are sniping at liberal sacred cows here, I may as well plink briefly at another one—gun control. It's all bullshit. The left plays into the parched red claws of the worst conservative elements when it makes a fool of itself over what it does not understand, when it succumbs to the righteous wailing of the anti-gun intelligentsia in the brownstones of Chelsea. Twice as many people own guns as vote in this country, and half of American households have at least one gun. Get over it. The guns are here to stay. Gun control and sexual privacy are just two of the dozens of political wedges that liberals drive in on behalf of the same elite class that has sent yet another generation off to die in the name of the country.

SCREAMING MAN HERE! DIE FOR THEIR COUNTRY? BAGEANT, YOU LOATHESOME, DOUBLE-DEALING GODDAMNED LIZARD! NOT A SINGLE CALLOW CORN-FED KANSAS STRIPPLING OR LOS ANGELES MEXICAN SCARFING THEIR MICROWAVED BURRITOS IN IRAQ HAS DIED FOR, OR HAD HIS ARMS BLOWN OFF FOR, HIS COUNTRY. THEY DIED (OR ARE TRYING TO MASTER THE ARTS OF LOVE WITH THAT SEXY NEW PROSTHETIC CLAW) IN SERVICE OF THE SYNDICATE. THEY DIED

AT THE ORDERS OF ITS CEO, PRESIDENT SPARKY AND HIS GANG OF
ADDLED COLD WAR DROOLERS. AND MAKE NO MISTAKE ABOUT IT!
THEY WILL SOON GO OFF TO IRAN WHISTLING THE THEME FROM
ROCKY AND SLEEP THE SLEEP OF ZOMBIES IN THE 100-DEGREE
DESERT NIGHTS BECAUSE, AHA! THE SYNDICATE'S MIND-SCRUBBING
MACHINERY IS FAULTLESS! FROM THE PLEDGE OF ALLEGIANCE IN
GRADE SCHOOL, TO THAT LAST SURPRISED LOOK ON THEIR FACES
WHEN THE I.E.D. SAYS "HELLO DARLING" IN FARSI, THEY WILL BE
DREAMING OF EAGLES, AND FLAGS, AND PARIS HILTON'S CROTCH.
BIRTH TO DEATH, THE MIND-SCRUBBER'S PROGRAMMING IS
FAULTLESS, I TELL YOU. FAULTLESS!

Anyway, the reason that liberals are sucker bait for every
wedge the Republican think tanks can hand them is because
liberals, like all other Americans, are conditioned to compete
against each other—even fellow liberals. In a monetized rat-
race society (best called The Company) that continually pits
its citizens/workers against one another in a toxic winner-take-
all rat race for quality education, health care, employment,
crime-free neighborhoods, and political attention of any sort,
and then dubs it mere "competition," as if it were a happy
game of badminton, *everybody*, rich or poor, feels existentially
threatened. Republican capitalists feel threatened that liberal
humanism might empower workers, which it would, if anybody
bothered to practice it. The gay man fears the common
homophobe, as if that dumb bastard has any more power than
he does. So he grabs the bullhorn at the Gay Pride rally and
publicly denounces the homophobe—who really couldn't
give a shit and won't hear the denunciation anyway—never
confronting the real enemy because, like the homophobe, he
has been conditioned to a combative personal response, instead
of a reasoned one, toward the guy down the street. CBS's
Sixty Minutes covers his "issue," for 15 minutes a year, thereby

validating it in a television-managed state. Divisive politics once again beats the snot out of reason.

Reason might dictate—just might, mind you—that issues such as secret torture sites, military star-chambers judging the citizenry, security-state data banks on tens of millions of Americans' private lives, or our destinies being bought and sold without our participation (or even knowledge) by corporate campaign contributions ought to have a higher priority than animal rights or abortion rights, at least for now. The fight for all these must be continual, of course; but, noble as these rights are, we have a better chance of achieving them or holding onto them if we are all rowing the societal boat together, away from the waterfall ahead. A gay marriage license hanging in your cubicle in the global labor gulag doesn't mean much.

A forensic search for signs of liberalism in America, true liberal unity of the kind that broadly underpins any humane and progressive society, shows it was DOA. Thanks to our birth-to-death indoctrination regarding "the American spirit of competition," the rats in the race are not inclined to run together or exercise their unified strength toward a common purpose, or even to consider it. Though the world is by no means a simple either/or proposition governed by the narrowest sort of struggle, we are conditioned to unquestioningly assume so. If we stop to think, or apply reason and then act on it, other rats will eat our lunch. That's what they are trained to do.

Luckily for the rat keepers of global capitalism, they have little to fear when it comes to American moths being attracted to the candle of reason. Reason is boring stuff in a nation—and, increasingly, a world—whose cultural glue is television, and whose main diversion is profoundly simplified emotionalism and conflict. In fact, in the American rat race, reason is not only a fatal weakness, but is also generally unavailable to a people who stay on guard every waking moment, ready to take on the next rat, then go home and watch more rats do each other in on television, in a steady diet of visible conflict, both overt and implied. Given that the human nervous system is programmed to respond instantly to conflict, there simply is no mental space left for much quiet thought to take root. Not when your nation's cultural values resemble those of Tamerlain or Aleric the Goth—tribal, hierarchical, aggressive, and acquisitive.

By contrast, I am sitting in my kitchen in the village of Hopkins, Belize, watching a lone Garifuna carpenter put a zinc roof on a nearby native cabana. Squatting barefooted on the roof joists, he saws and nails and chats all day with passersby on the sandy street below. A couple of times a day, one or another of them will voluntarily climb up to lend the carpenter a hand for a half-hour or so, then move on. Cooperation is an assumption, not a consideration. In the same loose spirit, neighbors often drift from house to house at mealtimes, making easy conversation and gossip, eating a little here, a little there, as they go along so as not to burden any particular household's meal. Next week the family sharing the food may be doing the visiting because their own refrigerator is empty. No stigma attached. In a culture marked by unemployment and food insecurity, such sharing of labor or food is a socially beneficial practice. Though no one here thinks about it, such practices represent a very reasonable social-support system in a country with almost no social-service resources. The elites, on the other hand, say the typically relaxed Belizean worker is lazy, and that the country would be more prosperous if people like the Garifuna would sweat harder to join the New World Order rat race, which profits the owning class leaders so handsomely. When the working people call for improvement, their demands are deemed unreasonable by the elites (though that doesn't prevent elites in government from promising these things at election time).

Whether in Belize or America, neither the owners of government nor their subset of social and financial managers are going to respond to any well-reasoned, socially beneficial cause unless they are forced to do so—with emphasis on the word "forced". Social progress and a humane environment is antithetical to the success of the owning and governing classes—both being exactly the same thing in a nation whose Constitution is essentially a guarantee of the rights of property. Things were that way from the beginning: creating a dynastic owning class, not just the Rockefellers, Bushes, and Kennedys, but thousands of discreet regional and local ones across the country which have been in place for a century or more—longer in places like the South. Regardless of what the written law says, the owning class chooses which laws will actually be enforced. Or abolished. For them, the long-term application of reason's kid brother, common sense, spells destruction.

On the other hand, it doesn't take much critical thinking to stomp the shit out of the weakest guy and grab his lunch money. Or his turf or his oil. If doing so should require some degree of thoughtfulness, we had best leave reason and thinking to more thoughtful leader-rats. And so Condi Rice and George Bush wrinkle their brows and try to look thoughtful, and pose for the cameras with a bright, vulpine stare. But not even the Republican leadership has ever believed that logic and reason were driving their game. Down inside, the Republican leadership is deeply realistic, even if it is of the tooth-and-claw reptilian-brain sort of realism: Eat, shit, kill, own the top of the rock where the sun is best. They've had the top of the rock for the two terms usually granted them before the game is up and the public throws them out—not because of any particular public wisdom, but because when theft and high crime becomes obscenely obvious to even the blindest beer-sucking idiot, it is always the Republicans who are in office. And now, even though the game is up, President Sparky and the neo-con Nefertiti have no choice but to keep on trying to look wise and leader-like, and keep on keeping on in the face of the brewing public backlash, just keep on prevaricating until the neo-con junta they rode into town with can get out of Dodge before the indictments come down—at which time, Sparky signs the pardons on his way out the door.

GODAMMIT, BAGEANT, DON'T MAKE THINGS MORE COMPLICATED THAN THEY ARE! THIS NATION OF FEEBS AND NOSE BORERS CAN'T EVEN SPELL PREVARICATE! THE "PUBLIC BACKLASH" AS YOU CALL IT … ALL THAT SQUEALING ABOUT THE BLOODY FOLLY IN IRAQ IS JUST SQUEALS FROM INSIDE THE SWINERY. THE UNLETTERED HORDES HAVE FIGURED OUT WE HAVE LOST A WAR. THAT A BUNCH OF GOAT-SKINNERS IN FLIP FLOPS IS KICKING OUR ASSES UP AND DOWN THE STREETS OF BAGHDAD LIKE A GODDAMNED SOCCER BALL. AND THEY SEE NOW THAT THEIR BOY, GEORGE ONE-NUTTED KING OF THE HUNS, TURNED OUT TO BE SIMPLE IN THE HEAD. COMPLETELY REPRESENTATIVE OF THE PEOPLE WHO VOTED FOR HIM. A LOSER!

True enough. But no matter. We live in, as Gore Vidal put it, "The United States of Amnesia," and President Sparky will later be canonized into Republican sainthood, alongside Ronald Reagan, and dozens of airports and highways will carry his name, until peak oil renders them dim relics resembling the Mayan ball courts of Tikal. The deal stands unless real catastrophe intervenes—either something natural, like a giant meteor splashing a thousand mile-wide hole in the Eastern Seaboard, or an unnatural one inflicted by the money elites themselves, such as a depression so deep that corn mush makes a dramatic comeback among the proles. Or, as the administration would have us believe, maybe an all-out nuclear war waged upon us by Kim Jong-il with both of his missiles. In any case, it must be a genuine catastrophe, meaning that it must come between Americans and their shopping malls. Otherwise, so long as voters can manage to hang onto their jobs and be convinced of their safety from people like the Korean Brat Boy, or the hapless, dimwitted Shoe Bomber, they will stick with the incumbent rat pack and its leader for at least eight years, even if their leader does stumble over three-syllable words and call the Greeks "Grecians." The armature of all politics is fear, whether there is danger or not—fear, and the mind-numbing monotony of the thinnest domestic platitudes.

Well, hell. Now that the Bush administration has played all the fear cards available—at least until he can bring a swarm of self-exploding Iranians down upon us—the 2008 Democratic presidential hopefuls are left to hoof the boards, peddling the moldiest of platitudes. They don't seem one bit embarrassed. Here you have candidates for leadership of the most powerful—and clearly dangerous—country in the world, and they have absolutely nothing of substance to say on real issues, domestic or foreign. On domestic issues they set their jaws for the cameras, and, with a steely glint in their eyes hinting of gravitas, deliver meaningless speeches in threadbare language about health care, taxes, and Social Security to millions of Europeans and Middle Easterners on CNN and Al Jazeera.

I say that because absolutely no one in America is listening, except the blogosphere and the congenital political junkies that television seems to have produced, along with the millions of sports fans and shopping-channel addicts. The record shows that neither party has done shit for over 40 years about any of those things, and probably never will, especially given that the country is (a) broke (shhhh, the mooks in the voting booths still think we are the richest nation in the world), and (b) so far in the hole we are a net debtor nation to countries such as Mexico; if the Empire manages to survive a bit longer, we may yet grovel before Yemen and Bolivia for a few bucks for a pint of gasoline for the Hummer and a cup of French roast.

Meanwhile, as I write this, John McCain gives out a love call to the Christian Right, promising to take down *Roe vs. Wade*, and lead America back down the happy road toward coat-hanger abortions. Like the one leading back to sexual repression, that road washed out long ago, which doesn't stop McCain and his kind from stoking illiterate white Christian nitwits to a frenzy, thereby sidestepping the issue of whether we are going to devalue the dollar and pay the Mexicans in cash, or simply open the borders and let millions of unemployed gringos do yard work and send much-needed pesos home to their families.

Same goes for foreign policy, another of those creatures the administration has rendered all but extinct, thanks to wardens and stewards such as John Bolton and the hard-faced Nefertiti in the $7,000 high heels (though I gotta admit that Condi has the kind of legs that nearly justify them). Oh, the Republicans have announced whose Persian ass we are going to attempt to kick next, but that is plain old thuggery, not foreign policy. Essentially it's a retread of the WMD ruse, only this time the claim is "Iranian intent," which neatly eliminates the problem of proof. "Hey, they are thinking about it, and thinking leads to doing. So that makes 'em a threat to Americans."

As we said earlier, the human nervous system is programmed to respond instantly to danger and violence, so thuggery smells like foreign policy to rats that have been kept on the treadmill of fear by the Republicans, and in the dark by both parties. And, besides, sending the Empire's legions into Persia will draw attention away from Iraq, just as Iraq draws attention away from the war now being lost in Afghanistan. In the United States of Amnesia, history is only eight-and-one-half minutes long, about the length of time between television commercials, and far less important than catching the second segment of *American Idol*. Given that it takes longer than that to even say hello to any foreign-policy issue, odds are good we will continue to hear zilch from the presidential candidates on the subject. And, besides, there are too many of both party's skeletons doing *La Danse Macabre* in that closet.

Like those "spider plants," sometimes called air plants, that hang from the trees outside my cabana window right now—the ones that sprawl gracefully from little jars of tap water in the apartments of solitary librarians and the elderly, subsisting apparently on nothing but air and some minuscule bits of nutrients to be obtained from water—American liberals seem to exist on bottled water and hope. Legend has it that American liberalism once had deep, traceable roots in farm populism, the struggle for dignity of immigrants, fair wages, and good working conditions for laborers, and other such noble principles. So noble, in fact, that even high-minded sons of the owning class—people like John Kennedy and Franklin Roosevelt—were drawn to them as a way to kill time between games of touch football at Hyannisport, and the search for the perfect Cuban cigar and accompanying highball, not to mention the prerequisite sexual dalliances with other birds following the flock of the famous. (Judith Campbell Exner once told me that JFK always had to be on the bottom due to his bad back, and that he cackled like a frat boy when they screwed on the desk of the Oval Office, as if thinking, she said, "Oh, if Bobby could see me now!")

At any rate, noble causes and party politics are antithetical these days. Beyond that, you must be rich, or at least very useful to the rich—like the Bush family was to the oil companies during its rise—to be a player in either party, both of which are faces of the only real party in this country, the party of business. Without a class base made up of real people, there can be no genuine political party. Without people from different classes defending their class interests, there can be no politics. Americans have been sold the idea that they are all somehow "middle class." Whether they are shoveling chicken shit for Tysons, a seven-buck-an-hour "dietary technician" at the local hospital, or hawking credit-card applications out of a telemarketing center in Nebraska, they are all now in the great middle class. Consequently, there are no politics in our political system—just business transactions taking place behind the curtain of a fraudulent democracy.

After 40 years of having their natural base absorbed by the amorphous middle class that isn't, and the meat of politics removed from the table, spider-plant liberals are left to find sustenance from the most minuscule nourishment. There are just enough tiny differences in the two parties to sustain ever-hopeful liberal voters, who have long accepted the thin gruel served by the Democratic political elite as the prelude to a promised feast. Of course, the feast never comes, because no Democrat is ever going to do more than "address" a problem, rather than solve it. In fact, for one of the Democratic elites to even acknowledge the existence of the most glaring sort of inequity sends good liberals into political insulin shock, so accustomed have their systems become to calorie-free ideas and "reality lite."

Al Gore makes a film about global warming, but dares not name the corporations that not only refuse to seek remedy, but insist on escalating the problem, and who just happen to fund both parties. Instead he tells the audience that they are personally to blame and must start sacrificing, hanging their clothes on lines, and so forth. Movies and documentaries being reality in this country, liberal America hails it as a turning point in our ravenous energy consumption, and drives the six blocks home from the Cineplex wondering where the hell you buy wooden clothespins, having never seen one in their entire suburban lives. Al Gore gets an Academy Award at the annual swarming of very rich swans living in a paradise, wherein they never even see their own laundry from the moment it drops from their gilded bodies.

Meanwhile, Hillary Clinton makes familiar noises about reforming health care, but flatly declares that the insurance companies which hold the entire nation to ransom "absolutely must be part of the solution." By that logic, when it comes to stopping the war in Iraq, Halliburton, Blackwater Security, 20,000 hired-gun mercenaries, and several thousand contractors presently cutting the fattest hog in their history must be involved in ending the war. Even SCREAMING MAN has more veracity and substance.

THE SCREAMING MAN HAS NEVER BEEN ACCUSED OF VERACITY! NOR ABSTENTION FROM ANY SUBSTANCE KNOWN TO CIVILIZED OR UNCIVILIZED MAN, NOR AVERSION TO ANY DEVIANT PRACTICE WHATSOEVER. (THEY DO NOT CALL HIM THE POL POT OF THE BOUDOIR FOR NOTHING!) FUTHERMORE, FOR A HEFTY FEE, SCREAMING MAN'S ENDORSEMENT, AND OR PHYSICAL PERSUASIVE EXPERTISE, IS AVAILABLE TO ANY VILE PERSONAGE OR POLITICAL PARTY, REGARDLESS OF THEIR CRIMES WHATSOEVER. ARE YOU LISTENING, HILLARY CLINTON? YOU'RE GONNA NEED HELP IN TAKING OUT THAT GREAT MOCHA HOPE OF THE DEMOCRATIC PARTY BEFORE NEXT NOVEMBER!

Right now, almost 70 percent of Americans, finally, mostly

for the wrong reasons, reject a senseless war that kills tens of thousands and bankrupts our children's children. In response, it took four years for the Democrats to come haltingly to the conclusion that it just might be a good idea to end it. And even now a large number are saying, "Let's test the water a bit more, maybe wait until the polls show 99 percent. Can't be too careful. And, besides, Iraq would descend into chaos and bloodshed if we pulled out."

Bloodshed and chaos? What do they think the Pentagon is conducting over there right now—a Red Cross community blood drive? And mention cutting the Pentagon back and spending a little of the dough on public education, and even the Dems begin to sound like Foghorn Leghorn in high dudgeon: "Whoa there, hoss! We gotta have thousands of nuklur waarheads ready to pop at any time. Somebody in the Middle East besides our strategic partner, po' defenseless little Israel, just might build one of their own."

How this "strategy" of reducing Israel's neighbors to rubble and guts serves you and me is a reasonable-enough question—one that can never be asked in the United States, although I can assure you that the media and the public here in Latin America openly ponder it. The question of why we continue to hone the teeth of the Middle East's meanest junkyard dog, but refuse to insist on a chain and muzzle, is left to the reader's speculation. Israeli belligerence is the third rail of American foreign policy that fries anyone with the balls to bring it up. Look at what recently happened to poor ole Jimmy Carter. Smoke is still curling up from his pasty old carcass. Will we ever see the day when an American politician says out loud what so many of us (and them) say privately?

Then there is the foreign-policy issue of the Third World and AIDS ...

AW RIGHT, BAGEANT! JUST SHUT UP AND LET SCREAMING MAN
DIRECT YOUR BOOGER HOOKS ACROSS THE KEYBOARD. LOOK, WHEN
IT COMES TO AIDS, LET'S CALL IT LIKE IT IS: EVERY WHITE MAN
IN AMERICA KNOWS THE WORLD IS TOO DAMNED CROWDED, TOO
DAMNED BLACK, AND FAR TOO FUCKING BROWN. AND AIDS IS THE
ONE THING THAT'S WORKING OUT RIGHT FOR THE WHITE MAN.
EVERY COUCH-BOUND BEER-SUCKING CRACKER KNOWS THAT IN
THE BACK OF WHAT MIND HE HAS. AND EVERY ARUBA-TANNED CPA
RUNNING THE FAMILY LEXU.S. THROUGH BUBBLES' CAR WASH IS
SECRETLY THINKING THE SAME THING — WHEN HE THINKS ABOUT
IT AT ALL. AND EVERY POLITICIAN SECRETLY KNOWS IT, TOO, EVEN
MOST OF THE BLACK ONES. SO THEY AIN'T GONNA BUST THE BANK
TO SAVE THE HOTTENTOTS IF THERE ARE NO VOTES IN IT.

THE BEAUTY OF IT IS THIS: THE WHITE GUY'S TEAM, AMERICA,
WINS BY DOING ABSOLUTELY NOTHING! THE WHOLE IDEA IS SO
GODDAMNED SICK NOBODY IN THE WESTERN WORLD WOULD DARE
ACCU.S.E HIM OF IT BECAU.S.E, HEY! THEY'VE THOUGHT THE SAME
THING. YESSIR, WHITEY HAS DRAWN THE "GET ONE GENOCIDE FOR
FREE" CARD IN HISTORY'S GREAT BOARD GAME. WHITEY DOESN'T
CATCH MANY BREAKS FROM HISTORY THESE DAYS. WHEN HE DOES,
HE'S GOTTA RIDE IT AND TRY NOT TO SMIRK. WHO SAYS WHITE MEN
DON'T DO SOLIDARITY?

Well, to be honest, those thoughts have crossed my mind,
too, though not with such glee. Anybody with the intelligence
of a flatworm can see AIDS is taking out a lot more black,
brown, and yellow asses than white ones. It comes down to
morals and how you really feel about it. If you happen to be
among that 5 percent of the world called Americans, who are
hording at least a quarter of the world's wealth, and you live in a
rigidly managed consumer state that hammers you to buy more
of everything, one that depicts the faraway 95 percent as either
French queers, terrorists, or HIV-positive semi-cannibals, well,

you are not likely to cultivate your inner Mother Teresa, are you?

Though dismal be the heart of man, we spider plants are feeling a bit hardier these days. Supreme manager of the Democratic political smoke-and-bubble machine that she is, Nancy Pelosi (at least to hear the echoes of the media tell it) is serving up one helluva bunch of appetizers—a cornucopia of proposed legislation. And as of this writing, there is even grappling on the floor of Congress to take away those same imperial powers that Democrats as well as Republicans granted our one-nutted cowboy king. But even if he is stripped of his Stetson crown and all the scepters of the Empire—meaning that those cattle prods of its "black site" torture chambers around the world are called home and smashed, and even if Guantanamo is leveled by the corps of engineers, and every prisoner is given a fair trial on television for all the world to see—we will only be approximately back to "Go." Back to where we started. Which was not a good place at all, since the system was already broken and was high-balling toward its own destruction financially, ecologically, and socially.

And so we sit patiently under the tent out here on the lawn, in the final dimming moments of the Empire. We've had the appetizers, and are waiting for the meat course: socialized medicine; a halving of the Pentagon's budget; nationwide public transit; a tripling of corporate taxation (which would still not put corporations where they were in the Fifties, when they paid 80 percent of America's bills and still made billions); an energy plan that works toward the elimination of the automobile and the closing of coal-fired plants; and universal, free higher education, just like in every other civilized first-world nation—none of which can even begin to happen without complete campaign-finance reform. That's some heavy meat and 'taters for any cook, including Nancy.

The band plays on, we fiddle with our napkins, and we wait. Cocktails are poured inside the grandly restored old homes in D.C.'s Georgetown district. The deal, the insiders agree, remains the same: Who buys the most campaign ads will almost certainly play Pied Piper to the most votes.

Meanwhile, not a soul under the tent has noticed that the lights in the kitchen have been turned off for a long, long time.

-13-

A Feral Dog Howls in Harvard Yard

[April 14, 2007]

If there is one bright spot in the bleak absurdity of slogging along in our new totalist American state, it is that ordinary working Americans are undisciplined as hell. We are genuine moral and intellectual slobs whose consciousness is pretty much glued onto an armature of noise, sports, sex, sugar, and saturated fats. Oh, we nod toward the government bullhorns of ideology, even throw beer cans and cheer when told we are winning some war or Olympic sports event. But when it comes right down to it, we could generally give a rat's ass about government institutions, and are congenitally more skeptical of government than most nations, especially nations that get things like good teeth and free higher education for their tax dollars.

Surely, there are governmental facts of life no working American can escape, like the IRS, but no ordinary person is dumb enough to actually trust political parties, banks, the courts, or the news media. Born with the organizational instincts and global awareness of a box turtle, we take the most torpid political path—we call it all bullshit, pay lip-service, vote occasionally, and then forget about our government altogether until April 15th of the next year.

As inhabitants (you couldn't really call what we practice citizenship) of a nation that is essentially one big workhouse/shopping compound, American life is simultaneously both easy for us and rather dangerous to the rest of the world. For instance, when the corporate state's CBS-ABC-FOX-NBC-XYZ television bullhorns told us some warthog named Saddam Hussein blew up the World Trade Center and probably fixed the NFL ratings, too, Tony the electrician said, "Well, OK then. Sure, go ahead and bomb the fucker." Then he flicked to the Home and Garden Channel, where the guy in the plaid shirt is explaining how to get a skylight installed without leaking. Thanks to American industrial molecular science, there's yet another new sticky-stuff miracle from DuPont, a tube of which costs about as much as the entire friggin' roof. After the obligatory DuPont public relations-sponsored tour of the plant where the goo is cooked up, plaid-shirt guy gives "application instructions," meaning he tells you how to squirt it out of the tube. And somewhere along the line, between the plant tour and watching the goo dry, Tony gave "informed consent" to the war in Iraq without even knowing it, or, for that matter, giving a shit.

This sort of life has its advantages, such as never having to analyze the institutions that manage us—not that we'd know how, even if we cared to. That's what television is for. Right? Given our short attention-spans, compliments of the business state's 100-channel national nerve system (three minutes into the show and the blonde hasn't taken her bra off or killed anybody yet, CLICK!), diversion fills the void of understanding as a nation of clueless mooks knocks around the new American emptiness, wandering the mall food courts, and maybe half-heartedly looking for a pair of size XXXL 50-inch-waist NBA basketball shorts (they actually make 'em), but generally is just bored.

But hold yer drawers there, hoss, because we nevertheless do possess a seed of existential angst, however tiny—this, despite the liberal intellectual managing class's and leftist profs' claims to the contrary. And that makes us potentially unmanageable politically speaking, potentially dangerous even. (It's the length of the fuse that is deceiving.) We may be being led around by our stomachs and our dicks, with our eyes taped shut, but we're not total ideological slaves yet. Because even the worst ideology requires at least a modicum of thought, and as a people with no authentic intellectual culture, we haven't enough collective intellect or education these days to pull it off.

Meanwhile, when it comes to pulling off, that small American class in charge of all things intellectual is doing just that—jerking off a whole nation. Admittedly, it's an unenviable job, but there are people selfless enough to do it. These poor intellectual bastards constitute the most servile class in America—the Empire's house niggers. It is their job to maintain the semblance of ideological control over the pizza-gobbling herd (America eats 126 acres of pizza a day!) for the Corporate States of America, which entertains no breach of official ideology—that collection of clichés and things that sound as if they ought to be true, according to our mercantile mythology and conditioning. So it is the American intellectual's gig to weave some philosophical and ideological basket of American Truth out of mercantile folklore and smoke in such a way as to appear to hold water when viewed at great distance by the squinting millions out there in the burboclaves, office campuses, construction sites, and fried-chicken joints. If the result were not so abysmally eye-glazing, tedious, and predictable, it would be an act of pure alchemy, truly spinning gold from chaff, turning mud bricks into bullion. Like we said, somebody's gotta do it, but the question remains as to why anyone would choose to. Answer: It beats working.

"Blessed are the thinking classes, for theirs is the kingdom of tenure."
—*Jesus to the Boston University philosophy department*

Though they never admit it, and especially to each other, these professors, book editors, intellectual critics, and social and economic "theorists" are very class conscious and privileged, and understand that they occupy their desk chairs at the pleasure of the Corporation. You don't have to stand back very far to see they have been the spin masters of the business class from the outset, and have either held America together or kept the fuck-job going from the beginning, depending upon the class from which you are viewing American history.

Of course, they are only human. Like any group of people with a class advantage, they prefer to keep on drinking cognac and pissing it out upstream from the rest of the Pepsi-swilling herd destined for bladder cancer. So this class sticks together, despite its prissy intellectual disputes in journals and critical publications. They produce "criticism" for the *New York Times Book Review*, or the *National Review*, etc., which may even be lively at times, and often full of that vacuous wit that garden-variety liberals so love because it revolves around a few threadbare names and dead ideas they learned during their college days or masters' degree indoctrination.

But the thinking classes' main job is to serve as intellectual hit-men for the ruling elites, the business class, which doesn't come all that hard for them, having all been stamped out of the same dough on the corporate system's university conveyor-belt. Most are utterly convinced that they are original and that they think for themselves—which, in the university scheme of things, means absorbing vast amounts of text, fermenting it in some sort of a second stomach, and regurgitating it as a concentrated cud, supposedly unique because they alone coughed it up. The few who understand that this in no way resembles original thought usually keep mum, and keep their jobs in publishing or academia. Or flee, screaming in despair, once they figure out what is going on.

Then, too, there is a huge number for whom America's university system is a sheltered workshop; people who simply could not survive in the real working world, which, miserable as it may be, nevertheless demands a modicum of practicality and some scant ability to socialize. I once dated a university professor with a doctorate in linguistics who, honest to God, let her Irish wolfhound shit all over the house and completely destroy every piece of furniture in her place until she was forced to sleep in the attic crawlspace in a sleeping bag, and actually did not understand why nobody ever accepted her dinner-party invitations. She was not, by the way, brilliant or eccentric—just completely helpless and out of it in her own little corner of academic goo-goo-land. Yet out there on the plains of Washington State University, hers was a reasonably respected intellect.

Now you can skin the cat (or that goddamned wolfhound) any way you choose, but if you want to be a really respected intellectual, you must serve business and power. You must serve the only apparatus capable of allowing you exposure enough to make a lunge at respect—which, after all, merely amounts to being allowed to create something scientifically useful to the Empire's goals or, in other cases, achieve that weird, localized hothouse-plant celebrity as an intellectual one finds on every campus. Either way, you'll never make as much money as say, Ann Coulter, who is infinitely more useful to the Empire and the business class that runs it than any intellectual can ever hope to be.

The United States has the most obsessive business class in the world. This would be no big deal if it did not direct the minds of the nation's population through its public-relations indoctrination industry. This is a matter of life and death for the financial pickle vendors, sub-prime mortgage shysters, and CitiBank, Morgan Stanley, and other high financiers who have come to actually own this country. There is only one threat to their empire of debt: people acting in the interests of ordinary society—which, in the rest of the world, is known as socialism. Consequently, we have no socialist politicians and no socialist journalists in our entire press and media, which is simply unimaginable in most civilized places like Europe. It is important that the working class thinks it has the self-determination they learned about in high school civics classes designed in the universities, that they feel any kind of individual power at all—which basically comes down the tepid power of consumer choice, which makes them malleable, and intolerant of any voice that suggests otherwise. But if even one iota of class awareness were allowed to flourish here, well, much of the American business class and the entire Yale University faculty would be hiding out in Argentina.

Without class interests and class awareness there can be no genuine politics or political parties. So, to the everlasting relief of the business classes, and with thanks to our university system's poli-sci, history, and social science departments, we have neither. Despite all the media's political white noise, we have a depoliticized society. It may be that the Internet is changing things. It surely is the most refreshing opportunity to come along, maybe in all of modern American history, and it does put heat on some political campaigns. No arguing that it influences certain influencers in society, to the degree that anything besides advertising influences anybody in the consumer republic. Problem is, though, how do you create critical political mass in a depoliticized society? Most people don't vote, and when it comes to actual participation in politics, opportunity is zilch. If you are not from the relatively privileged political and business segments, what the hell access is there for the individual to participate, except in one of the two business-based and -supported parties offered? Even at the local level—anyone who has tried to affect one of these parties locally knows you either play entirely by the party line or stand isolated, over in the corner of the Holiday Inn meeting room with your paper plate of stale salami and Triscuits, and keep your mouth shut and let the Rotary Club's big dogs bark. "Save the class-dissidence bullshit for your next Al-Qaeda cell meeting, buddy!"

It is 1958 and I am 12 years old, living on the edge of Niggertown in Winchester, Virginia, and hiding out in the Handley Public Library from the redneck bully kids. I am reading a somewhat pompous but erudite biography of a Harvard dean and wondering how such a mythical, magical being could possibly exist in the same country and on the same planet as me—a place where my dad came home from the gas station every night, skin penetrated by and forever smelling of motor oil and cigarettes. Yet this man in this book, this Harvard dean who apparently ate fish eggs called caviar (I looked it up in the dictionary) was a bulwark against something called McCarthyism, hated some people called communists, and was friends with a fellow named John Kennedy. His name was McGeorge Bundy, which meant absolutely nothing to me, neither at the time, nor even later when he became one of the Kennedy administration's gurus who launched the Bay of Pigs and cranked up the Vietnam War. Still, reading about him beat the hell out of being bloodied by the red-faced inbred yokels who plagued the 10-block walk home from school. That same year, I read Allen Ginsberg's "Howl," a copy of which was given me by an older kid, a fellow habitué of the decaying old Southern library, the queer son of the local insurance agent. It changed my life forever:

"America when will you be angelic? When will you take off your clothes? When will you look at yourself through the grave?"

Learning is a fickle thing. You never know which parts of it will turn out to be important, and you don't really need any credential or even much literacy to begin the journey. After reading "Howl" I was pretty sure I was a class dissident, even though the word was not even in use. Before a word is born, there is a mumbling in the heart that cries for a name.

All these years later, I find great comfort in the fact that there are any number of genuine class dissidents and original thinkers still nested within the university system, nursing happy-hour pitchers, writing poetry, and formulating perfectly rational antidotes to our national delusions, even though they serve now as proof of the great academy's tolerance for diverse ideas. They have been rendered eunuchs, but at least they are dissident eunuchs with health insurance. But I have always enjoyed living in or visiting major university communities. Just last week, I had one of the most meaningful evenings in ages with the dissident crowd at the University of Pennsylvania in Philly. Thankfully, such dissidents prefer to congregate there instead of, say, Bob Jones Cult College or wearing the secret Mormon underwear of Brigham Young University. It felt like old times. It felt free. Sort of. Still, though, there was a nagging feeling that these people were an endangered species. And also that they were actually philosophers and bards and artists—noble pursuits once esteemed by universities and the intellectual class—but somehow now fall under the category of dissidents, which, in America, is code for terrorist-sympathizing malcontents.

"From the viewpoint of university administrators, my puny philosophy department, and even the entire humanities division, looks rather like some vestigial organ. The business school is the heart, the natural sciences are the brain, and we, who read Plato and Descartes, Homer and Montaigne, are the appendix, just waiting to be excised once and for all."
—*Justin E. H. Smith, Concordia University philosophy professor*

Meanwhile, until the appendectomy happens, there are the nation's intellectual hall monitors to deal with. Most of America's intellectual class, like any that expects to maintain its privileges, must be self-policing. So real dissidents and original thinkers are ignored, and we watch B.F. Skinner's extinction-behavior practice put into action. Smile, and ignore the dissident to death professionally. Sometimes, though, in spite of the best pest-eradication efforts in the garden of academe, there sprouts a weed so completely antithetical to the great lie that he or she cannot be ignored. And if the offending party is particularly unlucky, he or she may be discovered by one of the political hacks sponsored to "elected office" by the Corporation—usually a Republican congressman looking for threats from within this very republic of eagles under God. Then all hell breaks loose. First, the dissident is publicly discredited and demonized by an organized media-lie campaign. After that, an appointed academic committee somehow discovers that his or her credentials, even after 25 years in the university system, are fraudulent and that there are some serious questions about his or her sexual appetites, not to mention his or her whereabouts on September 11.

I once thought I understood the ways in which America removes those who would point to the essential global criminality by which all Americans draw their ration of bread. But as I watched this process being conducted on my friend Ward Churchill, I realized how the extraction of these people from society has become an exquisitely brutal form of public surgery—certainly chilling on the face of it, but even more horrifying for the entertainment value it provided for the cheap seats in the Coliseum. I've known Church for over 30 years, and though I've never completely agreed with what I considered his somewhat violent take on things, I agree with him now. Not simply because the system took out another of my dissenting friends, but because for the first time I could see how the dismemberment of a thinking citizen's identity and life is conducted, tissue by tissue, through carefully sharpened lies and fraudulent moral and intellectual charges. In his starkest truth-telling about the genocide perpetrated upon indigenous peoples, and in his now-infamous description of the Empire's "little Eichmanns" occupying the World Trade Center towers, Church came too close to the truth about the kind of psychic violence that underpins The American Way, the unacknowledged kind that is executed by America's most servile class—the bureaucratic, managerial, and intellectual classes that maintain a system which could never survive the light of truth or anything resembling real justice.

It is because of guys like Church that the American intellectual establishment must conduct the self-policing of their own class. So a carefully nurtured and sustained system of intellectual critics finds faults, finds problems in the basic thesis or critical thinking or premise of any writer or thinker whose observations do not match the national hallucination being sold by the system's elites (to whom they must cater without appearing to cater). Even the supposed intellectual left does this. In fact, it probably does it best of all through its staunch assertions of the evils of free-market capitalism, even though free-market capitalism does not even exist and has never been practiced (more on that later). Most born into the establishment's intellectual class are born blind, rather like kangaroos or possums inside safe, dark, middle- or upper-middle-class marsupial pouches, where they experience nothing except what feels good as defined by the moist darkness of their nurture. And when they emerge, they feel entitled to be where they are and honestly cannot see the system itself, never giving it a thought until they go off to college and, between spring breaks and beer parties, learn to experience and define reality through texts.

Those who do see the system for what it is are either worn down by the sheer mass of our institutions, or they construct elaborate mental architecture to bridge over and avoid the truth. While their efforts are often applauded or taken up by fellow intellectuals—post-modernism has been the latest of these, and like all such constructions, contains a maybe one or two fly-shit-sized specks of truth—they are utterly lost in the national machinery of fabrication. Text is not reality. Hell, reality isn't even reality in this country.

It is not too hard to grasp why unlettered but intuitive—and not a little bit vengeful—Chinese peasants in their revolution killed, humiliated, and imprisoned the intellectuals. If Mao got one thing right, it was that those intellectuals who pretend to ignore the existence of class, or refuse to live at the level of the most common class, are actually class exploiters, and entertain the pretense at their own eventual peril. No amount of text, no amount of ideology or pretense, can ultimately protect us from reality—something which Americans are about to learn the hardest way possible.

When it comes to the state-sanctioned American intellectual establishment's support of charade and pretense, the biggest fraud of all has been the notion of capitalism and free markets. There never was a free market; as Howard Zinn has so often demonstrated, every single industrialized nation was built on protectionism from the beginning. Even a cursory study of economic history shows that not a single developed nation in the world has ever followed the rules of free-market capitalism. Not one. Early America built its textile industry on protectionism from the British. One hundred years later, our steel industry came about the same way.

That is not to say that the rules of free-market capitalism are never observed. The rules of free-market economics are for ramming down the throats of Third World or otherwise uncooperative peoples—especially those tracking crude oil through the marketplace on the soles of their sandals. Yet there is scarcely a college or university, or a business or school of that mumbo-jumbo ritual called "economics" in this nation, that does not teach "free-market history" and free-market "solutions" to such problems as the devastating eco-collapse in progress, or that millions of babies shit themselves to death from dysentery, or die for lack of a plain old drink of clean water.

Free-market capitalism may have been a fraud from the git-go, but at least there was once a version which accepted the notion that any market needed customers. Once upon a time, business in the industrialized world needed its citizen-laborers as customers, as consumers, which implied that they needed to be paid at least enough to buy the products of the businesses and corporations that beat their asses into submission along America's assembly lines and hog-slaughtering plants. That was called American opportunity and prosperity, and it looked pretty damned-good to millions of war-ravaged Urpeen furiners trying to decide whether to eat a wharf rat or the neighbor's cat for dinner. As for the Third World, they could eat dirt and do native dances for what few tourists existed then (otherwise called the rich), but mainly they had to stay out of the way of "our" natural resources in their countries.

At any rate, when the citizen labor-force, by their sheer numbers, held most of the dough in their calloused mitts, the business classes had no way of avoiding them. But now that so much of not just this nation's, but the world's, wealth has become concentrated in the hands of so few, that is no longer a problem for the rich. People are cheaper than ever and getting more plentiful by the minute. So work'em to death, kill'em, eat'em if you want to. Who the fuck cares? The international rich, the managers and controllers of the new financial globalism and the world's resources and the planet's labor forces—whether they are Asian "Confucian capitalists," masters of Colombian Narco-state fortunes or Chinese Tongs, New York or London brokerage and media barons, or Russian oligarchs—hold increasing and previously unimaginable concentrated wealth. Their customers look to be a replacement for the mass market, indeed even a better one, with fewer mass-distribution problems involved in supplying their higher-grade demand at top prices.

Until then, however, the real dough is still in the energy game, the big suckdown of hydrocarbons—that, plus convincing Americans to burn up their own seed corn. Academics, economists, and scientists offer "free-market solutions," such as ethyl alcohol from corn—which most readers here know requires more petroleum to grow than the energy it produces, and will deprive the rest of the world of much-needed food—just so Americans may continue motoring the suburban savannah lands, grazing on Subway Cold Cut Combos and Outback's Kookaburra Chicken Wings.

But even when the last Toyota Prius is forever moldering in the globally warmed deserts of Minneapolis, we proles will not be totally unprofitable creatures. Yesterday I read a gem of an economic paper asserting that in the emerging information, amusement, service, and "experience and attention economy," it is vital that "private business capture ownership and control of the public's knowledge and its attending rent streams." Apparently it's not bad enough that we become a third-rate gulag of impoverished nitwits. They are going to charge us for the privilege.

Oh, dammit to hell anyway. Like a lady in Philly told me last week, "Joe, you're always so grim about these things." She's right. It's not the end of the world. Just the opening act. There is still quite a bit of this ugly little drama to be played out. But I can say one thing with certainty: This may be, as the economic intellectuals assert, the new American "attention economy," but I sure as hell ain't gonna pay to watch.

14

Lost in the Hologram

[August 17, 2007]

"On television you see police cars surround the car of a 'terror suspect' ... When you learn he is a neurosurgeon whose wife and baby were in the car with him, you might think he probably just pulled over when the police seemed to want him to, but only if you were still capable of using your own brain. After all, his name is Mohammed and his wife wears a headscarf ... So maybe you'll just ignore what your brain was trying to say, which is that neurosurgeons have a lot invested in their careers ... But the media are so hard to ignore. Even when you make a point of ignoring them, they are always there, flickering around the edges, burning impressions you can't quite get rid of ... But it was all so tidy and comfortable in that TV/mainstream news site world. Meanwhile, though no evidence of guilt has been offered, the discussion zooms ahead. Why can't everyone else see it?"

—*Email from Jennifer in Los Angeles*

Needless to say, the Middle Eastern doctors accused of terrorism in Scotland may be guilty as hell. Mohammed Asha may be another one of your standard terror wogs who, as we all know by now, relish the idea of prison or perhaps blowing up his wife and baby for Allah.

But having been in the media business one way or another for almost 40 years, and having watched it increasingly take on a life of its own, I know that nothing of significance in the news is what it appears to be. This is not the result of some media conspiracy, mind you, but rather that the people working in the media have internalized the process so thoroughly they do not even know they are conditioned creatures in a larger corporate/state machine. Put simply, Katie Couric and the dumbshits grinding out your local paper actually believe they are in the news business. In today's system, everybody is a patsy for the new corporate global order of things—the well-coiffed talking head, the brain-dead audience, even the terrorists themselves. All play out their parts in our holographic image-and-information process.

All Americans, regardless of caste, live in a culture woven of self-referential illusions. Like a holographic simulation, each part refers exclusively back to the whole, and the whole refers exclusively back to the parts. All else is excluded by this simulated reality. Consequently, social realism in this country is a television commercial for America, a simulated republic of eagles and big-box stores, a good place to live so long as we never stray outside the hologram. The corporate simulacrum of life has penetrated us so deeply it now dominates the mind's interior landscape with its celebrities and commercial images. Within the hologram sparkles the culture-generating industry, spinning out our unreality like cotton candy.

The American media hologram forms our subconscious

opinions immediately and without our rational participation. Particularly when it comes to generating terrorist outlaws. For example, despite what we were told and most of us believe, Timothy McVeigh was a patriot, and was a more literate and intelligent person than most Americans; in truth, he more resembled Tom Paine than a terrorist. Chew on that one for a while ... or read Gore Vidal's *Perpetual War for Perpetual Peace*. Again, nothing significant is as presented by the American media. Watch television in countries with supposedly primitive media, and after a while you will be shocked at the technologically mediated and shape-shifted image of the world presented to Americans—how the hologram makes incongruous parts suddenly fit together and make sense in its own parallel universe.

For instance, a while back I saw a video clip of an ethanol-fueled automobile driving past waves of grain with the Rockies in the background and a rippling American flag ghosted into the sky. These four elements of the clip—food grain fields, the automotive industry, the natural beauty of the Rockies, and the national emblem—have not much to do with each in the natural world, but they have everything to do with one another in the context of corporate empire. Together, they indicate the national ethos. We accept such an image as naturally as the baby accepts the tit, and the idea of burning the earth's food to create gases that will turn the snowcapped mountains into desertified mountains is greeted happily as something newer and better than the old system of destroying the atmosphere and environment. Mentally we can identify separate elements, isolate things into categories. But the hologram nevertheless remains seamless in its interconnection of all things that benefit the corporate state generating it. Parsed, divided, and isolated, any part contains the entire logic (or governing illogic) of the whole—endless consumption.

In effect, the economic superstate generates a superhologram that offers only one channel—the shopping channel—and one sanctioned collective national experience in which every aspect is monetized and reduced to a consumer transaction. The economy becomes our life, our religion, and we are transfigured in its observance. In the absence of the sacred, buying becomes a spiritual act conducted by satellites in outer space via bank transfers. All things are purchasable and, indeed, access to anything of value is through purchase—even mood and consciousness, through psychopharmacology, to suppress our anxiety or enhance sexual performance, or cyberspace linkups to porn, palaver, and purchasing opportunities. But, most of all, the hologram generates and guides us.

Through advertising and marketing, the hologram combs the fields of instinct and human desire, arranging our wants and fears in the direction of commodities or institutions. No longer are advertising and marketing merely propaganda, which is all but dead. Digitally mediated brain experience now works far below the crude propaganda zone of influence, deep in the swamps of the limbic brain, reengineering and reshaping the realms of subjective human experience.

Yet we are the hologram, because we created it. In a relentlessly cycling feedback loop, we create and project the hologram out of our collective national psyche. The hologram in turn manages our collective psyche by regulating our terrors, cravings, and neurological passions through the production of wars, whores, politics, profits, and manna. Like legions of locusts, we pray before its productive engines of commerce, and under the shifting aurora borealis of the hologram's drama and spectacle. It is us. We are it. The psychology of the individual becomes irrelevant as the swarm relentlessly devours the earth.

Meanwhile, those bloody terrorist wogs are still up to no fucking good, that's for sure. They're everywhere these days, so somebody needs to keep an eye on that Palestinian meat-dealer down the street. As one reader responded, "The terrorists all look normal. That's the first thing you hear when one of them is caught. 'Oh, but he looked so normal,' his neighbors say. You'd never have guessed." Now, when so many apparently normal people—students, doctors, merchants, teachers, family men with ordinary lives—find themselves being accused of wickedness and evil, some even locked away in secret prisons and tortured, maybe it's time to start looking at the accusers more closely. When we do that, familiar terms come to mind, terms such as "mass psychosis", along with some less familiar ones such as "political psychosis".

Terrorists aside, the hologram offers us, and we have come to accept, plenty of now standard-issue American fears, such as identify theft and child molesters. My home in Winchester, Virginia, is located on a corner where neighborhood kids catch the school bus under a large maple tree. Thus some neighbors have asked me to keep an eye on the kids during the mornings. In addition, I leave the back door unlocked so they can run inside and call home should a predator accost them under that maple tree. Matters are not made any better by the fact that a guy in the apartment building across the street is on the Internet sex offenders' list. Nobody is safe in a country where, according to at least one "study," about 40 percent of adult men have sexual fantasies about children. It's a damned sick country. Hence the hundreds of child-protection organizations, TV shows, and pieces of legislation, all of which constitute a billion-dollar industry in this country. Just what are the chances of the kids at the bus stop being abducted by a stranger for sexual abuse or ransom? The truth is that a child is far more likely to be struck by lightning or slip on a rug, breaking his or her neck and dying instantly, than being kidnapped by a malevolent stranger. According to a U.S. Department of Justice study published in 2002, there were about 115 cases in 1999 that were considered stereotypical kidnappings—that is, a stranger took a child to hold for ransom or to kill. About 200,000 kids are snatched away from one parent by the other in the never-ending custody wars that clog the courtrooms and buy summer homes for lawyers. But the odds of pedophilic monsters or ransom artists grabbing your kid are not even worth worrying about, considering that there are nearly 300 million people in this country.

As for the registered sex offender across the street, I came to learn that he is a pothead and a pain in the ass as a neighbor. But he's not a child molester. He got on the list for mooning while drunk one night, which should be a lesson for anyone considering hanging his or her butt out a car window after a rock concert.

Still, it's a sick damned country all right. The government says so. The news says so. *Cold Case Files* says so. The *Today* show says so. Oprah says so. *Without a Trace* says so. In other words, the hologram says so. In the time it took you to read this paragraph, and while millions watch the cathartic media projection of their deepest nightmares, several dozen children died of famine or disease outside the hologram.

If the big picture is ominous, the little picture is comedic kitsch. In the 1970s, the hologram offered us "killer bees," a curiously "Africanized," aggressive species that "bred with every other kind of bee" as it moved up from the South—remember that seeping red area on the U.S. map indicating the spread of the insect in its killer apiary jihad to sting a nation to death? In truth, the bee's sting was no more toxic than any other bee's.

In the 1980s and 1990s we had the decade-long daycare sexual-abuse hysteria in a dozen states wherein children were reportedly used for prostitution and pornography, tortured, or made to watch snuff films. According to testimony, they were crawling through hidden tunnels toward Satanic worship chambers while witches soared overhead in hot air balloons at the McMartin Preschool in California, and they were being abused by clowns and robots in a secret room at the Fells Day Care Center, even as peanut butter was being spread on children's genitals at the Wee Care Nursery School in New Jersey. Numerous people spent years in prison before their cases were finally overturned, and they were set free to enjoy their bankruptcy. Again, no one stopped to look at the accusers more closely, or ask, "Does anyone else on the jury think this is too goddamned weird to be plausible? Aw, come on, folks—robots and clowns?" Such is the power of the media hologram. The most expensive jury trial in American history was about subterranean devil worship and witches in hot air balloons.

Another standard media holograph favorite is the case of The Missing Pretty White Girl, in which a young white woman is either missing, murdered, or maybe faking her own abduction. The hologram's finest hour may have been when it blended nationalism with armed feminine sexuality fantasy via the brave blonde Jessica Lynch, in a projection of her going down with automatic rifle blazing, then daringly rescued—oh, poor, wounded, little bird of our desire—by GI Joe action figures. If she had been an overweight lesbian, she'd still be in that hospital, and if she had been black, the media wouldn't have bothered to take the lens covers off the cameras. If the syndrome's appointed white girls turn out to be murdered, then we get the memorial websites, charity foundations, and maybe some sort of law passed, based upon the circumstances of the case, and named for the victim. However, you'll never see one called Tawanda Robinson's Law. Hologram don't sell no dark meat. Make a YouTube video, bitch!

And when the hologram gets hold of a real event, whoopee! We get a portrayal of a nation marked by school shootings (school shootings of teachers and fellow students took place in the 1800s, too—they just didn't have the firepower, not to mention the media, we have today), campus shooters, or the estranged killer husband or wife (a timeless favorite). None of the above are lurking around every corner, or any corner so far as I can tell. Then, too, I don't get out much.

It never ceases to amaze me how the hologram can sell even our own identities back to us in such tantalizing fashion. Regardless of politics, no one escapes it: "Ladies, buy your wardrobe at Target, and you too will be a slim, sexy humanitarian like Susan Sarandon." My eyeballs are in my lap every time that woman twists her stuff against the orange Target backdrop in the TV ad, while my wife growls from her armchair, "Buy me a quarter-million-dollar eye job, chin and butt tuck, and I'll shake all the damned booty you want, buster." I'm seriously considering her offer.

Of course, the entire American consumer shiteree is unsustainable. One day soon it will go bust, and the hologram will sell us the bust as a lifestyle. Renunciation of consumer goods and a monastic lifestyle will become a fad and then a major trend in America. Then it will be co-opted by the system and made expensive. The ozone hole will be so big we'll all be pedaling teensy cars that come with iron lungs as standard equipment. Renunciation will become a status symbol. All the beautiful people will be doing it.

Not that it will be the first time a worthwhile idea got

at least some small traction in the savagery of the American marketplace. Healthful organic foods and hemp fiber clothing were once merely a holistic hippie thing, but we've see them endure, even grow. And become expensive, of course. (Organic foodwise, I just bought a quart bottle of lemon berry juice with echinacea for nearly eight bucks, though I doubtlessly screwed up its healthful benefits by mixing it with cheap Aristocrat vodka—$9 a half gallon. I named the drink "The Echinacean Whore.") And hemp fiber clothing is a low-cost, practical solution to dozens of ecological problems. Just the other day I saw a $60 pair of hemp fiber, bibbed play shorts for the morally superior baby. Market capitalism can co-opt virtually any low-cost alternative and sell it right back at ridiculous prices.

Ah, for the good old days before the hologram and its hyperstimulation of "consumer affluence," the days of "America's teeming masses," that sweat-soaked, beer-farting mob of ordinary working Americans who didn't have a pot to piss in by today's standards, much less a credit card, but still knew bullshit when they saw it. Guys that looked like William Bendix and were unapologetic about earning their bread by their mitts and never heard of the word "lifestyle". Women in curlers who would have laughed Martha Stewart off the map. Them was Americans, bub!

Now, as walking advertisements for Nike and the Gap or Jenny Craig, and living by the grace of our Visa cards, we have become the artificial collective product of the corporately "administrated" modern state economy. Which makes us property of the government. One that is currently coughing blood in its last gasps, helped along toward its end by the rich white boy hubris of a gang of cowboying petro-crooks: "Put some purty muzak on the fog machine, Dick. We don't want the herd to stampede while we're packing up the loot. And, fer God sake, turn down that Baghdad gunfire noise in the hologram." Deploying 250 million televisions which absorb 11 years of the average America's lifespan, the hologram regulates the nation's neurological seasons—football season, which is delivered with its competitive passions, political election seasons, Christmas shopping season, but especially marketing seasons. It regulates the national mood, stirring our patriotic passions during wars and anxious vigilance against the threat of unseen terrorists who look absolutely normal. Together, we live within a media-generated belief system that functions as the operating instructions for society. It shows us how successful people supposedly behave, invest, and relate to each other. Through crime shows, it demonstrates what happens to us if we don't behave. It shows us who we should hate (Hugo Chavez and Fidel Castro, for starters). Anything outside of its parameters represents fear and psychological freefall.

Well, we can't have that happen, can we? So let us all close our eyes and let the one voice speak to the many. Take a deep breath, and exhale very slowly ... Let the soft electrical buzz engulf your mind, let that auroral drapery of flickering light play across the inside of your eyelids.

"This is the hologram speaking ..."

15

Nine Billion Little Feet

[February 8, 2008]

"John Raymond Castillo, age 91. Sunrise, January 14, 1917. Sunset, February 1, 2008. He leaves 21 children, 140 grandchildren, and 302 great-grandchildren."

—*Obituary announcement on Belize's LOVE Radio station*

"The population of Belize? Officially, it's about 300,000. But if you include all the kids, it's probably three million."

—*Greg, longtime expatriate American in Belize*

Hopkins Village, Belize

The din of squealing, laughing children is the background white noise of the Third World. In Belize, as in most of the Third World, 45 percent of all people are under the age of 16. About a dozen of that 45 percent swarm around me as I cut my toenails under the mango tree. A few are picking on the mangy, quarreling dogs, but the majority are drawn in close, giving advice about how to cut gnarly, old man-type toenails: "Saw dem off wid a file" seems to be the consensus.

What I see are children I help with homework and feed, and admonish about grades, unanxious and reasonably happy little members of the human race. They do not look much like a global migration or crushing planetary population pressure. Yet they are among the most incredible wave of both ever in human history.

Most families here have five or six kids, and their kids will have a similar number. I've yet to meet a native of the village who does not think half a dozen is a nice round number of offspring. My adopted family has six kids and four adults living on a 100 x 300-foot lot. This does not include the Guatemalan family of five living in a rented cabana at one corner of the lot. Assuming all the children reach adulthood and procreate, the tally in 10 years will be about 50 people of all ages trying to exist on this square of sewerage-soaked sand.

But, oh, were it that bright a future. As adults with families, these kids won't even have this spot on which to live at all, much less live as well as they live now. The resorts and condo rackets out of Canada, South Africa, and the U.S. are buying up these small plots. Unschooled in western financial concepts and sucked in by the developers' offers of more money than they have ever seen in their lives, locals sell. Usually they are broke within a year. In any case, their semi-literate children will join the next generation's issuance of dispossessed, poverty-stricken young adults headed for elsewhere. Just what the world does not need—not here in Central America, not in the Middle East, and not in Latin America or the U.S. But that's what we've got, and that's what we are going to get a lot more of.

Population growth is the rhino in the playpen, the root

cause of our approaching eco-disaster that no one honestly talks about. On the left we get an onslaught of information about what we must and must not do to prevent climate change. Good Democrats get Al Gore's advice, which somehow never mentions the corporations doing the damage. And all of America gets feel-good electric-car ads—buy your way out of the problem, or at least your guilt if you happen to have any. But nowhere do we get an honest discussion about population growth. If you care to, argue that climate change may or may not destroy us. But uncontrolled population growth is guaranteed to do the job. As an old Idaho rancher told me, "You can't run a hundred head of cattle on half an acre."

Most of the developed world remains clueless as to how all this will affect their own lives. But Americans in particular cannot get their head around the impact these billions will have on the lifestyles they are driven like rats in hell to sustain. About half of Americans ...

LOOKY HERE, BAGEANT, YOU PICKLED OLD GAS BAG. HALF OF AMERICANS LIVE UNDER THE GOOFBALL HALLUCINATION THEY CAN SEAL THE BORDERS WITH SILLY PUTTY, DRONE AIRCRAFT, AND MACHINE GUNS. THE OTHER HALF, LIBERALS OVERDOSED ON PROZAC AND WHITE WINE, IS LINED UP LIKE DOCKSIDE WHORES WAVING AT THE INCOMING FLEET. "LET'S WELCOME THEM ALL! AMERICA IS THE LAND OF IMMIGRANTS, SO HELL FUCKING YES, LET 'EM ALL IN!" YEA, RIGHT. LET EVERYBODY LIVE LIKE A FUCKING HAITIAN WHARF RAT IN THE NEW THIRD WORLD AMERICA. HELL, IT'S ALREADY STARTED. THEY'RE CROAKING 49 MILLION AMERICANS BECAUSE THEY CAN'T COME UP WITH THE BLACKMAIL DOUGH FOR HEALTH CARE. THEY'RE KICKIN HUNDREDS OF THOU.S.ANDS OUT OF THEIR PLYWOOD NESTING BOXES BECAUSE THEY CAN'T MAKE THE MONTHLY NUT. AMERICA IS ALREADY A THIRD WORLD COUNTRY WITH DRIVE-THROUGH FEEDING BOXES.

Meanwhile, both camps of a nation with no sense of history beyond its own state-sponsored founding fathers' mythology hasn't the slightest notion of how population migrations from areas of scarcity to areas of plenty have shaped human history perhaps more than any other force, including war (war is just more dramatic when it happens, and more entertaining to read about when it's over). The Vikings were a population shift from the limited arable-land resources of the north around the British coast to Normandy (and then back to England by way of William the Conqueror, a Viking descendant). So were the Huns, the Goths, the Vandals, the Irish in America, the Chinese into Tibet.

WELL, BUBBA, LET ME SPELL IT OUT FOR YOU IN CRAYONS. IT'S GETTING RIGHT BROWN OUT THERE IN HEARTLAND AMERICA. ALL THOSE SAWED-OFF LITTLE DARK-HAIRED FUCKERS HAVEN'T COME UP HERE TO BE LAWN ORNAMENTS. AND SINCE THEY EAT AND SHIT ABOUT THE SAME AMOUNT AS YOU DO, THERE'S GONNA BE SOME REDISTRIBUTION OF THE GOODIES. YOU'RE GONNA SEE A LOT OF AMERICAN BLUBBER PARKED IN LINE ALONGSIDE SALVADORANS WITH THEIR WHEELBARROWS FULL OF WORTHLESS GREENBACKS WAITING TO BUY BLACK BEANS AND MASA HARINA IN BULK — THEN HITCHING A RIDE HOME ON A FLATBED TRUCK LIKE THE REST OF THE WORLD SOUTH OF LOREDO DOES. OR MAYBE TAKING THE CHICKEN COOP FIREWOOD EXPRESS SURPLU.S. SCHOOL BU.S. BACK TO THE SAVAGE ARMED SUBURBS. A LITTLE TIP FROM THE OLE SCREAMING MAN: IF THERE IS A BILLY GOAT IN THE BACK OF THE BU.S., RIDE UP FRONT. IF THE DAMNED GOAT IS UP FRONT, RIDE ON THE ROOF. THERE IS U.S.UALLY SOMEBODY OR SOMETHING UP THERE TO HANG ONTO.

Meanwhile, the truth stays buried in the crapola. According to the UN's newest report on the planetary condition, crop production has improved but has not kept up with population. World cereal production per person peaked in the 1980s, and has since been decreasing. We have over six billion people now—there were far less than half that when I was born—and there will be roughly nine billion people by 2050. But the UN, being a world organization that has to please a couple of hundred governments, each beating its own national drum to its people, pretends there is a long-term solution other than to eliminate two-thirds of the world population within the above-mentioned kids' lifetimes. Thus, the UN issues "millennium development goals." This neatly sidesteps the fact that if the present six billion mouths and assholes running the world's resources through their gullets like shit through a goose is unsustainable, then nine billion of the same are waaaaaay beyond sustainable in any way worth calling human life.

For starters, it would take a doubling of world food production to (a) feed the current victims of hunger, and (b) feed the additional three billion. Theoretically, we're going to cut back. We'll feed the nine billion by some unarguably admirable means, like cutting waste, not overeating, biofuels, and ending meat consumption. Small problem here, Jackson: We're pretty much out of the phosphate fertilizer that is the foundation of world agriculture. The soil itself is collapsing in terms of human nutrition, as we use up its finite reserves of vital elements—iodine, chromium salts, and other complex materials that our six billion collective bodies need to function. And farming has already sucked down the world's water supply to the danger level. Yet, somehow, we are going to come up with *twice* the water we now use by 2050, global warming and drying be damned. The whole time we are fixing global warming, the population climbs.

Old Tom Malthus said that something like this was gonna happen, although he got some of the details wrong, which a person just might conceivably do in predicting the fate of human civilization a couple of hundred years in advance. Call me a softie here, but I tend to give the guy a break for getting it 90 percent right.

But then I'm no scientist. Supposedly sophisticated American scientists have been pissing on the grave of poor Tom at least since I was a kid in school. All my life, American capitalist economists have proclaimed that they've licked the population problem by using the world up faster. "A failed prophet of doom," I believe my high school teacher called Malthus. Even commies kicked Tom's dog around. Engels called him a barbarian. Marx couldn't handle Tom's action, either. Nor could practically anyone else, from John Stuart Mill to Allen Greenspan. And we still get the stale argument that "This planet isn't crowded; it is just mismanaged." Even the greens seem to believe that we can manage our way out of this fatal mess, if we just recycle, wear hemp, and vote for the candidate on the bicycle with the Celtic tattoo. The alternative geeks swear that nano tech is gonna pull us through. But last I heard, pandemic viruses were still smarter than carbon nanotubes. Something about rapid adaptability. Those little fuckers seem to be fast on their feet, so in a title match between nano tech (or any tech for that matter) managed in the ring by nerds, and natural evolutionary biology—which not only has mother nature holding the towels in its corner, but is also calling the fight—I'm damned sure betting on the biology.

At any rate, when it comes to the planet, now under new global corporate management, it looks to be managed to death—dirt, people, and all. The new management, kings and feudal lords of corporate finance to a man, peer down happily from the forty-fourth floor at six billion potential slave-wage employees, and wonder if you can feed 'em on dirt and kudzu.

Malthus must be thrashing inside his lead-lined English coffin right now, cackling, "Do the math, you fuckers!" But they won't. With the world's dough presently being loaded into their yachts bound for the Caymans, they don't have to. Not just yet, anyway. As for the guy on the bike with the Celtic tattoo, if he peddles long enough he's bound to run into some of those 49,671 human beings who were born while I was writing this.

AND WHILE HE'S SPEEDING HE CAN CLOSE HIS EYES AND MAKE A FUCKING WISH WITH TINKERBELL! THAT NINE BILLION WILL BE HUMPING AWAY TRYING TO CRACK THE TWELVE BILLION MARK. WHEN WE ARE ALL LIVING IN RENTAL STORAGE LOCKERS AND EATING PURINA PEOPLE CHOW, FUCKING WILL BE ONE OF THE LAST FREE PASTIMES LEFT, OTHER THAN LISTENING TO THE 24/7 ADVERTISING PIPED IN THROUGH OUR NECK CHIPS SELLING TEENSY STRAP-ON-YOUR-ASS RUBBER BAND-POWERED CARS. SO WE'RE GONNA HAVE EITHER HOMELAND SECURITY FUCK POLICE, OR FORCED STERILIZATION BY ICE PICK.

Actually, SCREAMING MAN is not so far off the mark. Human sterilizing crops are being researched, and I'm not entirely sure I'm agin it, partner, so long as they make the white people eat the stuff first.

In the meantime, the air is getting rather balmy in places it shouldn't. Such as the North Pole. So the corporate and financial lizards at the top of the world rock, in a last-ditch effort to milk out a few bloody trillion dollars more, have come up with a plan: carbon emissions-trading.

Just as in a Mafia handshake and kiss-on-the-neck "business agreement," there are no escape clauses in the laws of physics. In either case, the rules cannot be bent, though your ass may well end up worse than bent if you try to escape the debt you have racked up, be it in greenbacks or the green life-supporting stuff of our planet. Both are finite and vital. Which means you get killed if you try to scam the game, and you certainly don't get to write yourself an escape clause after the fact. But that doesn't keep the high-rolling carnie hucksters we call legislators from trying.

Naturally, they like carbon trading. To my mind at least, making a profit off the fact that you did not piss into the community-drinking gourd is the kind of logic that only obsessive, property-based western world governments and corporations could come up with. It assumes that (a) poisoning everyone else in the human fishbowl is a right to start with, and (b) that right is a property which can be bought and sold between corporate poisoners.

Traded or not, there will be plenty of carbon around, so don't worry about not getting your fair share. In fact, we could park every car on the planet and be assured of a nice, steady supply of carbon pollution for our great-great-great grandchildren. Turns out that, decades ahead of an already grim global-warming schedule, biological repositories of carbon are beginning to release enough of the stuff to tide us over so our progeny can gasp for breath as they skateboard piggyback to and from their barracks at the Manpower gulag. Anyway, we can monetize pollution, and trade our commonly shared hemlock back and forth, and we can call it a "partial solution and a progressive step forward." But it's still hemlock. Yet economists assure us that it makes good sense to propertize, then buy and sell catastrophe in the market of calamity.

LOOK HERE, SPORT. THEY'RE POLISHING A TURD SO THEY CAN SHAKE DOWN THE YOKELS. AND THE DUMB MAMMY-JAMMING PUBLIC BUYS IT! HELL, AN ECONOMIST SAID IT AND AN ECOLOGIST AGREED, SO IT MUST BE A GOOD IDEA, RIGHT? BUT WHEN ALL THOSE MOOKS WITHOUT ECONOMICS DEGREES FIGURE OUT THAT TURD IS NEVER GONNA SHINE, THE GAME WILL BE UP. ESPECIALLY WHEN THEY BEGIN TO ASSOCIATE POLLUTION WITH THE FACT THAT THEIR KIDS ARE BEING BORN WITH 177 TEETH AND AN I.Q. OF 33.

Civilization's most fatal folly was monetization and propertizing of the natural world that is humanity's great commons. In fact, those two things—monetization and propertization—have come to mean civilization from the perspective of most ordinary people over the increasingly brutal centuries that they have enabled. If modern cumulative civilization is not perceived as being very brutal by, say, the average hedge-fund manager or Russian oligarch with a cell phone jacked into one ear while hurtling through the earth's commons in a new BMW toward either the Outback Steakhouse or an appointment with his mistress, well, theirs is certainly a minority perspective. Ask any indigenous person.

"Commons" may be the current precious little term embraced by environmentally concerned American writers and activists—including me—but it rests on old European "ours together and my own private" concepts of the earth. That green foliage stuff whizzing by our windshields is more than commonly shared space. It is our commonly shared oxygenic and chlorophylic blood. And the "dirt" scraped and hammered into sterility and smothered under the asphalt is the armature, the bones, of our existence. It was never possible for anyone to "own" any part of this so-called common, a word that only exists so someone else—usually a less than nice fellow surrounded by thugs in armor and whatnot—could call a piece of it his private property. You dared kill and eat one of my grouse! Die, peasant motherfucker!

But once the delusion set in, and the peasants were allowed to scratch out a living on "their own" miserable, designated little square, there was no turning back. Especially if you were European or a derivative thereof, and ultimately ended up on the winning side of the delusion, otherwise called empire. But there never was a "mine and theirs" when it comes to breathing clean air or drinking clean water. It only appeared so to propertized minds and cultures busy conquering and killing and pillaging other people's natural worlds. And thanks to feudalism's greatest shape-shifting trick of all, capitalism, there ain't much left to pillage.

For Americans, this is particularly ironic, especially in terms of politics. Just as we started ballyhooing the triumph of America consumer capitalism over communism, the world's ecology started backing up like a redneck septic tank. And Castro's Cuba, of all places, emerged as a beacon of relatively petroleum-free eco-enlightenment, organic farming, and clean air — thanks to our 45-year embargo and the Ruskies turning off cigarland's oil spigot in 1990. And now, despite its toxic track record, we find that China, the same goddamned anthill people who flat-out starved 30 million people (there's population control for ya) to make way for a great leap forward, is running the two largest eco-reclamation projects on earth — the Natural Forest Protection and the Sloping Land Conversion programs. These are admirable efforts in the world's eyes, even if the air over their cities is still so foul that buzzards fly into it and drop dead. It certainly beats the U.S. refusing to stop in at the Kyoto Conference, not even for the hors d'oeuvres. Or going to the Bali Eco Summit just to pick fights with the French. George Bush might claim to be from Texas, but he plays global poker like a drunk. Meanwhile, the Chinese are still reaping the benefits of offing those 30 million because — voila! — they never reproduced. Are those guys inscrutable or what?

So what are we all-American guys to do but drive around the suburbs looking for fried chicken, watching the weeds grow up on the foreclosed lawns, and slobber into our cell phones regarding our geographic location, having lost all sense of historical and moral location? "I'm going down Shirley Drive.

Where are you?" "Me? I'm eating a pizza and watching some hot blonde on *Animal Planet* smootch upon bonobo chimps. It's educational. Kinda sexy, too, in a weird way." Now this, folks, is called our "socio-economic environment." It may be social, and it may be economic, but it sure as hell ain't much of an environment. Unless you happen to be a chimp. Of course, like the chimps, we are "prime apes." And, as such, we're supposed to have big brains that account for our "success as a species." We're gonna have to rethink that one. I'm not seeing much success here, hoss. Are you?

Sad lot that we are as a species, not everyone is a moral pig. Millions of individuals, some governments even, are unnerved by what is happening. In America, the best among us are outraged, and protest that officialdom has failed us. Unfortunately, we are officialdom, indirectly as that may be. Because we are mankind, and mankind is all inclusive, organically and forever—forever having turned out to be rather shorter than we thought. If officialdom has failed us, it is because we have failed ourselves, and, in many respects, our official governments provide us with a collective excuse not to act personally.

Mainly, though, aware Americans are watching and waiting for someone else to make an important move. Guts are nonexistent in Americans these days, programmed out of us during the posh captivity of the "cheap oil fiesta" that drove our grotesque and brief civilization. Still, if ever there were a time to show some guts, it's now. Not by protesting—which has become a security-state-supervised liberal pussy sport—but by giving up the material life, the consumer life. Damned-near all of it. Including all those leftie and alternative books from Amazon—sitting on our asses reading, and drinking green tea, just because we can afford to, is just another type of inaction and consumerism. It's the only real act of protest possible for the prisoners of our consumption-driven monolith. True, you'll be just one iPodless and carless little guy throwing a single stone at the United States of Jabba the Hutt. But assuming you're still capable of any kind of life after the Stelazine mind-conditioning we've all been administered for past 40 years, I've got folding cash that says you will own your life in a way that seemed previously impossible. Hanging onto or chasing the bling is over with, anyway — as dead as the economy. The Olive Garden and Circuit City are still open, true, but only because the hair and nails still grow on Jabba's corpse. Would somebody please quit pretending he's alive, and yank the feeding tube?

Scoffers abound, those lurching, undead cud-chewers whose best lick is: "Aw, if things were really that bad, somebody would be doing something about it." Asked who that somebody might be, they usually come up with "the government." Or science, or, the stupidest of all, the Free Market Solution. In other words, they haven't the slightest fucking notion other than that there is some great governmental or commercial force that governs their destiny —one so vast that, like God, they don't have to understand it, just swear by it and trust it. What it is, of course, is good old-fashioned pillage. But even Alaric the Goth limited pillage to three days—with an extra day of rape thrown in if it had been a particularly good siege.

In Hopkins Village, one can find examples of everything that is both destroying the world (scarcely a villager here would not live the American lifestyle if given half a chance) and good about the world (this morning, I took a bath in the sea at dawn, then ate fresh papaya with one of the kids now supervising my pedicure). Americans constitute 5 percent of the world's population, but consume at least 28 percent of the world's resources. This is a primary contributor to the fact that the kids around me — Kirky, Lian, Ebony, Dennis, and the rest — have no future. Is that our fault? You and I are but two of 300 million Americans. Yet just because one's contribution to global misery seems small, it does not mean exemption from responsibility. If I took part in the mass stoning of a child, would I be less guilty because the stone I threw was smaller than the rest?

Compassion figures somewhere in all this. Or is supposed to, anyway. Without it, we are lost. Being born American, I have as little as anyone else. Last week, a young Garifuna woman in our village, a neighbor and friend, lost her baby son in a terrible truck crash. That night, with neighbors gathered round her in the dim light of her shack, her grief was beyond grief. Unable even to walk, she lay on the bed issuing a low, feral, gurgling howl. And as I stood there, packed in among the black faces, I felt nothing, except a strong sense of looking at a *National Geographic* documentary of exotic dark people mourning in a strange setting. That's what American media does to human consciousness. It provides inhuman reference points in the brain/mind to replace experience and feeling. As a people who demonstrably show no guts and even less compassion about the rest of the world, we are in real trouble.

Comfortable as we have been in our plenitude, and confident as we have been in our providence—or perhaps because of these things—we Americans are now at the most critical and terrible moral and ethical juncture in our history. Do we care at all about anybody but ourselves? Is the reader, who has never met Ebony, Lian, Kirky, or Dennis, responsible for accommodating any kind of future for them? Are we responsible for feeding them adequately, full well knowing that the world has far too many babies anyway?

Not many Americans would eat a cheeseburger in front of a starving African child. But is it OK to eat the cheeseburger behind the child's back, out of sight of the child? How far must we get from the starving child to make it OK? What if we worked very hard to buy that cheeseburger? Does hard work justify everything? What is our responsibility? Or are we just helpless in the face of such things?

That we look to other people—politicians, police, and supposed experts—to solve our problems demonstrates that we have learned to be helpless. This is even called "learned helplessness." But none of us is helpless. The fact is that, at any given moment in any given day, we can do something to help eliminate world misery and disparity. As any Third World priest can tell you, this is done mostly face to face, people helping other people one at a time. But America's strictly enforced and fearful class lines prevent us from even associating with those we can actively help—the single mother, the felon just released from prison, the Mexican with four kids who empties your office waste-basket at night.

Americans and people of the developed world are in an unusual position. We can help by doing nothing—simply by sitting on our asses and not buying stuff, not driving to the Gap or the organic market, not turning on our televisions, which is the ultimate act of protest, since it both denies access to our minds by corporate interests, and denies media monoliths that all-important sea of eyeballs. We can refuse to consume. By not consuming we can create our own economic cutbacks. Otherwise, economic cutbacks are not going to happen, and endless war is the inevitable outcome. People will be killed so others survive: advanced nations with sophisticated weaponry will kill off the people from weaker nations so as to grab their land and resources. It happens. And if we let it get that far (well, much farther, since we're already doing it), Americans will be in favor because we live here and not in a poor country. Evil as it sounds, we will have no choice because it is human to prefer to see others die and our own families survive. Morals never get in the way of ultimate survival. In the end, there is no other way except universal legislation to push our bloated material standard of living back three generations. Clearly, democracy cannot make this happen—unless it is the democracy of the human heart, that internal thing which seeks justice.

Overcoming our worst instincts is hard enough. But we also have an array of genuine enemies lined up before us—many, but not all, of our own making. Being the toughest kid on the global block, we long ago chose a geo-strategic struggle for dwindling energy resources rather than conservation of them. Simply because we could. The richest and strongest among us, the global schoolyard bullies, the ones with the power, who are holding all our national wealth —they hold the wealth, we hold the debt—are seeing the same thing coming down the pike that we see, and are building their forts around the planetary neighborhood, consolidating as much wealth and power among as few people as possible.

Yet no one is much alarmed by this because they are incapable of being alarmed by anything except what the state message tells them to be alarmed about—mainly terrorism, which is a form of chickens coming home to roost. America is moreover a nation of state-supervised zombies. This used to scare the piss out of me, but now they have been the national furniture for so long that they are merely depressing. Especially considering that, despite the Republican historical rewrite of the era, we—meaning my generation—had a real crack at turning this thing around during the Sixties. And we failed. We failed ourselves, and failed our children. And as if that were not enough, we failed the planet and humanity itself. Fucking up doesn't come bigger than that. I spent at least a decade nailing the bling. The only excuse I can offer is that I didn't know any better. And I didn't. But somehow that seems so lame.

I'm trying to atone. Yes, that is the right word here—atone—for my part in this unholy mess. I try to live on about $4,000 to $5,000 a year, and come close to pulling it off. I share the rest with the world's needy, almost never drive, and refuse to own a cell phone or anything else that requires earth-killing batteries, other than the laptop that now provides my livelihood … yada yada, you know the drill. Lest I sound holier than thou, let me confess to my continuing part in fucking up the earth's food chain due to a love of pork. But, on the whole, I'm not too ashamed these days of my role in the continuing disaster called America, though there is more I could do. Almost weekly, I seriously consider refusing to pay income taxes as an act of personal resistance. But I ain't Joan Baez and this ain't the Sixties, and I'm scared shitless of going it alone. (Work with me here, people!) Besides that, my wife is unenthusiastic about the idea of her geezer playing dress-ups in the Big House. The relatives would talk.

Thus, I am moreover just waiting it out. Either I'll watch my sorry-assed species walk right off that cliff, or I will croak first. Crappy set of choices. Meanwhile, on a good day I realize that I've still got horses to break, ball games to fix, and beer to drink.

Stay strong.

-16-

The Audacity of Depression

[April 4, 2008]

One of the best things about the hundred-or-so book festivals in America is that, with luck, a writer can manage to get drunk with some of his or her readers. And, with more luck, the readers pick up the tab. Bear in mind that 90 percent of all real writers, people for whom writing is their sole income, spend much of their time counting their change in the rest room of the hotels where they are being put up while on tour. Believe me, there are better rackets than writing.

So here I am at the Virginia Festival of the Book, copping a smoke on the back dining patio of the Omni Hotel in Charlottesville with one of my readers—a somewhat elegant sixty-plus blonde who runs a small public library financial-support group down in ancient, marshy Northumberland County, Virginia. Created in 1648, it is the area that James A. Michener wrote about in *Chesapeake*, and a place where, she tells me, periwinkles that were planted three hundred years ago on the graves of slaves still bloom. My wife, a historical librarian doing colonial African–American research, tells me that these periwinkle-marked slave graves can be found throughout Virginia.

Immensely energetic, and a lifelong activist for literacy and informed thought, this cigarette-voiced Northumberland librarian has built the county's new little library, and even managed to coax enough money out of the local government for two employees. In a county with a population of 12,000, that's no small political feat.

At the moment, though, politically speaking, the Obama-Hillary dirt fight is in full fury, so I asked the obligatory question of the week, "Who will you vote for?"

"Oh, Obama, I guess. It's so hard to get excited over the elections. Lately I've been just plain depressed," she said.

"About what?"

"Oh, just everything. It seems to have become so pointless in America, as if we are entering a Dark Age. I've come to wonder why I do anything at all."

On that melancholy note, we return to the lounge to join my wife for that last drink. The next one is always, of course, the "last one," in the early stages of these situations before all pretense is dropped, and people start taking off their clothes or falling off those infernal high stools that replaced good old-fashioned chairs—the kind where your feet reach the floor at all times and with arms you can grip if the room starts spinning.

Over the past couple of years I've had hundreds of encounters with reading Americans—and by encounters I mean conversations, not falling off chairs—which is to say, with book-loving, thinking people like the Northumberland librarian, people of every stripe. They have ranged from a good-ole-boy Texas electrician, who took me to a real smoke-choked pool-table-and-concrete-floor joint, to professors of literature, and to Washington policy wonks who actually use the little red cocktail napkin that accompanies their martinis.

During this period, I have noticed a change in the nature of discussion with these previously unmet readers. Four years ago, much of it centered on the outrageousness of the Bush administration, on the stomach-turning criminality of the Iraq War, on Cheney, the Fanged Man of Wax, with a little rage at our planetary ecocide thrown into the mix. In other words, about what you might expect from a baby-roasting, alien, commie readership such as mine, made up of such folks as school teachers, union members, sociology profs, and other congenital malcontents, the sort of people who resent things like student strip-searches in public high schools (HR 5295, *The Student Teacher Safety Act of 2006*, which, to its credit, at least bans cavity searches by faculty. You gotta be a cop to do that in our public schools), and other subversive types.

Lately, though, I don't hear so much outrage. In fact, the readers seem to be suffering from what someone aptly called "rage fatigue." Which is another way of saying that the bastards have simply worn us out. And it's true.

I am not kidding when I say that rage-fatigue victims have fallen into a continuing mid-level depression. (Looks to me like the whole country has, but then I'm no mental-health expert.) The less depressed victims can be found lurking near the edges of the Obama cult, consoling themselves that a soothing and/ or charismatic orator is better than nothing. Obama may yet be borne through the White House portico by a Democratic host of seraphim, but he cannot do much without the consent of a bought and paid-for Congress. Only George Bush can do that, and we can only hope that God broke the mold after he made

George. And like whoever else wins the presidency, Obama can never acknowledge any significant truth, such as that the nation is waaaaay beyond being just broke, and is even a net-debtor nation to Mexico, or that the greatest touch-me-not in the U.S. political flower-garden, the "American lifestyle," is toast. But then, we really do not expect political truth, but rather entertainment in a system where, as Frank Zappa said, politics is merely "the entertainment branch of industry."

Still, millions of Americans do grasp at The Audacity of Hope, a meaningless marketing slogan of the publishing industry if ever there was one. At least it has the word "audacity" in it, something that millions of folks are having trouble conjuring up the least shred of these days. And there is good old-fashioned "hope," of course—that murky, undefined belief that some unknown force or magical, unseen power will reverse the national condition—will deliver us from what every bit of evidence indicates is irreversible, if not politically, then economically and ecologically: Collapse.

Compounding everything is the fact that it is quite human and even pragmatic to passively accept reality as it is. Until it's too late to do anything. As my late friend Virgil the philosophical backhoe operator summed it up: "If we fucked everything up so bad tryin' to do our best, maybe we oughtta just leave'er be for a while. Quit thinking about it so much."

More Band-Aids for the trained chickens, please!

Virgil may be popping open a Keystone Light lager somewhere in heaven, or in maybe a much warmer venue. I dunno. But people are thinking about it more than ever. Among sentient people everywhere there is a deep, visceral unease, and among those most aware there is genuinely acute suffering. I hear this expressed quite articulately, not only in places such as this Omni Hotel "writers' lounge," but in working-class and middle-class living rooms, and in emails from Americans and from around the world.

Naturally, the bunny-and-cupcake set of Americans are still oblivious, or at least pretend to be. But even at the more inchoate and private level, there is a growing awareness that things are going very wrong, and doing so on an incomprehensively massive and complex scale. There is the feeling that even if what is happening could be made comprehensible to the majority of humanity, to all those people just trying to keep afloat on the planet—from Zimbabwe to Flint, Michigan—overall it is unstoppable. Unfixable, except in the fleeting media/politics Band-Aid sense, and then only in locales rich enough to afford the illusionary Band-Aid fixes that politicians dream up when they write their campaign "plans for change."

All of which is horseshit, of course, since real change would entail undoing most of the machinery of planetary destruction and extreme pressure to standardize humanity that we have come to know as modern civilization and mass society—halting, then reversing, the momentum that this monolith has achieved.

We now live as the technoculture's subjects, not its masters, and will do so from here on out as viral technology mediates, homogenizes, and monetizes human experience worldwide, in ever-more-remote corners. I watch it regularly in the Third World, where the power of gadgets such as cell phones is wiping out the core foundations of indigenous or longstanding cultures within a decade or two. The global machine's technological nervous system and production musculature, the techno grid now embedded in the world, grows in quantum fashion to control every aspect of our lives more deeply and more thoroughly than is imaginable by the folks living those lives. It's so pervasive that we don't feel it at all.

For instance, I just hit the ATM in this hotel for 40 bucks.

And in doing so, I joined the Manhattan book editor, the black Carib village fisherman in Dangriga, Central America, and the taxi driver in Capetown, South Africa in performing the same activity. We all stand submissively before the global ATM network like trained chickens pecking the correct colored buttons to release our grains of corn. Freedom and, to a large extent, joy, as we understand it in our common technoculture, is mostly just the grid's monetized consumer offerings, each with its own type of packaging, its own technologically produced overlay of commercial skin. These choices, by the way, do not include the non-uniform products or experience, unauthorized products or joys such as hashish or deviant sex. Not officially, at least, but perhaps when technoculture solves the uniform packaging and delivery problem ...

American philosopher John Zerzan has a simple thesis: civilization is pathological, and needs to be dismantled. In his essay "Seize the Day," Zerzan writes that if anybody solves this problem, it will be the Japanese. There seem to be no bigger suckers for technoculture than the people who have given the world plastic dirt ("half as dense as and a thousand times cleaner than real dirt"), the UFO-detecting keychain, the online lie-detector, and the hydroelectric toilet, which "assesses what variety of waste you've just put into it". Technoculture is stressful enough, but obsessing over how clean or dense dirt is, and assessing the varieties of your bodily waste (last time I looked, there were only two) well, there may be a certain justice in the Japanese suffering the highest levels of anxiety, stress, and depression.

Zerzan believes it's so bad that, according to Dr. Kunio Kitamura, director of the Japan Family Planning Association, Japanese "people simply aren't having sex", and the suicide rate has been rising rapidly. Personally, I am not having much sex either, but that has not yet pushed me to toward suicidalism, and probably never will. After reaching the age of 60, sex became perhaps my fifth-highest priority, just below the availability of cheap beer or maybe even a double bourbon after 6.00 p.m.—which, of course, has a helluva lot to do with that fifth priority and its likelihood. All of which is more than you cared to know, I am sure.

"Eventually the system will reach a point—the word that provides the social cue is 'integration'—where the universal dependence of all moments on all other moments makes the talk of causality obsolete. It is idle to search for what might have been a cause within a monolithic society. Only that society itself remain the cause."
—*Theodor Adorno*

In other words, Teddy boy, a totalitarian society. Not a nice word, according to our Western Civ instructors. An ironic one, too, considering that Americans and Europeans sowed so much of its original seed. But the reality is that totalitarian society (dubbed "Totoland" in my household, in a grim effort toward mockery: Dear Dorothy, fuck you and your little dog, too! Signed, Bill Gates) is already here. And most of the planet accepts that, as long as nobody next door is getting beheaded, and at least some grains of corn keep dropping out of that ATM machine. Such is the belief in technology's supposed production efficiency in dealing with the supply-and-demand problems of this world's six billion.

That belief will remain because the technology will remain—until it collapses, along with the corporate aristocracy that makes and owns it. Otherwise, it cannot be dismantled without dismantling the world as we have made it, and we cannot undo our own evolutionary species' trajectory. Regardless of what the New Agers and Earth-worshipping goddess-cultists believe, we cannot haul six billion people back into pre-technology, or support them in any natural, sustainable fashion. Most of the world's common people accept this, however unconsciously—thus the lack of protests and counter-efforts on any meaningful scale. The new totalitarianism is its own justification, and nobody in America or Europe is going to kick up much sand so long as the Darfurs and Haitis remain on the goddamned TV screen, where they belong.

At the same time, those empowered to do what little can be done, the world's aristocrats, do what they have always done: surf the crest of power and wealth, with their dicks pointed into the sunset of their civilization and their heads up their asses. A delighted nation cheers as a brunette corporate aspirant sucks on Donald Trump's pant leg on *The Donald Trump Show*. ("Ya gotta really want it, baby!") As a hobby, the guy owns the Miss Universe organization, and the Miss U.S.A and Miss Teen U.S.A pageants. He'll never want for pants-suckers.

Meanwhile, I've got 40 ATM bucks that have to last me two days at this book bash.

A new Dark Age? Hell, why not?

I've painted a grim picture, for sure, made worse by claiming that hope is a sucker's game, even a religion, for millions of "people of faith" who believe that hope and faith are the same thing. Ah, hope! That fuzzy-hearted Hallmark world of mass-produced sentiment and emotions, even about "bereavement"—a world where thinking is regarded as a rat in the larder of bourgeois smugness. Thinking gnaws away at everything so relentlessly, until it finally breaks a tooth on one truth or another. And one of those truths is that the technology enabling those digital greeting-cards that play "Happy Birthday" is systematically destroying nature, and toxifying and maiming the millions of drudgery-filled souls whose sole purpose for existence is industrial.

I'm convinced that we are watching what Jean-Francois Lyotard called "a new barbarism, illiteracy and impoverishment of language, new poverty, merciless remodeling of opinion by media, immiseration of the mind, obsolescence of the soul," in action. I could be wrong—my wife and kids assure me I am wrong about most things. But I have at least one scholarly author-type on my side, Dr. Morris Berman, who argues that we are indeed seeing the approach of a new Dark Age. I'm willing to bet that the tens of millions living on less than a dollar a day, or any of the women and children sold into the world's multibillion-dollar sex-slave trafficking (including those under American auspices of Dyncorp, and Halliburton subsidiaries like KBR), feel that it's here already. Not that anyone is asking them or anyone else in the Third World.

Living as I do much of the year in a Third World village, watching daily the cost of the American lifestyle on the village's people, the technocultural cheapening of their lives, their physical hunger, I feel guilty even being in such a posh hotel as the Omni. I should be back in Central America finishing up the water-and-sanitation project I recently started there (and probably would be, if I were not out of money). Yet through the patio's glass door I can see the people round my table—the Northumberland librarian, the writer Tom Miller, whose moving testimonies of Latino immigrants open up worlds unseen by white Americans, and my own good wife, who brings to life the truth of slavery by excavating memories in an amnesiac America ... These are people who understand that human life is short and history is long, and that their humanly elegant efforts will not only go unheralded by that history, but will mostly go unacknowledged in their own darkening time, and will be all but eradicated by the sheer impoverishment of language and literacy in their native country during a New American Dark Age that comes cloaked in glittering technology instead of a coarse woolen cowl. Such unassuming and dedicated people are among our best.

This sordid American drama, the one I am calling a Dark Age, will in all likelihood not be completed until well into this century or the next, with a slew of increasingly nasty episodes along the way. Everyone here in the hotel lounge will say goodbye to this world long before America says the Big Goodbye.

Until then, we are left to play out the game, day by day. That being the case, we should elect to play it out with the best among us, the ones on humanity's side, that hidden and unheralded aristocracy—those quiet lamp-lighters making their way through the deepening dusk of American civilization.

E.M. Forster described them as:

Not an aristocracy of power, but an aristocracy of the sensitive, considerate and the plucky. Its members are to be found in all nations and classes and through the ages, and they know each other when they meet ...

Authority, seeing their value, tries to net them and to utilize them. ... But they slip through the net and are gone; when the door is shut they are no longer in the room; their temple is the Holiness of the Heart's Imagination, and their kingdom, though they never possess it, is the wide-open world.

In this, they are deathless. Like periwinkles.

17

Old Dogs and Hard Time

[June 13, 2008]

Late at night, through my window by the computer, I can see my neighbor Stokes bicycling at 10.00 p.m. to the local convenience store to buy groceries. Not only is that an expensive way to feed oneself, but it is the only way for old Stokes to cop some grub without getting thrown in jail. Seriously. As a convicted sex offender, he is not allowed to come in proximity to young women in a supermarket checkout line. Nor is he allowed to visit a park, or even his own grandchild—even though he is not a child molester, by the court's own admission. He is not allowed to drink a beer. In fact, he is not even allowed to read *Playboy* magazine.

A dozen-or-so years ago, Stokes, now 66 with a gray ponytail, an altogether gentle soul who labors under the illusion that he looks like Willie Nelson (and even has a framed photo of Willie on his wall to invite comparison), got caught by police in, shall we say, "a vehicular sexual incident" with a married woman. They were both drunk. Big deal. That happens in beer joints. To make a long story short, by the time they got to court, the lady's testimony was that it was all against her will—which, being a married woman, solved a lot of problems for her. That resulted in Stokes being convicted as a sex offender while his public defender all but slept through the trial.

To make matters worse, Stokes had an unregistered handgun stashed in his car. Stupid, I know, but rednecks are often like that, and I'd be willing to bet there are more unregistered handguns than registered ones around here. This may horrify urban liberals; but, legal or not, it is the common practice of tens of thousands of people down here in the southern climes of our great nation. Not to mention common nationwide to many thousands more cab drivers, night clerks, hotel parking-valets, bill collectors, repo men, single women, and God only knows how many others. At any rate, thanks to the gun, which he never touched, Stokes was prosecuted for armed abduction for sexual purposes, and did 10 years.

He's been out for years now. But he was released into an entirely different world than the one he left—one which seems scripted by Adam Smith and Hanging Judge Roy Bean. As a convicted felon, he has been released from prison to serve a new sentence as a profit center for our economy. In truth, he has been one from the day he was charged.

First off, he was a profit center for the prison where he served his time. Now it is fairly common knowledge that America's burgeoning system of privatized prisons, "super jails," and related services has been a boon for corporations such as Corrections Corporation of America, the Geo Group, Inc. (formerly Wackenhut Corrections Corporation.), and their investors. Prisoner-leasing programs such as Florida's, which rents out prison labor for less than 50 cents an hour to private industry in the name of "job training," make building more prisons an attractive option for state governments and investors. It also makes recidivism desirable, since it assures the prison labor pool. Somewhere between 1 and 2 percent of Americans are behind bars, locked up at any given time; and as many more are on probation or under state monitoring, capitalist-style punishment is obviously a solid financial investment.

Now I am not about to screech here that our prison system is anywhere near that created by Uncle Joe Stalin. We do not have nine million people in it, and we do not get sent there for being late for work at the factory, our factories having been outsourced. However, after 1929, Stalin's prison camps were transformed into an economic machine. And in order to fulfill the camps' economic goals, more and more prisoners were required, just as more prisoners are required to fulfill the investor goals of Corrections Corporation of America and Geo Group. In any case, convictions are profitable, and the more of them there are, the more money both private interests and the State take in.

That in itself is way the hell past just being strange. But throw in the term "sex offender" and get on the registered sex offender list (which seems to be mostly filled with Johns who solicited prostitutes, though you'd never know it by the way they name the offense), and it all gets really weird. Chilling, even. This is partly because of the taboo and stigma associated, but mostly for the bizarre monitoring rules, and the money involved in enforcement. For example, Stokes must pay a couple of hundred a month for counseling, group therapy, and so on, until they tell him he can stop doing so. This therapy mainly amounts to listening to the stories of more serious offenders such as child molesters even though he is not one, but is being treated by the law as if he were. Such is the fate of being legally shackled to any of dozens of types of "certified sex offender treatment providers"—an ever-expanding industry, they tell me.

He also must pay for registration as an offender, for blood and saliva samples, fingerprints, palm prints, police registration of his Internet address (within 30 minutes of obtaining it), and so on with the Department of State Police and the Sex Offenders Registry, providing a new photo, address, etc., for 10 years, effectively the rest of Stokes' life, not to mention registering with the local cops wherever he lives. After five years he may petition the court for relief from having to re-register monthly. He cannot leave the state. He is supposed to inform employers of his status as a sex offender. So he cannot get a normal job, and subsists on handyman work. In the end, he generates about $400 a month for one post-incarceration entity or another, whether he has a job or not.

Stokes' designated handlers tell him that the system would smile upon him if he would get more formal 8.00 a.m.–5.00 p.m. employment, something that could be more easily tracked and taxed. Would that it were so easy for a 66-year-old man in this country. So he replies, "I'm retired, dammit. I got the same right to live on my Social Security, if I can manage to, as anyone else."

Yes, but it's not much of a life for someone who once worked a skilled job setting up lights and stage gear in large arenas and performance venues. Now he lives in a basement workshop of an overcrowded apartment building/rooming house, in a space that is supposed to pass for an apartment but doesn't even come close. For that privilege he pays $600 a month, and is allowed by the landlord to work off part of it as a handyman.

Stokes tells me he could get out from under much of this by satisfying the court—and here's the legal wording—with "clear and convincing evidence that due to his physical condition he no longer poses a menace to the health and safety of others".

"You could cut your dick off," I suggested.

"Sometimes I wish I had," he sighs.

In any case, I am pretty damned convinced that parole is a racket, just like incarceration has become a racket, just as everything in this whole goddamned country is a racket in disguise, from home mortgages to health care. If it is vital to ordinary citizens, it's a racket. But fear is the biggest racket of all. Even our rightful fear of sex offenders gets harnessed to the objectives of the corporate and political elites, woven into the weft and warp of the national delusion we call "the fabric of our society"—the freedom-loving one that currently has 2.2 million of its own citizens locked up, and another 2 million walking around under strict post-incarceration supervision and monitoring.

At this writing, there are supposed to be 117 registered sex offenders in this burg of 24,000 from which I write, Winchester, Virginia—and yet there are only 61 in the surrounding county, which has a population of 73,000. Let me make a wild speculation here, and say there may be a difference in the way that justice is administered in the two localities.

As if Stokes needed to catch any more bad breaks, his situation got worse. It seems he had the outrageous gall to get himself a dog. Stokes came upon a rather large black female mutt recently, who looked like she had a little retriever in her, according to Stokes, though I could never see it. She was bone-skinny, partially blind, and being neglected and abused by an old alcoholic woman down the street.

That dog, named Beulah, just loved Stokes. He lovingly fed her, and she stayed by his side constantly and obediently. But she kept getting skinnier and skinnier, no matter how much he fed her. For a while we speculated it was worms, but I've seen enough dogs to know that something worse was at work. Stokes spent money he didn't have on expensive worm medicine. But he surely did not have $150 for a vet and tests, and in a nation where uninsured folks are left to die slowly because they cannot pay cash, there was damned-sure no more mercy for dogs. Mercy, too, has been privatized, and costs money. Meanwhile, old Beulah was hanging out in the backyard in a friendly fashion, weak and sick as she was, sniffing around and getting petted by all who came her way. Dogs are like that—uncomplaining and decent unto death. I've had several who passed that way. She was old and getting ready to die, sure as God made little green apples. Broke as Stokes is, this certainly was not going to be a veterinarian-administered death, with a canine Kevorkian attending. And being a paroled felon, for damned-sure Stokes was not going to produce a gun and shoot her, which is the way we put old dogs out of their misery back in our day.

A situation like that is bound to draw the animal-control officer's attention, and rightfully so, given the outward appearance of the situation. So Stokes was busted. An examination showed that Beulah had diabetes. Seems they'll get a vet to examine a dog to get a conviction, but not to save a dog's life. Whereupon Stokes was charged with animal abuse by the animal-control officer of our city police department. "You should never have let that dog get in this condition; you should have taken her to a veterinarian!" Now Stokes has a court appearance on the docket for animal cruelty. And, of course, no money for a lawyer. That's where the compassion of a lonely old man for another sentient being will get you—smack dab in the jaws of our justice system.

I hold middle-class America responsible for this deformed thing we now call justice. And I've wanted to write an article about the sex-abuse crime-industry scam in this country, and proposed it to several magazines. Every one of them said that sex abusers are too unsympathetic as characters for them to publish such an article. I pointed out that these are real people, not characters in a fictional work. The editors added that they were afraid the public might mistake such a story as being supportive of real sex offenders.

Governments and states exist to control people, and for no other reason. If justice is achieved somewhere in the process, it's an added bonus. But control, above all else, is necessary for modern civilization to exist. The population grows by the minute, increasing social pressure on humanity. More rules and more control are required to keep order. Order is defined as the way we think others should behave—or imagine them to misbehave. We support the state's police machinery, and the massive incarceration of our fellow citizens, so long as they are being imprisoned for the right reasons. They should pay. Every action in a capitalist world must produce money. So they should pay in cash.

Last week I was in Minneapolis, and spent a couple of nights getting drunk with a friend, an apartment-building owner, who in his younger years did hard time for burglary. Things were somewhat different then, he avowed. In the Fifties and Sixties, a prisoner may or may not have worked off his "debt to society." But in these times, he says, "The system demands that you just deliver payment in cash. It's more efficient. But not fundamentally different. Back then, the rich still profited for our crimes more than we did. We stole $10,000 worth of stuff. Next day in the paper, we found that the guy we burglarized claimed it was $30,000 worth for insurance purposes. Getting robbed was a winning situation for him. He made 20K on us."

It's also a winning situation for the 20 percent of Americans in what we call the middle class—those actually living the middle-class life as advertised by the commercial and financial state's marketing department. It works well for Stokes' psychologist, his piss-tester, his lie-detector service contractor, the people with the sex-offender website contract, and all good citizens with investments on Wall Street. The psychologist needs money to send his kid on the private school trip to Italy this summer. The contractor providing the sex-abuser services just built a summer home down on the eastern shore of Virginia. The state police officer running the sex-abuser monitoring program will retire in six years—his investments need to earn another $50,000 in that time ...

But hold on!

Honest to God, as I conclude writing this—and I swear on a stack of friggin' Bibles—a police prowl car and two of the department's animal-control officers in a police truck just parked in front of Stokes' place across my driveway. They get out after rifling through some papers on a clipboard and talking on cell phones.

Now they have walked over to Stokes' back door. He comes out, and they sit him down in a lawn chair while they stand over him, wearing dark sunglasses, hands on hips, lips moving. And the neighbors are all peeking out of their blinds, watching the cops accost the registered sex offender (once he was on the Internet registry, word got around here fast). They are probably looking at the animal-control officers' truck and thinking, "Oh my gawd! Bestiality, too?

Any way you look at it, this cannot be good. Not for Stokes, not for you or me, or for anyone else less than enamored with the idea of a police state.

And Stokes? As he told me only yesterday, "I'm a goddamned magnet for bad luck."

No, he's not. He's just one more anonymous human profit-center to be squeezed, one more grape to be crushed in a grotesque blood-and-money press that has no mercy.

18

Meet the Leftnecks

[September 2, 2008]

This piece was first published in The Guardian *(U.K.).*

The last of the paper cups had scarcely been swept up after the Democratic convention when American liberals got the bad news. While they had been celebrating Barack Obama's steamroller ride to the Democratic nomination, their candidate's lead over his Republican rival had evaporated, leaving John McCain five points ahead in Reuters/Zogby polls.

Meanwhile McCain's popularity in the red-state heartland took another jump with his selection of the moose-shooting ex-beauty queen, Alaskan governor Sarah Palin, as his vice-presidential running mate. The war hero and the gun advocate "hockey mom" are obviously reaching American heartlanders: at some point the left is going to have to learn to reach the same people, especially in the swing states. And to do that they are going to have to learn to speak "redneck".

A third of Americans live in the geographic "redneck" south, and more than 50 percent in the cultural south—in places with white southern Scots–Irish values such as western Pennsylvania, central Missouri and southern Illinois, eastern Connecticut, northern New Hampshire, and others never seen as southern. When you look at people in what has come to be called the red-state heartland, most of their values are traditional white Scots–Irish values.

They hold the key to any national election, yet the liberal and alternative media never speak to, or for, them. Progressives dominate the Internet, politically speaking, but use it to talk to one another in a closed, politically correct conversation that by definition excludes others, particularly rednecks. I had an editor once, an old-school shot-and-a-beer newsman, who told me, "Joe, don't become a stenographer for the powerful, regardless of their politics or party." I still believe that. It's humanity and a nation we're obligated to, not political junkyism or political correctness.

Especially political correctness that excludes millions who do not see the world in terms of social politics. For instance, if I say on National Public Radio that "rednecks don't vote in their own interests because they are misled by the gun lobby", liberal middle-class America agrees with me. Proof is in the sales of my book. It's been normal practice so long that we rednecks are immune to it, and have come to take a certain defiant pride in the label.

I am an Appalachian native who grew up dirt-eating poor. Yet I have managed to live a couple of decades in the middle class as a news reporter, magazine editor, and publishing executive. I know the liberal middle class is condescending to working-class redneck culture—which is insulting, but not a crime. The real crime is the way corporate conservatives lie to my people, screw us blind, kill us in wars, and keep us in economic serfdom.

The good news is that many lower-working-class people are starting to figure that out. If we bothered to cover redneck culture, we'd be surprised to find how many progressive rednecks, what I call leftnecks, are out there. America's media caste, however, is put off by the way these folks look and sound, and by their unpredictable opinions. It's happy to deal with the rural red-state working class as long as it remains out there somewhere in "the heartland", a place to be polled and surveyed by Gallup to fuel self-absorbed political punditry.

Those in the media are granted entitlement to be the one voice, defining America to the many. And they keep that entitlement as long as they maintain false objectivity and keep working-class people politically in the dark. That is not difficult. Every daily newspaper has a business section, but none has a labour section. My European friends, this is no accident. No accident at all.

-19-

Escape from the Zombie Food Court

[April 3, 2009]

Joe Bageant spoke at Berea College in Berea, Kentucky, Eastern Kentucky University at Lexington, and the Adler School of Professional Psychology in Chicago, where he was invited to speak on American consciousness and what he dubbed "The American Hologram" in his book Deer Hunting with Jesus. *This is a text version of the talks he gave, assembled from his remarks at all three schools.*

I've just returned from several months in Central America. And the day I returned I had iguana eggs for breakfast, airline pretzels for lunch, and a $7 shot of Jack Daniels for dinner at Houston Airport, where I spent two hours listening to a Christian religious fanatic talk about Obama running a worldwide child-porn ring out of the White House. Entering the country shoeless through airport homeland security, and holding up my pants because they don't let old men wear suspenders through security, well, I knew I was back home in the land of the free.

Anyway, here I am with you good people, asking myself the first logical question: What the hell is a redneck writer supposed to say to a prestigious school of psychology? Why am I here, of all places? It is intimidating as hell. But Janna Henning and Sharrod Taylor here have reassured me that all I need to do is talk about what I write about. And what I write about is Americans, and why we think and behave the way we so. To do that here today I am forced to talk about three things—corporations, television, and spirituality.

No matter how smart we may think we are, the larger world cannot and does not exist for most of us in this room, except through media and maybe through the shallow experience of tourism—or, in the minority instance, we may know of it through higher education. The world, however, is not a cultural history course, a *National Geographic* special, or a recreational destination. It is a real place with many fast-developing disasters, economic and ecological collapse being just two. The more aware among us grasp that there is much at stake. Yet even the most informed and educated Americans have cultural conditioning working against them round the clock.

As psych students, most of you understand that there is no way you can escape being conditioned by your society, one way or another. You are as conditioned as any trained chicken in a carnival. So am I. When we go to the ATM and punch the buttons to make cash fall out, we are doing the same thing as the chickens that peck the colored buttons to make corn drop from the feeder. You will not do a single thing today, tomorrow, or the next day that you have not been generally indoctrinated and deeply conditioned to do—mostly along class lines.

For instance, as university students, you are among the 20 percent or so of Americans indoctrinated and conditioned to be the administrating and operating class of the American Empire in some form or another—in the business of managing the other 75 percent in innumerable ways. Psychologists, teachers, lawyers, social workers, doctors, accountants, sociologists, mental health workers, clergy—all are in the business of coordinating and managing the greater mass of working-class citizenry by the Empire's approved methods, and toward the same end: maximum profitability for a corporate-based state.

Yet it all seems so normal. Certainly, the psychologists who have prescribed so much Prozac that it now shows up in the piss of penguins, saw what they did as necessary. And the doctors who enable the profitable blackmail practiced by the medical industries see it all as part of the most technologically advanced medical system in the world. And the teacher who sees no problem with 20 percent of her fourth graders being on Ritalin, in the name of "appropriate behavior," is happy to have control of her classroom. None of these feel like dupes or pawns of a corporate state. It seems like just the way things are. Just modern American reality. Which is a corporate-generated reality.

Given the financialization of all aspects of our culture and lives, even our so-called leisure time, it is not an exaggeration to say that true democracy is dead and that a corporate financial state has now arrived. If you can get your head around that, it's not hard to see an ever-merging global corporate system masquerading electronically and digitally as a nation called the United States. Or Japan, for that matter. The corporation now animates us from within our very selves through management of the needs hierarchy in goods and information.

As students, even in such an enlightened institution as this one, you are being subjected to at least some of the pedagogy of the corporate management of society for maximum profit. Unarguably, your training will help many fellow human beings. But, in the larger scheme of things, you are part of an institution, the American psycho-socio-medical complex, and thus authorized to manage public consciousness, one person at a time. Remember that the entire pedagogy in which you are immersed is itself immersed in a corporate financial state. Even if some of what you do is alternative psychology, that is a reaction to the state, and therefore a result of it. It's still part of the financialization of consciousness. And I might add that none of you expect to work for nothing.

This financialization of our consciousness under American-style capitalism has become all we know. That's why we fear its loss. Hence the bailouts of the thousands of "zombie banks," dead but still walking, thanks to the people's taxpayer-offerings to the money god so that banks will not die. We believe that we dare not let corporations die. Corporations feed us. They entertain us. Corporations occupy one full half of the waking hours of our lives, through employment, either directly or indirectly. They heal us when we are sick. So it's easy to see why the corporations feel like a friendly, benevolent entity in the larger American consciousness. Corporations are, of course, deathless and faceless machines, and have no soul or human emotions. That we look to them for so much makes us a corporate cult, and makes corporations a fetish of our culture. Yet to us, they are like the weather—just there.

All of us live together in this corporate-fetish cult. We agree upon and consent to its reality, just as the Aztecs agreed upon Quetzalcoatl, and the lost people of Easter Island agreed that the great stone effigies of their remote island had significance.

Strangely enough, even as part of a population-mass operating under unified corporate-management machinery, most Americans believe they are unique individuals, significantly different from every other person around them. More than any other people I have met, Americans fear the loss of their uniqueness. Yet you and I are not unique in the least. Despite the American yada yada about individualism, you are not special. Nor am I. Just because we come from the manufacturer equipped with individual consciousness does not make us the center of any unique world, private or public, material, intellectual, or spiritual. The fact is, you will seldom if ever make any significant material or lifestyle choices of your own in your entire life. If you don't buy that house, someone else will. If you don't marry him, someone else will. If you don't become a psychologist, lawyer, clergyman, or telemarketer, someone else will. We are all replaceable parts in the machinery of a capitalist economy. "Oh, but we have unique feelings and emotions that are important," we say. Psychologists specialize in this notion. Yet I venture to say that none of us will ever feel an emotion that someone long dead has not felt, or some as-yet-unborn person will not feel. We are swimmers in an ancient, rushing river of humanity—you, me, the people in my Central American village, the child in Bangladesh, and the millionaire frat boys who run our financial and governmental institutions with such adolescent carelessness. All of our lives will eventually be absorbed without leaving a trace.

Still, though, for Western peoples in particular, there is the restless inner cultural need to differentiate our lives from the other swimmers. Most of us, especially as educated people in the Western World, will never beat that one.

Fortunately, though, we can meaningfully differentiate our lives (at least in the Western sense) in the way that we choose to employ our consciousness. Which is to say, to own our consciousness. If we exercise enough personal courage, we can possess the freedom to discover real meaning and value in our all-too-brief lives. We either wake up to life or we do not. We are either in charge of our own awareness or we let someone else manage it by default. That we have a choice is damned good news.

The bad news is that we nevertheless remain one of the most controlled peoples on the planet, especially regarding control of our consciousness, public and private. And the control is tightening. I know it doesn't feel like that to most Americans. But therein rests the proof. Everything feels normal; everybody else around us is doing the same things, so it must be OK. This is a sort of Stockholm syndrome of the soul, in which the prisoner identifies with the values of his or her captors—which in our case, of course, is the American corporate state and its manufactured popular culture.

When we feel that such a life is normal, even desirable, and we act accordingly, we become helpless. Learned helplessness. For instance, most Americans believe there is little they can do in personally dealing with the most important moral and material crises ever faced, both in America and across the planet—beginning with ecocide, war-making, and the grotesque deformation of the democratic process we have settled for. Citizenship has been reduced to simple consumer group-consciousness. Consequently, even though Americans make up only 6 percent of the planet's population, we use 36 percent of the planet's resources. We interpret that experience as normal and desirable, and as evidence of being the most advanced nation in the world. Despite this, our lives have been reduced to a mere marketing demographic.

Let me digress for just a moment, to tell you about how life is outside that demographic. I live much of the year in the Third World country of Belize, Central America, a nation so damned poor that our cash bounces. True, it ain't Zimbabwe or the Sudan—there are no dying people in the streets. But food security is easily the biggest problem, and growing by the day.

Yet, despite our meager and diminishing resources down there, and much government corruption, people are still citizens, not marketing demographics—not yet, anyway. They are citizens who struggle toward a just society. They have even made more progress than the United States in some respects. For instance, we have a level of free medical care for the poor, though we lack much equipment and facilities; maternity pay, if either you or your spouse are employed; retirement on Social Security at the age of 60; and worker rights, such as mandatory accrued severance pay for workers, even temporary workers. Most Belizeans own their homes outright, and all citizens are entitled to a free piece of land upon which to build one. Employment is scarce, and that has a down side: Many folks waste a lot of valuable time having sex, perhaps because they have too much time on their hands. The Jehovah's Witnesses missionaries are working hard to fix that problem.

Anyway, American and Canadian tourists drive by in their rented SUVs, and you can see by their expressions they are scared as hell of those bare-footed black folks in the sand around them. Central America sure ain't heaven. But life there is not what we Americans are told about the Third World, either. It's not a flyblown, dangerous place run by murdering drug lords, and full of miserable people. It's just a whole lot of very poor people trying to get by and make a decent society.

I mention these things because it's a good example of how North Americans live in a parallel universe in which they are conditioned to see everything in terms of consumer goods and "safety," as defined by police control. Conditioned to believe they have the best lives on the planet by every measure. So when they see our village and its veneer of "tropical grunge," they experience fear. Anything outside the parameters of the cultural hallucination they call "the First World" represents fear and a psychological free-fall.

Yet, even if we think in that sort of outdated terminology (First, Second, and Third World, and most Americans do), America is a Second World nation. We have no universal, free health care (don't kid yourself about the plan underway)—no guarantee of anything, really, except competitive struggle with one another for work and money and career status, if you are one of those conditioned to think of your job and feudal debt-enslavement as a "career." With high infant-mortality rates, abysmal educational scores, a poor diet, no national public-transportation system, crumbling infrastructure, and a collapsed economy, even by our own definition we are a Second World nation.

But there is a shiny commercial skin that covers everything American, a thin layer of glossy, throwaway technology that leads the citizenry to believe otherwise. That slick commercial skin, the bright-colored signs for Circuit City and The Gap (rest in peace), the clear plastic that covers every product from CDs to pre-cut vegetables, the friendly yellow-and-red wrapper on the burger inside its bright-red paper box, the glossy branding of every item and experience—these things are the supposed tangible evidence that the conditioned illusion, the one I call The American Hologram, is indeed real. If it's bright and shiny and new, it must be better. Right? It's the complete opposite of tropical grunge.

Last week when I got back to the States, I took a shower in an American friend's new $30,000 gleaming, remodeled bathroom. It felt like a surgical operating-room experience, compared to wading into the Caribbean surf in the tropical dusk with a bar of soap. Like a parallel universe straight out of *The Matrix*.

So how is it that we Americans came to live in such a parallel universe? How is it that we prefer such things as Facebook (don't get me wrong, I'm on Facebook, too), and riding around the suburbs with an iPod plugged into our brain looking for fried chicken in a Styrofoam box? Why prefer these expensive, earth-destroying things over love and laughter with real people, and making real human music together with other human beings—lifting our voices together, dancing and enjoying the world that was given to us? Absolutely for free.

And the answer is this: We are suffering a mass national hallucination. Americans, regardless of income or social position, now live in a culture entirely perceived inside a self-referential media hologram of a nation and world that does not exist. Our national reality is staged and held together by media—chiefly movie and television images. We live in a "theater state."

In our theater state, we know the world through media productions that are edited and shaped to instruct us on how to look and behave and view the outside world. As in all staged productions and illusions, everyone we see is an actor. There are the television actors portraying what supposedly represents reality. Non-actors in Congress perform in front of the cameras, as the American Empire's cultural machinery weaves and spins out our cultural mythology.

Cultural myth-production is an enormous industry in America. It is very similar to the national projects of pyramid-building in Egypt, or cathedral-building in medieval Europe. And in our obsession with violence and punishment, two characteristics of a consensual police-state reality, we are certainly similar to the kind of prison-camp building that went on in Stalinist Russia. Actually, we're pretty good in that department, too. Consider that one-fourth of all the incarcerated people on earth are in U.S. prisons—U.S. citizens imprisoned by their own government.

In any case, the media culture's production of martyrs, good guys, and bad guys, fallen heroes and concept outlaws, is not just big corporate business. It is the armature of our cultural behavior. It tells us who to fear (Middle Eastern terrorists, Mr. Chavez in Venezuela, and foreign-made pharmaceuticals), who to scorn (again, the same candidates, along with Britney Spears for her lousy child-rearing skills). Our daily news is the modern version of Roman Coliseum shows. Elections are personality combat, chariot races, not examinations of solutions being offered.

What are being offered are monkey models. Man as a social animal necessarily mimics the behavior he sees around him, whether by real people or moving images of people. Consequently, we know how to act because television and other media tell us what to do. Television is the software, the operating instructions, for our society. Thus, social realism for us is a television commercial for the American lifestyle: what's new to wear, what to eat, who's cool (Obama), what and whom to fear (that perennial evil booger, Castro), or who to admire (Bill Gates, pure American genius at work). This societal media software tells us what music our digitized corporate complex is selling, but you never see images of ordinary families sitting around in the evenings making music together, or creating songs of their own based upon their own lives and coming from their own hearts. Because that music cannot be bought and sold, and is not profitable. I think about that when the children and their parents sing and dance on the sand in front of my shack in Central America. We Americans are not offered that choice.

So, instead of a daily life in the flesh, belly to belly and soul to soul, lived out in the streets and parks and public places, in love and in the workplace, we get 40-inch televisions, YouTube, Cineplexes, and the myths spun out by Hollywood.

Now, for a national mythology to work, it has to be accessible to everyone all the time; it has to be all in one bundle. For example, in North Korea, it is wrapped up in a single man, Kim. In America, as we have said, it is the media, and Hollywood in particular. Hollywood accommodates imperial myths, melting-pot myths, hegemonic military-masculinity myths, and glamour myths. It articulates our culture's social imaginary — what Rosemary Hennessy described in her book *Profit and Pleasure: sexual identities in late capitalism*, as "the prevailing images a society needs to project about itself in order to maintain certain features of its organization." And the features of our media mythology are terrifying when you think about them.

As a writer friend says, it is like watching *Man on Fire*, with Denzel Washington's tragic pose and his truthful bullets, and his willingness to saw the fingers off Mexicans to get the information on time to protect us from The Evil. It is the absorption of that electronic mythology that allowed us to co-sign the torture at Abu Ghraib.

Incidentally, speaking of Abu Ghraib, I am a friend of Ray Hardy, lawyer to Lynndie England, the leash girl of Abu Ghraib. He has copies of thousands of other, far more grisly, Abu Ghraib photos. Believe me, they picked the gentlest ones to release. When the media and government people made that selection, they were managing your consciousness. What you know and don't know. Keeping you calmer by withholding the truth — rather like not upsetting little children so they will continue to quietly behave the way you want.

But, like children, the American public got bored with the subject of torture long ago, so we quit seeing the victims. Plenty of new evidence has been coming out for years since Lynndie's famous pics from Abu Ghraib. But the short American attention span, created by our rapid-fire media, says, "Move on to the next hologram please. Whoa! Stop the remote. Nice butt shot of Sarah Palin there!"

The result is that Americans we cannot achieve the cathexis we need. By Freudian definition, cathexis is the ground-zero psychic and emotional attachment to the world that cannot be argued with. As Lisa A. Lewis wrote in her 1992 book *The Adoring Audience: fan culture and popular media*, it is "beyond ideological challenge because it is called into existence affectively." Americans are conditioned to reject any affective attachment that does not have a happy ending. And, in that, we remain mostly a nation of children. We never get to grow up.

So we tell ourselves the *Little Golden Book* of fairy tales—that we are a great and compassionate people, and that we are personally innocent of any of our government's horrific crimes abroad. Guiltless as individuals. And we do remain innocent, in a sense, as long as we cannot see beyond the media hologram. But it is a terrible kind of self-inflicted innocence that can come to no good. We are a nation of latchkey kids babysat by an electronic hallucination, the national hologram.

You may or may not watch much television, but the average American spends almost one-third of his or her waking life doing so. The neurological implications of this are so profound that they cannot even be comprehended in words, much less described by them. Television constitutes our reality, just like water constitutes the environment in a goldfish bowl. It's everywhere and affects everything, even when we are not watching it. Television regulates our national perceptions and our interior ideations of who we Americans are. It schedules our cultural illusions of choice. It preselects candidates in our elections. By the way, as much as I like Obama, I fully understand that he is there because he was selected by the illusion-producing machinery of television, and by citizens under its influence. It is hard to underestimate the strength of these illusions.

TV regulates holiday-marketing opportunities and the national neurological seasons. It tells us that, "It's Christmas! Time to shop!" Or that, "It's election season, time to vote." Or that, "It's football season, let us rally passions and buy beer and cheer." Or that America's major deity, "The Economy," is suffering badly. "Sacred temples on Wall Street make great sickness upon the land!" Or, most ominous of all, that, "It's time to make war! Again."

It is fair to say that television and the American culture are the same thing. More than any other factor, it is the glue of society and the mediator of our experience. American culture is stone-cold dead without it. If all the TVs in America went black, so would most of America's collective consciousness and knowledge, because corporate media have replaced nearly all other previous forms of accumulated knowledge.

Especially the ancient forms, such as contemplation of the natural world, and the study and care of the soul. And I do not mean "soul" in the religious sense, either. I mean the deeper self, the one you go to sleep with every night.

The media have colonized our inner lives like a virus. The virus is not going away. This commoditization of our human consciousness is probably the most astounding, most chilling, accomplishment of American capitalist culture.

Capitalist society, however, can only survive by defying the laws of thermodynamics, through endlessly expanding growth, buying and using more of everything, every year and forever. Thus the cult of radical consumerism. It has been the deadliest cult of all because, so far, it has always triumphed, and has now spread around the earth and its nations.

Why has it been so viral, so attractive to so many for so long? How did it come to grip the consciousness of so much of mankind, from Beijing to Bangladesh? Thuggish enforcement accounts for part of it, of course. But it has succeeded, too, because it requires no effort—no critical thinking, not even literacy—just passive consumption. The easy addiction to consumption is probably hardwired into us. Every one of us will go right out of this door tonight and continue to play out our lives as contributors to ecocide and global warming, mainly because it's easier. And, besides, we are not offered any other real options, and we don't know any other way. Nor can we ever know any other way without making a great effort.

How to make that effort? (Assuming you even want to.) As I said, consuming images and goods, or buying your identity at Old Navy or a retro-clothing shop, takes no real effort or thought. Just money. Text messaging your whereabouts at the mall may be a technological wonder, but you're still absolutely nowhere if you are just one more oral-grooved organism in the food court at the mall moving in a swarm toward a Quiznos sandwich shop.

So how do you escape the programming of the food court, and, I might include, escape even those parts of this school that may serve more to indoctrinate than enlighten you? All pedagogy, even the best, is nevertheless about control. How does one escape such a total system?

In a word, service. Humble and thoughtful service to the world. It is heartening that we do have concerned Americans studying to alleviate the great suffering of so much of humanity. I have no proof of it, but it seems like earnest idealism is making a comeback since its decline following the optimistic 1960s.

People and institutions such as this one are attempting to move American society forward again, to heal us of our national sickness to the extent you can, after decades of regression, not to mention repression. Of course, to solve problems you must first identify them.

Let me say here that one of the most profound things I have learned from the Third World, perhaps the only thing I have learned—and, as psychologists, you've surely heard it before—is this: The diagnosis is not the disease. Which is why our prescribed treatment never seems to work in places like Africa. Or even in the Bronx or South Philly.

Even our most well-intentioned thinking, and our study of the afflictions of Africa and Latin America, of American inner cities or Appalachia, suffers from hubris, because whatever approach we adopt is necessarily the product of the Western propertized and monetized thinking that caused the problem in the first place. So now we study our victims with great piety, and supposedly teach them solutions to the problems we continue to cause for them. Western people studying globalization's horrific effects, or rape in Africa, or world poverty, are doing so under the assumption that such things can be dealt with through some social mechanistic means, through analysis and unbiased reason and rational, value-free science. Or by a network of officially sanctioned agencies.

For years, I have wanted to see the opposite take place—to see well-fed, educated Americans learn from the poor of the earth. I'd like to see them do what Gandhi advised: Let the poor be the teachers. Go among them with nothing, with one set of clothing and no money, keep your mouth shut, and do your best not to affect anything (which is impossible, I know. But you can come, as they say, "close enough for government work").

Then just let the world happen to you, like they do in the so-called "passive societies," instead of trying to happen to it in typical Western fashion. Don't try to "improve" things. Maybe practice milpa agriculture with Mayans on the Guatemalan border, watching corn grow for three months. Fish in a lonely dugout, sun-up to sun-down, in the dying reefs of the Caribbean, with only a meal or two of fish as your reward. Do such things for a month or two.

First, you will experience boredom, and then will come an internal psychic violence and anger, much like the experience of *zazen*, or sitting meditation, as the layers of your mind-conditioning peel away. Don't quit—keep at it, endure it, to the end. And when you return you will find that deeply experiencing a non-conditioned reality changes things forever. What you have experienced will animate whatever intellectual life you have developed. Or negate much of it. But in serious, intelligent people, experiencing a non-manufactured reality usually gives lifelong meaning and insight to the work. You will have experienced the eternal verities of the world and mankind at ground zero. And you will find that the healthy social structures which our well-intentioned Western minds seek are already inherent in the psyche of mankind, but imprisoned. And you will come to the startling realization that you and I are the unknowing captors.

In conclusion, I would point out that the high technological imprisonment of our consciousness has been fairly recent. There are still those among us who remember when it was not so entrapped. A few of us still know what it was like to experience non-manufactured realities—life outside our mass-produced kitsch culture. Particularly some aging Sixties types, who sought to pass through the doors of perception. Many made it through. But in my travels to places such as this one, I also meet a new breed of younger people, who get it completely. I meet them in the more advanced psychological venues such as the Adler School of Professional Psychology.

And especially in the ecological movement.

They already seem to know what it took me a lifetime to learn: that each of us is but one strand in the vast organic web of flesh and blood chlorophyll. All things and all beings are inextricably connected at the most profound level. Any physicist will confirm this. We are bound by its every wave and particle, all of us—the lonely night clerk at Motel 6 and the leviathans of the deep, the sleeping grandmother in New Haven, Connecticut, and the maimed Iraqi child in Kirkuk. It can be understood by anyone, though, simply by owning one's own consciousness. And in doing so we find that ownership and domination are both temporary and meaningless. And that the animating spirit of the earth is real and within us and claimable.

The purpose of life is to know this. Einstein glimpsed it. Lao-Tzu knew it. So did Saint Francis. But you and I are not supposed to. It would shatter the revered, digitized, super-sized, utterly meaningless hologram—the one that mesmerizes us, and mediates our every experience, but isolates us from universal humanness and its coursing energies. Such as love. Mercy. Compassion. Existential pain. Hunger. Or the unmitigated joy of simply being alive that one finds in children everywhere, even among the poorest. Most of the human race still lives in that realm.

Blessed is the one who joins them. Because he or she learns that the truth is not relative, and that because the human mind seeks balance, social justice is not only inescapable in the long run, but inevitable. I won't be around for that; but on a clear day, if I squint real hard, I can see down that road ahead. And on that road I can see the long chain of decent human beings like yourselves walking toward the light. And for your very presence on this earth and in this room, I am grateful. Thank you all from the bottom of my heart.

-20-

A Redneck View of the Obamarama

[May 25, 2009]

The original version of this article appeared on the website of the Australian Broadcasting Corporation.

When it comes to expressing plain truths, few are as gifted as American rednecks. During recent travels in the Appalachian communities of West Virginia, Tennessee, and Kentucky, I've collected scores of their comments on our national condition and especially on President Barack Obama.

In America, all successful politicians are, first and foremost, successfully marketed brands. In fact, Barack Obama was named *Advertising Age*'s 2008 marketer of the year. George W. Bush's brand may have "collapsed," as they say on Madison Avenue, but things don't change much. Rednecks instinctively know this.

"It don't matter who gets to warm his butt in the White House chair," says a West Virginia trucker. "The top dogs eat high on the hog, and the little dogs eat the tails and ears. That's what them bailouts is all about, and that's the way it is, no matter who's president. So you might as well vote for the guy who looks like the most fun because you gonna be watching his ass on television for the next eight years."

Yup, rednecks do have a way of getting right down to the bone of the matter. For example, the news shows us Obama in an auto plant … Obama talking to the troops in Iraq … Obama ladling out grub in a soup kitchen. That's the stuff of urban-liberal wet dreams. But a fellow over in the mountains of Mineral County, West Virginia, a guy named Pinch, who sells fence posts, poles, and firewood out of his backyard, puts it like this: "Nothing against Obama, mind you, but the last time I looked, the car plants was dead meat. Obama has never even come close to serving in the military, except for serving up that batch of hash in Baghdad. And there he was with his wife in a soup kitchen, for God's sake! Things has got so bad that we've got soup kitchens all over this country now. So, two millionaires in their armored limo drop by a soup kitchen, and this is supposed to make me feel good about my country?"

To be sure, the Obama brand is a feel-good brand. Like those Hallmark talking, digital greeting-cards we geezers send one another that say, "You're still sexy, baby!" Or "How's it hanging, stud?" We know, of course, that the only things hanging are our beer bellies and the fat on our upper arms. But it makes us feel good anyway. For about ten seconds.

What makes us feel good in the long term is getting back to the true meaning of being an American—buying stuff and racking up debt. Still, who'd have ever thought we'd see the president of the United States on television telling us there's never been a better time to refinance our homes, or to buy a car (which is exactly what he did last month)?

Hawking home refinancing seems a bit unpresidential to some of us. But then, too, this is America, where, by order of President Bush, we struck back hard at the 9/11 terrorists by going shopping. In any case, a local mortgage-lender here in Winchester, Virginia, is running ads with pictures of Obama and quoting him on the virtue of debt. That lender is one cast-iron Obama-hating Republican. So maybe Obama is truly a uniter after all.

As to America's working-class debt serfdom, some of us were resigned to that a long time ago. My former neighbor, Fat Larry (whose real name is Myron, and is thus happy enough to be called Fat Larry), says: "Hey, look, I don't care if Obama is putting us in debt. I was already in hock for the rest of my life before they started hollering about a 'debt crisis'". Nor is he opposed to accepting a handout: "Obama can let a smidgen of them trillions land in my poke anytime. Right now, I got no problems that fifty thousand bucks wouldn't fix."

Not to worry, Larry! According to our media, the cavalry is on the way to our rescue. Arrival time is estimated to be in two years. That's when employment is supposed to start coming back, after another year or so of continued job losses.

Meanwhile, Obama is humping the pump in an effort to re-inflate an economy that every day looks more like a balloon with a .55 caliber bullet hole in it. He's even tried to get some of the escaped air back into the balloon by making corporations return a few billion dollars of the trillions in bailout money that disappeared the minute it crossed their paws. "Seems to me," says Fat Larry, "he should'a give the money back to me. It was mine to start with."

Personally, I really cannot bitch too much about Obama's giveaways. At the end of this month he's sending me a $250 check—stimulus money being handed out to us retirees—which is about the only good thing I have encountered so far about getting old.

Indeed, it's cause for celebration. So I'm gonna call ole Larry and we're going out to get so damned stimulated we can't walk home.

Postscript: Aw hell! The front page of today's newspaper tells me that the $250 stimulus payment is only a loan from the government, and that I will have to pay it back next April. In this new America, we are all issued debt, whether we ask for it or not (sigh).

21

The Devil and Mr. Obama

[December 8, 2009]

Patrick Ward, associate editor of the U.K.'s Socialist
Review, *asked Joe to write a piece for the party publication.
This is a copyedited but unabridged text of that submission.*

Well, lookee here! An invite from my limey comrades to recap
Barack Obama's first year in office. Well, comrades, I can do
this thing two ways. I can simply state that the great mocha
hope turned out to be a Trojan horse for Wall Street and the
Pentagon. Or I can lay in an all-night stock of tequila, limes,
and reefer, and puke up the entire miserable tale like some
5,000-word tequila-purged Congolese stomach worm. I have
chosen to do the latter.

As you may know, Obama's public-approval ratings are
taking a beating. Millions of his former cult members have
awakened with a splitting hangover to find their pockets
turned inside out and eviction notices on the doors of their
4,000-square-foot subprime, mortgaged, cardboard fuck boxes.

Many who voted for Obama out of disgust for the Bush regime are now listening to the Republicans again on their car radios as they drive around looking for a suitable place to hide their vehicles from the repo man. Don't construe this as support for the Republicans. It's just the standard ping-ponging of disappointment and disgust that comes after the honeymoon is over with any administration. Most Americans' party affiliations are the same as they were when Bush was elected. After all, Obama did not get elected on a landslide by any means; he got 51 percent of the vote.

Right now, his approval ratings are in the 40th percentile and would be headed for the basement of the league were it not for the residual effect of the Kool-Aid love fest a year ago. However, millions of American liberals remain faithful, and believe Obama will arise from the dead in the third year and ascend to glory. You will find them at *The Huffington Post*.

This frustrating ping-pong game in which the margin of first-time, disenchanted, and undecided voters are batted back and forth has become the whole of American elections. That makes both the Republican and Democratic Parties very happy, since it keeps the game down to fighting the enemy they know—each other—as opposed to being forced to deal with the real issues, or, worse yet, an independent or third-party candidate who might have a solution or two.

Thus, the game is limited to players sitting between two political parties. One is the Republican Party, which believes we should hand over our lives and resources directly to the local Chamber of Commerce, so the chamber can deliver them to the big corporations. The other, the Democratic Party, believes we should hand over our lives and resources to a Democratic administration—so it alone can deliver our asses to the big dogs who own the country. In the big picture it's always about who gets to deliver the money to the Wall Street hyena pack.

Americans may be starting to get the big picture about politics, money, and corporate power. But I doubt it. Given that most still believe the war on terrorism is real, and that terrorists always just happen to be found near gas and oil deposits, there is plenty of room left to blow more smoke up their asses. Especially considering how we are conditioned to go into blind fits of patriotism at the sight of the flag, or an eagle, or any mention of "our heroes," even if the heroes happen to be killing and maiming Muslim babies at the moment. Patriotism is a cataract that blinds us to all national discrepancies.

Much of the rest of the world seems plagued with similar cataracts that keep it from noticing the chasm of discrepancy between what Obama says and what he does. The Nobel Committee awarded the 2009 Peace Prize to the very person who dropped the most bombs and killed the most poor people on the planet during that year—the same guy who started a new war in Pakistan, beefed up the war in Afghanistan, and continues to threaten Iran with attack unless Iran cops to phony U.S.–Israeli charges of secret nuclear-weapons facilities. It's weapons of mass destruction all over again. Somewhere in the whole fracas, the fact that Iran has been calling for a nuclear-free zone in the Middle East since 1974 has been forgotten. Iran has also been consistent in its position that "petroleum is a noble material, much too valuable to burn for electricity," and that nuclear energy makes much more sense, given that our food supply, whether we like it or not, is fundamentally dependent upon petrochemicals and will remain so until the earth's population is reduced to at least half of what it is now. The Iranian attitude has been to use the shrinking petroleum deposits as judiciously as possible.

To which oilman George Bush replied that, "There will be consequences for Iran's attitude." Obama has reinforced Bush's sentiment, stating that not only will there be consequences, but that a military strike on Iran "is not out of the question." Although the use of nuclear weapons is in direct opposition to the Muslim faith, 71 million Iranians must have shuddered and paused to think: "Maybe an Iranian bomb isn't such a bad idea after all."

Under cover of being the first "black" president, Obama is looking to best one of the Bush administration's records. And that is causing unshirted hell for anybody two shades darker than a paper bag, particularly if they are wearing sandals (Obama himself being only one shade darker than the bag, and given to wearing size-11 black Cole Haans). So far, two million Pakistanis have been, in official U.S. State Department jargon, "displaced" by U.S.-backed bombing and gunfire—which will surely displace a fellow if anything will. A significant portion of them are "living with host families". Translation: packed into crowded houses ten to a room, wiping out food and water supplies, crashing already fragile sanitation infrastructure, and serving as a giant human Petri dish for intestinal and respiratory diseases. Many more are still living in the "conflict area." Makes it sound like living next door to a neighborhood domestic squabble, doesn't it? God only knows how many more innocent people will yet be killed in the conflict area of Obama's "war of necessity." You know, the "good war"—the war that is supposed to offset the interminable, bad one in Iraq, where we continue to occupy and build more bases.

Then there are Obama's noble efforts to fight terrorism by beefing up troop "deployment" in Afghanistan. Deployment may be construed to mean an American-style armed gangbang, in which everybody piles on some wretched flea-bitten hamlets for all they are worth, with periodic breaks for pizza and video games.

Now if you look at the deployment of U.S. forces in Afghanistan, compared to NATO country forces there, you'll find them in a nice even line along what could easily be mistaken for an oil pipeline route—one that taps into the natural-gas deposits in Uzbekistan and Turkmenistan and, by the purest coincidence, just happens to bypass nearby Russia and Iran. But we all know that, "It's about fighting terrorism over there so we won't have to fight it here!" That still plays in Peoria, so we're sticking with it.

At the moment, the out-of-pocket cost of America's wars in Iraq and Afghanistan is $900 billion. Interest on the debt incurred, plus the waste of productive resources on the war, pushes the cost to three thousand billion dollars (according to Nobel economist Joseph Stiglitz). By comparison, the entire 2009 government budget for elementary and secondary education is slightly above $800 billion. Or, to look at it another way, how far would three thousand billion dollars go toward establishing energy independence? As Harvard monetary expert Linda Bilmes points out, there is "no benefit whatsoever for any American whose income does not derive from the military/ security complex." I sent an email to Obama pointing this out, suggesting that we pull out of Afghanistan, grab the opium, and run. I got a nice reply saying that my president is grateful for the input. So there ya go.

Lately there has been a ruckus about our little "slap shop" in Guantanamo Bay, Cuba. Despite Obama's promises to close down "Cigarland," it is still open for business. Word has it that Cigarland may be moved to an "underused" maximum-security prison (one would think a scarcity of criminals for a maximum-security prison would be good news, but what do I know?) in the desperately broke community of Thompson, Illinois. Locals there tell the national press, "Sure, put it in our backyard. No problem." Or, "This town is in the prison business. Prisons-R-Us." Or more bluntly, "We know how to handle these creeps, and we need the jobs."

It's the kind of job creation that Stalin would have understood.

But at least the recession is over. This, according to Obama's monetary point-man, Ben Bernanke, chairman of the Federal Reserve Bank. For British readers unfamiliar with the U.S. system, the Federal Reserve is not a government agency, despite its agency-like name. "The Fed" is an offshore private banking cartel that decides just how much bogus currency can be printed and circulated profitably for bankers without wrecking their Ponzi schemes. And the chairman of that august body has announced that the recession is over. Well, hallelujah! We can quit rolling our own cigs, buy ready-mades, and run recklessly through the Dollar Store scooping up dented canned goods and cheap Chinese tube socks.

That makes us luckier than the three-and-a-half million Americans, most of whom led normal lives a few years ago, who are now homeless. That includes one million school children sleeping in tents, shelters, and other makeshift arrangements, and trying to look presentable each morning at schools that have not even the mercy to let them use the school showers. By the administration's own calculation, the number of homeless and people out of work will continue to escalate at least into the next year. Home foreclosures, and therefore homelessness, "has not topped out yet," says Obama.

But Bernanke has announced that the recession is over. So there you have it. A grateful nation breathes a sigh of relief. And besides, he is right about it being over. The recession is over for the most important members of a capitalist society, the oligarchs and banksters, who have made fortunes off this recession, thanks to our unique economic system, and may now return to their standard garden-variety usury.

Economic systems are merely belief systems. I didn't say that—John Maynard Keynes did. For instance, if the early Assyrians believed a shekel was worth a jar of wheat, it was worth a jar of wheat. American-style capitalism eventually stretched belief to the absolute limits of fantasy—to the snapping point, as regards general credulity. Nobody abroad still believes the dollar is worth folding up and sticking in a wallet, certainly not worth exchanging for a good old-fashioned shekel. However, be it shekels or dollars or euros, there is no economic system at all if there is no production. And there is no production if there are no jobs. Hence the obsession with unemployment rates.

The U.S. Ministry of Truth has announced that our unemployment rate is at 10 percent. I've yet to meet an American who does not know that the official unemployment rate is a complete fiction. One-half of the unemployed—the half that has been unemployed for more than one year—are simply erased from the official count. Poof! The real rate is somewhere around 20 percent. But if we acknowledged that, we'd have to admit to being on par with Europe's unemployment rate. And by diddle damned, we can never do that. Every American fully understands that the purpose of life is to hang onto one meaningless job or another—two of them if possible. And by the state's official numbers, more Americans have a white-knuckled grip on life's purpose than any of those pussy socialist European nations with their free healthcare, low infant-mortality rates, and ridiculously long vacations.

But the bad news, which the Obama administration openly acknowledges, is this: Unemployment will in all likelihood go higher. And nobody on earth knows how to reduce it (although no one in the administration is about to acknowledge that). The factories are all but gone, and they are not coming back—not unless American workers are willing to work 13 hours a day for two Chinese yuan an hour, which is about 31 cents. What U.S. factories remain are laying workers off due to high interest rates, and are waiting for a lower interest-rate policy before deciding if it is feasible to call any workers back into production.

During their wait they can watch hell freeze over. Banks know a fatter hog when they see it. And that hog is the consumer-credit business (nobody has figured out yet that consumers need paychecks before they can consume anything, on credit or otherwise). To that end, the Federal Reserve has logically set a low interest-rate policy. And, in true accordance with banking logic, the banks took the Fed's money, then raised the annual percentage rate on credit-card purchases and cash advances, and on balances that have a penalty rate because of late payment. Next, they raised the late fee. What the hell? If Americans are on the ropes, struggling to make their payments on time, the logical thing to do is to stick it to them. Bleed 'em for all they're worth. It's an American free-market tradition. We, the people, do not complain. We expect no mercy. America is a business, and the American concept of business is pure ruthlessness.

A Deutsche Bank analyst tells me a near-term worst effect is yet to come: bank failures and home foreclosures have not peaked. A commercial real-estate bust is coming down the pike. He says that, while there will be some minor periodic upswings, the fraudulent value of the dollar is now evident as it falls against every other currency, even the Russian ruble (13 percent), except for those unlucky enough to be pegged to the U.S. dollar. As former assistant secretary of Treasury,

Paul Craig Roberts, says: "What sort of recovery is it when the safest investment an American can make is to bet against the U.S. dollar?" My Deutsche Bank friend, who is younger and has a family to think about, has taken what he considers more appropriate action. He's buying gold and moving to an undeveloped Central American country.

But Mr. Bernanke assures us that the worst is indeed over. Despite the outside world's serious doubts, Bernanke's announcement just might fly in the U.S. We believe whatever our Ministry of Truth tells us. We believed that debt was wealth, didn't we? And we believed in WMDs, and have come to believe warfare is a prerequisite to peace.

The saddest thing is that Americans are cultivated like mushrooms from birth to death, kept in the dark and fed horseshit. Consequently, they haven't the slightest idea that there is an alternative to the system in which they labor at the pleasure of corporate and financial elites who own both their government and their every waking hour. That alternative is democratic socialism: self-governance for the broadest common good. Which the Ministry of Truth has defined for them as fascism.

Healthcare and environment? Ha-ha-ha-ha-ha-ha-ha-ha-ha-ha-ha-ha.

I would guess that you have heard about the "debate" over "healthcare reform in America." There really wasn't much debate—just a lot of thuggish behavior and wild tales of geriatric death panels by the right, and groveling capitulation on the left. The "reform" turned out to be a $70 billion-a-year giveaway to the insurance companies, by forcing those 45 million folks who cannot afford insurance at all to buy it anyway. Taxpayer dollars will make up the difference between what can be wrung out of the working poor, and what insurance corporations can demand and get because they have a throat lock on both of the other parties involved — the doctors and the patients. As for the doctors, they have played it so cool that butter wouldn't melt in their mouths, and have successfully avoided the question of whether their quarter-million-dollar-and-up incomes just might be contributing to the exorbitant cost of healthcare. Even with a majority in Congress, the best Obama and the Democratic Party's corporate lapdogs could come up with was a total handover to the insurance industry. If this smells a bit suspicious, it is the sweat of cold fear that your olfactory sense is registering. The insurance companies have always made it clear that they have billions to spend in defeating and destroying any elected official not on their side.

As for environmental legislation, under the Obama administration environmentalism is pretty much reduced to "cap and trade." In the truest spirit of capitalism, corporations will be able to sell their pollution for a profit, instead of ending it. And even this legislation barely made it through the House of Representatives. Moreover, environmental legislation has had the snot knocked out of it by the economic crash, and opinion polls now show that the American public believes the price is too dear. It should be interesting to see what price their children will be willing to pay for oxygen and water.

Just when you think your country has reached the limits of raw shame and the outer banks of rogue internationalism occupied by Korea's Kim Jong-Il and Sudan's Omar al-Bashir, it surprises you with some new and worse outrage. America's latest is right up there with holocaust denial in sheer, unmitigated, abrasive gall — putting the kibosh on the UN's Goldstone Report. The report documents Israeli war crimes in the Gaza ghetto, where 1.5 million Palestinians have been held miserable hostages by Israel. Admittedly, the leadership both in Gaza and

Israel is nothing short of a pack of criminals. But the Israeli attack on civilians and civilian infrastructure such as hospitals and schools, using illegal munitions such as skin-melting white phosphorus, was a war crime by every definition. The UN and the world agree that it meets and exceeds the Nuremberg standard that the U.S. established in order to execute Nazis. But, as any American will tell you, the United States has never considered itself part of the rest of the world or in any way obliged to join it. So the rest of the world was not surprised when the U.S. House of Representatives voted 344 to 36 to condemn the Goldstone Report. The Obama administration has promised Zionist groups that it will never let the report get to the criminal court. The perps are safe. Zionists everywhere threw their hats in the air and cheered. The AIPAC boys at the back of the room nodded in approval: "Now tell us, Congressmen, who's yer daddy?"

I might add at this point that I am not one of those conspiracy freaks who see Zionist plots behind everything. The Zionists are but one of many backstage operators with a death grip on some aspect of U.S. policy. Frankly, of all the greaseballs and thugs muscling U.S. domestic and international policy, I fear Wall Street and the bankers far more than I fear any Zionist (except maybe that spooky, shape-shifting motherfucker, Rahm Emanuel. Brrrr!).

In any case, most Americans have never heard of the attack on Gaza or the Goldstone Report. They were prevented from hearing the outside world's news coverage of the grisly two-week-long specter. Residing in a free Central American country at the time, I was fortunate (or unfortunate) enough to hear the daily dispatches from inside Gaza, despite Israeli efforts to suppress them. About the only place the Zionist misinformation machinery really worked was in the United States, where it successfully repressed media coverage of Israeli atrocities and genocide. Not that it required great effort. American politicians and media long ago learned, as a client state of Zion, to look the other way. Or, if that is not possible, to support one of the prepackaged lies conveniently provided for the U.S. media by the Likudnik media-management apparatus. "And besides, weren't the Palestinians the fuckers who danced in the streets after 9/11? Screw 'em! We now return to Cable News coverage of last night's *America's Got Talent* winners, the ZOOperstars!"

The same day the assault on Gaza began, January 4, 2009, President-elect Obama announced that he would create or save three or four million jobs during his first two years in office. Ninety percent of them were to be in the private sector, of which about 400,000 would be in building roads, bridges, schools, and broadband lines. Another 400,000 were predicted in solar panels, wind turbines, fuel-efficient cars, and one million in healthcare and education. The key term here was "jobs saved." Any job not lost apparently goes in the jobs-created column. I'm rather math impaired, but it seems to me that with real unemployment at about 20 percent and rising, and job losses predicted by the administration to continue for at least another year, it's hard to see how the claim can be made. I suppose that as long as three million jobs remain in the U.S. economy, Obama can claim to have saved them. I'd be the first to admit it's all over my head, and a damned-good example of why I am not suited for public office. Then, too, I never did understand Bill Clinton's surplus, either. Political math is done in some fourth-dimension anti-space where terrestrial rules do not apply.

So Obama's plan lines more corporate pockets than those of the working man. This being America, however, Obama was charged by conservatives with having an anti-capitalist socialist agenda. These businessmen conservatives are more than happy to take the money. But the rule of thumb in America is "Show No Gratitude! Bite the living hell out of any hand that feeds you, on the chance that it may give up more. Maybe even drop everything it is holding so you can grab it up and run while a crowd gathers to stone the alleged socialist."

But the truth is that Obama's jobs would have done nothing to help the economy "recover" anyway. There is no economy left to recover. It has moved to China and India. Things such as road projects do not generate capital. Under capitalism, roads are worthless unless they make money, and they can do no economic good if there is nothing being manufactured to haul on them.

Likewise, education that does not contribute to the gross national product (otherwise known as corporate interests) by producing higher wages to exponentially pump up American consumer fetishism is considered worthless. And, let's face it, higher education has become, for the most part, another racket. The student is saddled with massive loan debt (again, there is the odor of hyena-banker spoor in the air) on the promise of eventual higher wages—or at least a belief that the graduate will work in a nice, warm, dry video store, and never have to ball sod. Unfortunately, the number of jobs that require "college-educated" Americans—quite an oxymoron, given the caliber of U.S. colleges these days—is shrinking right along with the Empire. All those jobs middle-managing the Republic, such as helping us cheat on our taxes, brainwashing the school kids, and devising sales strategies for beer, grow scarcer by the day. Even book editing and reading medical scans are being outsourced to Asia. There's a nasty rumor that American medical scans are being read in India by trained Buddhist temple monkeys to save rupees. The U.S. healthcare industry has been mum on the subject.

Obama's recovery plan depends on going deeper in hock to the Chinese. For Christ sake, aren't there any of our tax dollars lying around anyplace other than in Wall Street vaults? Apparently not. So the Treasury Department keeps cranking out more funny money to make payments on the pawn ticket for the Empire. Rather like those doddering old Englishmen one meets on estates in rural Kent sporting "The Queen's Own" military ties, we still prefer to think of ourselves as an empire.

But the Chinese are looking askance, questioning the wisdom of pouring more money down a rat hole, based upon the U.S. Treasury's allegation that the other end of the rat hole comes out somewhere in China and not on Wall Street. Chinese talk-shows publicly question American loans, when upcoming powerhouses such as Brazil are so ripe for investment. You can bet that if it's on television in China, the public is being issued an official, state-sanctioned opinion they may feel free to hold as their own.

In the end, the campaign rattle and prattle about Obama's recovery plan turned out to be moot anyway. Wall Street moved in and heavied up on the whole damned country, in one of the ballsiest heists in American history. It was a stroke of pure genius, as theft goes. Following a meeting of the Five Families—Citicorp, Bank of America, Morgan Chase, Wachovia, Taunus Corp.—the financial cartels said, "The rip-off is in. We got it all. Now if you don't hand over all the people's savings and assets so we can loan it back to them, the whole flaming ball of shit you call the services and information economy is gonna come down on everybody's asses like a giant meteor. So you can load three trillion bucks for now into the armored cars lined up out front, and nobody will get hurt. Or you can watch the national economy shrivel up until the schmucks out there in the cul-de-sacs and cardboard condos can't even put together a cab fare for their ride to the poor house. It's your call, Barack."

There are still a few delusional souls out there who believe that Obama is trying to do his honest best to fulfill campaign promises, but just cannot get past the pack of vampire financial corporations and cold-blooded Republican lizards. Which is true, in a sense. He cannot get past the Wall Street pack because he is running in the middle of it. Obama has had a nefarious relationship with Wall Street's power players for years. It is no accident that Wall Street got to select the members of the president's financial cabinet. My mutton-eating friends, it's a sad and sordid tale, one I have neither the space nor the stomach to cover here—especially since better journalists such as Matt Taibbi and others have written extensively about it in detail.

Last I heard, the banks never un-assed the dough. Never let it circulate in the people's hands, or even through business loans. Instead, they declared a profit, divvied it up in bonuses, and congratulated themselves. Indeed, this was the sort of sheer brilliance we have come to expect from the Yale/Harvard MBA crowd. Getting rich by going broke—then getting even richer by sticking up the U.S. government and the entire American public, and eventually the entire world, leaving a 1.5 quadrillion-dollar cloud of toxic derivatives girding the world, to hoover up more money for them before imploding like a dark star. And, indeed, the derivatives are even astronomical in nature. They represent a $180,000 debt-load for every man, woman, and child on earth (although I cannot understand why, if the money isn't real, we should consider the debt real). It is impossible to produce our way out of this calamity. There aren't even enough resources left on earth to sustain that scale of production.

For now, the financial mobsters have retired to Tuscan villas to savor their haul. The poor schmucks out there in the U.S. heartland are left to devise new ways of hiding the family ride from the repo man. Never once, though, do they doubt capitalism. They figure it is all just a big financial accident. Fate. And that we will somehow "work our way out of it," like we always have. These things happen in a dynamic free-market economy.

To backtrack, that was when there was the smell of long green dollar bills flying out of the public treasury. Insurance racketeers moved in with their own muscle to fill the void left by the Wall Street gang. The insurance syndicate dispatched its made men and soldiers throughout the halls of Congress, and, voila! They were able to pass off the aforementioned $70 billion-a-year political blackmail job as "reform legislation." Say what you want to about my country, but pillage and looting have never been so elegantly ritualized, institutionalized, and executed.

Realistic people on the left have long known that the last act of American strong-arm capitalism would be a massive at-gunpoint redistribution of wealth from the public to the owning class through the private financial sector—which the owning class happens to own. But few would have expected it to be executed under a Democratic majority in both the House and the Senate. Or under a Democratic administration honchoed by the first black president. One liberal blogger wondered aloud, "Imagine what the Republicans would have done had John McCain been elected?"

The same thing, brother. The same thing. Only with a different cover story. Both parties exist at the pleasure of the same crime syndicates.

As I remember, it was a Mexican diplomat who once told me

that graft, theft, and bribery are socialized in his and other Latin American countries—democratically distributed throughout much of society. But in America, he said, this sort of criminal activity is legislatively institutionalized. Only the elites are allowed to practice usury, theft, insurance blackmail, and other forms of non-violent looting (violent looting being reserved for oil-bearing Middle Eastern countries). The first step in building one of these rackets is to become a legally recognized interest group, in order to access the key congressional players you wish to bribe or strong-arm into acquiescence or complicity.

The banking mob, the insurance mob, and other criminally organized legislative muscle men, cartels, and commodity syndicates are all officially sanctioned as "interest groups," operating alongside hundreds of others in that whorehouse by the Potomac River.

To list just a few, there are environmental interest groups such as the Sierra Club, which exists so its officers can draw fat salaries and meet movie-star environmentalists. There is an interest group for education, which exists to assure the mediocrity of our public schools. Munitions manufacturers comprise an interest group. Gambling casinos and tobacco corporations are interest groups. There is an interest group to force-feed us corn sugar, in order to sustain midwestern Republican farmers and ensure the future of the ever-expanding weight loss and diabetes industries. There are even lobby groups to protect the interests of syndicates in other countries, such as Israel. There is an interest group for everything except us ordinary American pudwhackers—the folks who just want to raise families in peace, and maybe have modest financial security in old age. And there are thousands of interest groups whose purpose is to make damned sure we never get either one.

Yesterday I watched a CNN host ask two experts: "Is stepping up the war in Afghanistan really the best use of our tax dollars?" The killing, maiming, and displacement of untold thousands is discussed in terms of the best use of capital. A dehumanized and monetized capitalist society sees everything in dollars and cents, and return on investment. Even infant mortality is rated that way, though seldom does anyone admit it. Saving a black ghetto baby has a low return on investment, according to some human-services analysts, as regards their lifetime contribution to the gross national product. I actually heard an expert on a television panel show say this.

Yet Americans sitting in front of their TV sets do not find this one bit odd. Or even mean-spirited—much less an indication of a cruel society. No American thinks of himself or herself as cruel, or connected in any way with the world's largest human and environmental killing-machine. No American doubts his inalienable right to drive around, or run air conditioning, or drink wine from grapes grown in Chile at the expense of a national war on the environment and those of the world's people who have been born without energy resources. If there are things such as cruelty and injustice, we, the people, aren't the ones doing it. We, the voters and taxpayers, are not the CIA snatching people off to Uzbekistan and Turkmenistan to be raped with broken bottles and boiled alive to extract those "terrorist confessions" that keep the war on terror alive. We simply finance such operations.

And accountability? Well, on the very slight chance that someday the world will hold America accountable (which will never happen so long as we possess more armaments that the rest of the world combined and are quite clearly willing to use them toward our own ends), we, the people, can express our shock and disgust as citizens. We good people would never,

never, never have approved of all those awful acts. And besides, there is not much the ordinary person can do about such things anyway. Right?

Maybe not. But it was Americans who so loudly proclaimed that complicity through silence is no defense, when we rubbed the German people's noses in the grisly filth of the concentration camps and hung their national leaders.

We haven't heard much from George W. Bush since he packed up his comics and moved to Dallas. But his policies remain like dog-piss stains to stink up the Obama White House. Rendition and assassinations continue, as does warrantless spying on the citizenry, along with other civil liberties' violations in the name of the "war on terror."

All of these are terrible things for a president who ran on reform and change to continue to do. But it is the thing that Barack Obama and his party did not do, the thing they did not insist upon, that will have the greatest continuing effect on this country. Obama and the Democrats refused to prosecute Bush and Cheney, ensuring that:

1. No quail hunter in Georgia will ever be safe as long as Cheney's pacemaker still functions; and
2. The precedents set by the most criminal administration in U.S. history remain. Until they are confronted and rectified, America will not have the opportunity to heal and recover. Honestly speaking, though, the patient has been dead since the 2000 election fraud went unchallenged.

Obama's election was the only chance that America had to hold the Bush Republicans accountable for their crimes. Now it's gone.

Opportunities to exercise moral principles as a nation and a people are rare to begin with, and fast vanishing. At some point they will be extinguished by the exigencies of human species' survival. It doesn't take a prophet to know this. Anyone paying attention to planetary population, resource depletion, and the eco-collapse understands it in the gut. The mounting worldwide competition for human survival will not allow for much high-mindedness. So we should exercise principles and administer justice while principles and justice are still possible.

There are endless rationalizations proffered as to why Obama has not come within a mile of fulfilling the promise and potential of his presidency, and the Democratic Party is writing more of them every day. Disappointed Democratic voters grab at them, and desperately defend each one on Internet forums and in letters to the editor. But we must use our own personal capabilities as free, rational human beings to assess Obama, and decide why he is failing. Or not failing. To hell with highly crafted official explanations about "wars of necessity" and trillion-dollar blackmail payments.

George W. Bush left office wearing the same smirk he came in with. Perhaps it's congenital. But if Bush was smirking when he left office, he must now be convulsed in crazed, hysterical laughter. His gang not only got clean away, but Obama carries on the dark Bush–Cheney legacy. And, almost as if to top the whole black escapade with a cherry of irony, the most inarticulate president in American history is now on the motivational speaking circuit at $200,000 a pop. Never let it be said that the Devil does not care for his own.

Will Americans ever rise up in defense of their own common wellbeing through such things as education, health, and a productive, peace-caring society? Nope. Because it has been seen to that socialism—the administration of the nation solely for the common good and benefit of all the people, without preference or privilege—doesn't stand a chance in America. For over a century, those who have attempted to further socialism have been shot, hanged, burned alive in their beds on Christmas Eve, imprisoned, falsely accused of crimes and falsely convicted, and demonized by the capitalist elites of the corporate state. The cause of socialism has effectively been wiped out in the U.S. Few Americans can even define the word. Most think it is a political system, whereas it is a social philosophy. Hell, these days, half the socialists themselves think it is entirely a political system.

But even if Americans were to understand socialism, they are too terrified to ever admit to its virtues, much less to publicly support the cause. And without free and open public participation in some democratic form of socialism, regardless of the name or label given to it, there can be no recognition of the people's common welfare and good. And so the most egalitarian social philosophy ever conceived dies within a nation, with very little chance of being reborn—because such an ideal, by its definition, cannot exist within the narrow mindset of bankers and oligarchs.

Bush smirks, Obama break-dances in and around the minefield of his false promises, and Wall Street's CEO bonuses are higher than ever.

Like I said, the Devil does take care of his own.

22

Live from Planet Norte

[June 27, 2010]

Starting with the Homeland Security probe at Washington's Reagan Airport, arrival back to the United States resembles an alien abduction to a planet of bright lights, strange beings, and incomprehensible behavior. The featureless mysophobic landscape of D.C.'s Virginia suburbs seems to indicate that homogeneity and sterility are the native religions — especially after having spent eight months in Mexico's pungent atmosphere of funky, sensual, open-air markets, rotting vegetation, smoking street food grills, sweat, agave nectar, and ghost orchids.

The uniformity on Planet Norte is striking. Each person is a unit, installed in life-support boxes in the suburbs and cities; all are fed, clothed by the same closed-loop corporate industrial system. Everywhere you look, inhabitants are plugged in at the brainstem to screens downloading their state-approved daily consciousness updates. iPods, Blackberries, notebook computers, monitors in cubicles, and the ubiquitous TV screens in lobbies, bars, and waiting rooms, even in taxicabs, mentally knead the public brain and condition its reactions to non-Americanness. Which may be defined as anything that does not come from of Washington, D.C., Microsoft, or Wal-Mart.

For such a big country, the "American experience" is extremely narrow and provincial, leaving its people with approximately the same comprehension of the outside world as an oyster bed. Yet there is that relentless busyness of Nortenians—the sort of constant movement which indicates that all parties are busy-busy-busy, but offers no clue as to just what they are busy at.

We can be sure, however, that it has to do with consuming. Everything in America has to do with consuming. So much so that we find not the slightest embarrassment in calling ourselves "the consumer society." Which is probably just as well, since calling ourselves something such as "the just society" might have been aiming a bit too high. Especially for a nation that never did find enough popular support to pass any of the 200 anti-lynching bills brought before its Congress (even Franklin Roosevelt refused to back them).

On the other hand, there is no disputing that we do reduce all things to consumption. Or acquiring money for consumption. Or paying down the debt for past consumption. It keeps things simple, and stamps them as authentically American.

For example, now faced with what may be the biggest ecological disaster in human history, I'm hearing average Americans up here talk of the oil "spill" in the Gulf of Mexico (when they speak of it at all—TV gives the illusion that those outside the Gulf region give a shit), in terms of its effect on: (a) the price of seafood; and (b) jobs in tourism and fishing. Only trolls stunted by generations of inbred American-style capitalism could do such a thing: reduce a massive oceanic dead zone to the cost of a shrimp cocktail or a car payment.

Meanwhile, even as capitalism shows every sign of collapsing upon them under the weight of its sheer non-sustainability, Norteamericanos wait like patient, not-too-bright children for its "recovery." Recovery, of course, is that time when they can once again run through the malls and outlet stores, the car lots, and the fried-chicken palaces, eating, grabbing, and consuming. No doubt, something resembling a recovery will be staged for their benefit, thereby goosing their pocketbooks at least one more time before the rest of the world forecloses on the country.

On Planet Norte, nothing is finite. Not even money, which, under the flag of the consumer society, you can keep borrowing forever. Equally limitless is oil, infinite quantities of which are being hidden from us by a consortium of energy companies. Several people here in the States have told me that the size of the Gulf oil spill is proof that there is plenty of oil still in the ground, and that this "peak oil stuff" is a scare tactic, an excuse to keep the price up. They were dead serious.

Considering the inexhaustibility of Planet Norte, it's no surprise its inhabitants have never doubted the "American Dream," the promise that every generation of Americans can be fatter and richer, and burn up more resources, than the previous one, ad infinitum.

All of which makes folks like me, and probably you, too, want to run away, pulling out our hair and screaming, "What the fuck has happened to these people? From the start, it was clear that Americans were never going to win any prizes for insight. But this is ridiculous. Is it the hormones in the meat? Pollution? A brain-eating fungus? How on God's (once) green earth can a nation so frigging 'out of it' manage to survive each day—much less constitute a continuing threat to the rest of the world?"

However, you must hand it to us that, so far, we have managed to sustain this culture of "I want it all, everything, the whole shebang, and I want it right now!" Except for the liberal and leftie websites and organizations, few seriously question it. When your designated role as a citizen is to live out a round-the-clock materialistic wet dream, why would anybody want to question it? Besides, seeing is believing. So reality is a titty tuck or a Dodge truck. Thank God it's Friday, and go ahead, do it, put another trip to Cancun on the plastic. It's a limitless world, baby!

In my little casita back in Mexico, limits are very real. Because the price per unit escalates with increased usage, we have to pay serious attention to electricity. So does the government. Our municipality is so conscious of every kilowatt that traffic lights have no green or orange phase—which saves on expensive bulbs, too—and it seems to work out just fine. You get one streetlight per block. Water is available to our village's neighborhoods only every other day, so it has to be stored in rooftop tanks. Once the water is in the tank, gravity eliminates the need for further electric pumps. Every single plastic bag, large or small, is used for household trash, and then hung on the front gate to be collected. You accept limits every day in Mexico, and live within them.

But for that 20 percent or so of the planet living in the (over) developed Western nations—thanks to colonial plundering for resources and, later, world banking scams—the limits of the natural world have never sunk in. Not really. Oh, ecological limits can be intellectually real to us, and we can have discussions about them. And being comparatively rich, we can build wind turbines and solar panels, and tell ourselves smug lies about "sustainable energy" and "green solutions." However, in our daily world, the affective one that governs our behavior, the one that tells us what we honestly need to deal with and what we do not, there are no apparent limits or potential end of anything. For example, if you wanted a glass of iced water right now, you could walk over to a refrigerator and get it. Most of the world cannot.

We assume much. We assume that when we get up every morning, the coffee maker will come on and the car will start. We assume that everything imaginable is available for a price, even if we cannot come up with that price. But we never really worry about having food or clothing, other than its style and type. Our biggest concerns turn on such things as who will win the World Cup or be eliminated from *American Idol*. The social and political environment assures us that we can afford to be consumed by these trivialities. The world of Americans has been like this for generations. So how could it possibly come to an end? Lest one have doubts, every voice of authority tells us that no matter how bad things may seem at times, they always "return to normal."

This theme of engorgement and spectacle endures—thrives, really—year after year, despite even the slowly unfolding world economic collapse. But it is Americans in particular who become stupider by any historical measure of intelligence. Millions pay money to visit Branson, Missouri. Or the Holy Land Experience, the Christian theme park in Orlando, where you can have the improbable experience of "fun with the world's most popular Biblical characters" (Hmmmm, maybe Mary Magdalene), and watch Jesus get crucified daily. And just when you think you've seen every possible insult to the democratic process that a degraded society can vomit up, some new one comes hurtling in your direction. Like those fat women in pink sweatpants leering from our TV screens, dangling teabags, and vowing revenge for they know not what.

For a thinking person, a low-grade depression settles in, alongside an unspoken fatalism about the future of the human race—particularly the American portion. That's the point I reached a year or so ago. I would probably be ashamed to admit it, if I did not receive hundreds of emails from readers who feel the same way.

If nothing else, though, in the process of building our own gilded rat-cage, we have shown that old saw about democracy eventually leading to mediocrity to be true. Especially if you keep dumbing down all the rats. After all, Dan Quayle, Donald Trump, and George W. Bush hold advanced degrees from top universities in law, finance, and business. The head rats, our "leaders" (if it is even possible to lead anybody anywhere inside a cage), have proven to be as mediocre and clueless as anyone else. Which is sort of proof that we are a democracy, if we want to look at it that way. While it is a myth that virtually anybody can grow up to be president, we have demonstrated that nitwits have more than a fighting chance. During my 40 years of writing media ass-wipe for the public, I have interviewed many of "the best of my generation" and, believe me, most of them were not much.

Naturally, they believe they are far superior by virtue of having made it to an elevated point in the gilded cage, closer to the feed, water, and sex. Because they believe it, and the media—sycophants waiting for quotes—echoes their belief, discussing their every brain fart, we tend to believe it, too. Nothing shakes our belief, not even staring directly into the face of a congenital liar and nitwit like Sarah Palin, or a careening set of brainless balls like Donald Trump, or a retarded jackal like George W. Bush. Americans are unable to explain why such people "rise to the top" in our country. We just accept that they do, and assume that America's process of natural selection—the survival of the wealthiest—is at work. These people are rich; therefore, they should run the country. God said so. It's a uniquely American principal of governance, which in itself, makes the case for our stupidity.

Yet, despite such intellectual and moral torpor, some of the numbest bozos are beginning to suspect that the wheels are coming off their "have everything" society. One clue is that every time they check, they have less than before. "There's other signs, too," concludes our bozo. "You gotcher radical Muslims blowing shit up, or plotting to. China holds the mortgage on our asses. Who wouda ever thunk it? The bodies of our fallen heroes are being tossed out of the revered Arlington Cemetery into the landfill. You got yer freshwater fish with three eyes, obese high school kids droppin' dead of heart attacks, meth epidemics out in the boondocks, and wild coyotes moving into big cities. It's all just too goddamned much!" And so, right in the middle of the morning commute, our bozo pulls over onto the roadside berm, puts his hands up against the windshield, and screams. "*Aaaaaaagh!* Is anybody in control here, for Christ sake?"

Control, huh? Nothing could be easier to obtain. Just sit back and allow those who want total control of the government to have it. The Republican Party is sure to come up with a candidate willing to pistol whip this country into shape. And that solution looks more attractive by the day. As violent competition for survival increases and resources diminish, the public demands more government control—control of borders, drug lords with entire armies of their own, pillaging by banks. Who else but the government is capable of beating all those sociopathic freaks out there into submission?

No less a personage than Thomas Jefferson pointed out that, whether for good or evil, controlling the people is the main thing all governments do best. Both Jefferson and Stalin understood this. They also understood that government control is a one-way street—it never voluntarily contracts, never shrinks. Government grows incrementally in the best of times, and balloons exponentially during the worst. When the people are anxious or fearful, when the have-nots are coming out of the woodwork for their share, and there is a genuine risk of losing something, the citizens always demand more government control. Given enough time, all government control, regardless of type or stripe, metastasizes—whether into the religious control of a theocratic state or the democratic totalitarianism of the United States.

Although totalitarian democracy is well solidified in the U.S., it is difficult, if not impossible, for its citizens or the outside world to name the beast, due to the outward appearance of freedom. Petty liberties are left intact. The process of orderly elections is maintained, thus retaining the world's general respect as a free country. After all, the people do "exercise their will" by voting.

Beyond that, the people have no further participation in, or effect upon, the government's decision-making process regarding the public's will. From that point onward, an economic, political, and military elite interpret the general will as what best fits their own interests. A media elite then sells their decisions, such as war or destruction of the social safety-net, as the people's choice. Wars are packaged and marketed as "Operation Iraqi Freedom," fought by "our heroes." Policies kicking the slats from under the old, the poor, and the weak are sold as "eliminating wasteful, unfair entitlements," such as eldercare and child nutrition. Everybody knows that words such as "entitlements," "eldercare," and "child nutrition" are code words in capitalism-speak. Eldercare wastes money on worn-out old fuckers who can no longer work and pay their own way. Child nutrition is just a nigger/wetback feeding program that causes them to multiply even more, draining off valuable funds that the already rich could have put to better use.

Liberty nonetheless abounds in a totalitarian democracy. Open elections verify majority rule. The slaves are free to elect their masters, and that is enough to satisfy most folks in the land of the free. That, along with 100-plus cable channels to keep us entertained inside the cage. We know we are powerless, but better the devil you know than evil socialism, where you are not allowed to take out a second mortgage on your cage.

What's a little totalitarian oppression, anyway?

In the big picture, however, the hardening of our totalitarian state is a piffle, compared to what drives the people to accept such a state. That driver is the escalating social pressures of six billion humans, and the ecocide caused by our disastrous hydrocarbon culture. Would that the state and its media allow the public enough information to make the connection between things like global warming, peak oil, desertification, and the state's wars we pay for and die in.

From the dawn of agriculture, human civilization has been a net subtraction from the environment on which we depend for life. Consider what once existed, and what little of it is left. Consider the burgeoning hordes everywhere burning, smelting, polluting, and generally devouring what remains. Where is that leading us?

You don't need to call Harvard's environmental science department for the answer (even though the profs and scientists there maintain the charade that we do, to protect their rackets). Despite the rule of scientism and the fashionable modern disdain for human intuition, common sense is still a viable option. Does common sense and experience tell you that all six billion of us are suddenly going to come to Jesus and save the planet? Suddenly be seized by the spirit of universal cooperation and pagan love for Gaia? Are those billions going to quit doing what our species has done for about 15,000 years —attacking nature first with the stone axe, then the plow, and later with atomic energy?

Call me a grim old fatalist, but I just do not see the human race turning things around. Not because humans are inherently evil (although pimping Gaia to death comes close), but because we are what we are. In any case, we are not going to stop eating, shitting, burning up stuff to stay warm, or following the genetic imperative to breed. How can we solve the problem when we are the problem, other than by self-extinction?

So here it is, top of the ninth round, and Gaia is on the ropes with cuts over both eyes, and no referee on the mat. *Homo sapiens* is moving in for the killer punch. It's been an ugly fight. But the truth is that there will be no winner. Certainly not man, considering that his triumph results in the specter of human self-extinction, die-off, or at least massive die-back.

Informed and globally conscious people are sickened, heartbroken, by the spectral truth. But to use the same Neal Cassady quote for the second time this year: "To have seen a specter is not everything."

In fact, it even has a good side: Transformation. Once you honestly accept what you have seen, you are changed, released from the previous stress and fear. Like so many feared experiences, it has its own psychodynamic, and is about "coming out the other side" of the experience. Accepting such a truth—especially for pathologically optimistic, cheer-stressed Americans—shatters many painfully held illusions. The chief one is that we are the animating force behind all significant change, and that the massive damage we do is "progress". In their place grows a new inner awareness. Although it does not conform to any popular definition as such, the easiest way to describe it is "spiritual." Who in these times, you may ask, believes in the spirit as an animating force of mankind? My answer is: Those who can be still enough to see that spirit moving.

With it comes the awareness and acceptance of forces far more powerful than our puny anthropocentric illusions of planetary authority. We can arrive at this understanding by way of logic and reason. The mind is a cumbersome and inefficient way to go about escaping the traps you build with your mind but, yes, it can be done. Most educated people in this science-worshipping age prefer the convoluted path of logic and rational exercise over calmly opening one's eyes and heart to the world before us, as wiser men have done for thousands of years.

Edwin Arnold reminds us in *The Light of Asia* that, when it comes to sinking a string of thought into that fathomless void, "Who asks doth err / Who answers, errs," because, as any searcher by way of mortal mind discovers, "Veil after veil will lift—but there must be / Veil upon veil behind."

Either way, there never was any guarantee that we would like the universal truth. And the truth is that the universe is busy enough hurling toward its destiny, and does not give a rat's ass what we do or do not like. Or whether a smear of biology on a speck of cosmic dust manages to poison itself to death.

So stay strong. Transcend. Find reasons to love.

Nobody ever gets out of this world alive, anyway.

-23-

Waltzing at the Doomsday Ball

[July 6, 2010]

Ajijic, Jalisco, Mexico

As an Anglo–European white guy from a very long line of white guys, I want to thank all the brown, black, yellow, and red people for a marvelous three-century joy ride. During the past 300 years of the industrial age, as Europeans, and later as Americans, we have managed to consume infinitely more than we ever produced, thanks to colonialism, crooked deals with despotic potentates, and good old gunboats and grapeshot. Yes, we have lived, and still live, extravagant lifestyles far above the rest of you. And so, my sincere thanks to all of you folks around the world working in sweatshops, or living on two bucks a day, even though you sit on vast oil-deposits. And to those outside my window here in Mexico this morning, the two guys pruning the retired gringo's hedges with what look like pocketknives, I say, keep up the good work. It's the world's cheap-labor guys like you—the black, brown, and yellow folks who take it up the shorts—who make capitalism look like it actually works. So keep on humping. Remember: We've got predator drones.

After twelve generations of lavish living at the expense of the rest of the world, it is understandable that citizens of the so-called developed countries have come to consider it quite normal. In fact, Americans expect it to become plusher in the future, increasingly chocked with techno gadgetry, whiz-bang processed foodstuffs, automobiles, entertainments, inordinately large living-spaces—forever.

We've had plenty of encouragement, especially in recent times. Before our hyper-monetized economy metastasized, things such as housing values went through the sky, and the cost of basics, food, etc. went through the basement floor, compared to the rest of the world. The game got so cheap and fast that relative fundamental value went right out the window and hasn't been seen since. For example, it would be very difficult to make Americans understand that a loaf of bread or a dozen eggs have more inherent value than an iPhone. Yet, at ground zero of human-species economics, where the only currency is the calorie, that is still true.

Such is the triumph of the money economy that nothing can be valued by any other measure, despite the fact that nobody knows what money is worth these days. This is due in part to the international finance jerk-off, in which the world's governments print truckloads of worthless money so they can lend it out. The idea here is that incoming repayment in some other, more valuable, currency will cover their own bad paper. In turn, the debtor nations print their own bogus money to repay the loans. So you have institutions lending money they do not have to institutions unable to repay the loans. All this is based on the bullshit theory that tangible wealth is being created by the world's financial institutions, through interest on the debt. Money making money.

As my friend, the physicist and political activist George Salzman writes:

> Everyone in these "professional" institutions dealing in money lives a fundamentally dishonest life. Never mind "regulating" interest rates. We must do away with interest, with the very idea of "money making money". We must recognize that what is termed "Western Civilization" is in fact an anti-civilization, a global social structure of death and destruction. However, the charade of ever-increasing debt can be kept up only as long as the public remains ignorant. Once ecological limits have been reached, the capitalist political game is up.

You can see why I love this guy.

Capitalism wouldn't be around today, at least not in its current pathogenic form, if it had not caught a couple of lucky breaks. The first, of course, was the expansion of bloodsucking colonialism to give it transfusions of unearned wealth, enabling "investors" to profit by artificial means (death, oppression, and slavery). But the biggest break was being driven to stratospheric heights by inordinate quantities of available hydrocarbon energy. Inordinate, but nevertheless finite. Consequently, the 100-year-long oil suckdown that put industrial countries in the tall cotton now threatens to take back from the subsequent beneficiary generation everything it gave. The Hummers, the golf courses, the big-box stores, cruising at 35,000 feet over the Atlantic — everything.

You'd never know that, to look around at Americans or Canadians, who have not the slightest qualms about living in that 3,500-square-foot vinyl-sided fuck box, if they can manage to make the mortgage nut, or unashamedly buying a quadruple-X-large Raiders' jersey because, hey, a guy's gotta eat, right? Why don't I deserve a nice ride, a swimming pool, and a flat screen? I worked for it. (Sure you did, buddy—your $12,000 Visa/MasterCard tab is proof of that).

The doomers and the peak-oilers gag, and they call it American denial. Personally, I think it is somewhat unfair to say that most Americans and Canadians are in denial. They simply don't have a fucking clue about what is really happening to them and their world. Everything they have been taught about working, money, and "quality of life" constitutes the planet's greatest problem—overshoot. Understanding this trashes our most basic assumptions, and requires a complete reversal in contemporary thought and practice about how we live in the world. When was the last time you saw any individual, much less an entire nation, do that?

Compounding our ignorance and naiveté are the officials and experts—the politicians, media elites, and especially economists—who interpret the world for us and govern the course of things. The go-to guys. They don't know, either. But they've got the lingo down.

Somehow or other, it all has to do with the economy, which none of us understands, despite round-the-clock media jabbering on the subject. Somehow it has to do with this great big spring on Wall Street called "the market" that's gotta be kept wound up, and interest rates at something called The Fed, which have got to be kept pushed down. The industry of crystal-gazing and hairball-rubbing surrounding these entities is called economics.

The following may be old news to some who studied economics in college. However, I did not. And, for me at least, this gets to the heart of our dilemma (if "dilemma" is the right word for economic, environmental, and species collapse). Here goes:

The human economy is made up of three parts: nature, work, and money. But since nobody would pay people like Allen Greenspan or Milton Friedman millions of dollars if they talked just like the rest of us, economists and academics refer to these three parts as the primary, secondary, and tertiary economies.

Of these, nature—the world's ecosystems and natural capital—is by far the most important. It comprises about three-quarters of the total value of economic activity. (See Richard Costanza et al., in *An Introduction to Ecological Economics*, 1997.) To Western economists, nature—when it is even given a thought—is considered to be limitless.

The second part, work, is the labor required to produce goods and services from natural resources. Work creates real value through the efficient use of both human and natural-resource energy. A potato is just a potato until people sweating over belt lines and giant fryers turn it into Tater Tots.

The third economy, the tertiary economy, involves the production and exchange of money. This includes anything that can be exchanged for money, whether it is gold, or mortgages bundled as securities, or derivatives—in short, any paperwork device that can be rigged up in such a fashion that money will stick to it. Feel free to take a wild-assed guess about which of the three economies causes the most grief in this world.

To an economist, work—the stuff that eats up at least a third of our earthly lives—is merely a "factor" called labor. Work is considered an unfortunate cost in creating added value. Adding value, along with exploiting nature's resources, is the basis for all real-world profits. Without labor, the money economy could not gin up paper wealth in its virtual economy. Somewhere, somebody's gotta do some real-world work before bankers and investment brokers can go into their offices and pretend to work at "creating and managing wealth."

Paying the workers in society to produce real wealth costs money. Capitalists hate any sort of cost, as it represents money that has somehow escaped their coffers. So, when any behemoth corporation hands out thousands of pink slips on a Friday, Wall Street cheers, and "the market" goes up. No ordinary mortal has ever seen "the market." But traders on the floor of 11 Wall Street, people who've deemed themselves more than mortal by virtue of their $110 Vanitas silk undershorts, assure us that the market does exist. No tours of the New York Stock exchange are permitted, so we have to take their word for it.

In any case, in the money economy, eliminating costs—even if those costs happen to be feeding human beings, citizens of the Empire—is sublime. That is why economists in the tertiary economy can declare a "jobless recovery" with a straight face. By their lights, the perfect recovery would necessarily be 100 percent jobless. The human costs of generating profit would be entirely eliminated.

Say what you will about the tertiary "money economy," but one thing is certain. It's virulent. Right now, finance makes up 42 percent of GDP, and is rising. Traditionally that figure has been around 9 percent. Fifty-eight percent of the economy is "services." When it comes to the service economy, most people think of fried-chicken buckets and "customer service" call centers harassing debtors or selling credit cards. However, much of the so-called service economy consists of the "services" of sub-corporations and entities owned and operated by monopolies in communications, electronic access, and energy. They are designed for the sole purpose of robbing the people incrementally. Borrow a magnifying glass, and try to read the backside of your cable and electric bill. Billing you is a "service" for which you pay. So is what the guy does who cuts off your lights if you don't.

And manufacturing? Ten percent. Mostly producing big-ticket items such as salad shooters, as near as I can tell.

Still, though, the foundation of the world, including our entire economic structure, is nature. This is clear to anyone who has ever planted a garden, hiked in the woods, gone fishing, or been gnawed on by chiggers. *In vis est exordium quod terminus.* ('In nature is the beginning and the end.')

Yet not one in a thousand economists takes nature into account. Nature has no place in contemporary economics, or in the economic policy of today's industrial nations. Again, like the general American public, these economists are not in denial. They simply don't know it's there. Historically, nature has never been considered even momentarily because economists, like the public, never figured they would run out of it. With the Gulf oil "spill" at full throttle, the terrible destruction of nature is becoming obvious. But no economist who values his or her career wants to start figuring the cost of ecocide into pricing analysis. For God's sake, man, it's a cost!

With industrial society chewing the ass out of Mama Nature for three centuries, something had to give, and it has. Capitalists, however, remain unimpressed by global warming, or melting polar ice-caps, or Southwestern desert armadillos showing up in Canada, or hurricanes getting bigger and more numerous every year. They are impressed by the potential dough in the so-called green economy. In fact, last night I watched an economist on CNN say that if the government had let the free market take care of the BP gulf catastrophe, it would not be the clusterfuck it is now. Now *that* might qualify as denial. In the meantime, anthropogenic ecocide and resource depletion, coupled with the pressures of six billion mouths and asses across the globe, have started to produce—surprise surprise, Sheriff Taylor!—very real effects on world economies. (How could they not?) So far, though, in the simplistic see-Spot-run American mind, it's all about dead pelicans and oiled-up hotel beaches.

When the U.S., and then the world's money economy started to crumble, the first thing capitalist economists could think of to do was to monkey with the paper. That's all they knew how to do. It was unthinkable that the tertiary virtual economy, that great backroom fraud of debt manipulation and fiat money, might have finally reached the limits of the material earth to support. That the money economy's gaming of workers and Mother Nature might itself be the problem never occurred to the world's economic movers and shakers. It still hasn't. (Except for Chavez, Morales, Castro, and Lula). Jobs disappeared, homes went to foreclosure, and personal debt was at staggering all-time highs. America's working folks were taking it square in the face. Not that economists or financial kingpins cared much, one way or the other. In the capitalist financial world, everything is an opportunity.

Cancer? Build cancer hospital chains.

Pollution? Sell pollution credits.

The country gone bankrupt? "Nothing to do," cried the mad hatters of finance, "but print more money, and give gobs of cash to the banks! Yes, yes, yes! Borrow astronomical amounts of the stuff and bribe every fat-cat financial corporation up and down The Street!" All of which came down to creating more debt for the common people to work off. They seem willing enough to do it, too—if only they had jobs.

Along with the E.U., Japan, and the rest of the industrial world, the U.S. continues to flood the market with cheap credit. That would be hunky dory, if it was actually wealth for anybody but a banker. The real problems are debt and fraud, and tripling the debt in order to cover up the fraud. And pretending there are no natural costs of our actions, that we do not have to rob the natural world to crank up the money world through debt.

No matter what economists tell us abut getting the credit industry moving again, papering over debt with more debt will not pollinate our food crops when the last honeybee is dead. I suggest that we put the economists out there in the fields, hand-pollinating crops like they do in China. They seem to know all about the subject, and have placed a monetary value of $12 billion on the pollination accomplished by bees in the U.S. Can you imagine the fucking arrogance? All bees do is make our fruit and vegetable supply possible. Anyway, if we cannot use the economists for pollinators (odds are they are too damned whacked to do that job), we could also stuff them down the blowhole of the Deepwater Horizon spill. For the first time in history, economists would be visibly useful.

Speaking of China: Since there is no way to pick up the turd of American capitalism by the clean end, much less polish it, American economists have pointed east, and set up a yow-yow about China as "the emerging giant," the "next global industrial superpower." Many Chinese are willing to ride their bicycles 10 miles to work through poisonous yellow-green air, and others in the "emerging middle class" are willing to wade into debt up to their nipples; this is offered as evidence of the viability of industrial capitalism. All it proves is that governments and economists never learn. In the quest of getting something for nothing, China follows the previous fools right into the smog and off the cliff.

The main feature of capitalism is the seductive assertion that you can get something for nothing in this world. That you can manufacture wealth through money manipulation, and that it is

OK to steal and hold captive the people's medium of exchange, and then charge them out the ass for access. And that you can do so with a clear conscience—which you can, if you are the kind of sleazy prick who has inherited or stolen enough wealth to get into the game.

Even so, to keep a rigged game going, you must keep the suckers believing that they can, and eventually will, benefit from the game. Also, that it is the only game in town. Legitimizing public theft means indoctrinating the public with all sorts of market mystique and hocus-pocus. They must be convinced that there is such a thing as an "investment" for the average schmuck drawing a paycheck (and there is, sort of, between the crashes and the bubbles). It requires a unified economic rationale for government and industry policies, and it is the economist's job to pump out this rationale. Historically, they have seldom hesitated to get down on their knees to do so.

Capitalism is about one thing: aggregating the surplus productive value of the public for private interests. As I have said, it is about creating state-sanctioned "investments" for the workers who produce the real wealth—things like home "ownership" and mortgages, or stock investments and funds to absorb their retirement savings. That crushing 30-year mortgage with two refis is an investment. So is that 401(k) melting like a snow cone at the beach.

As the people's wealth accumulates, it is steadily siphoned off by government and elite private forces. From time to time, it is openly plundered for their benefit by way of various bubbles, depressions, or recessions, and other forms of theft passed off as unavoidable acts of nature/God. These periodic raids and draw-downs of the people's wealth are attributed to "business cycles." Past periodic raids and thefts are heralded as being proof of the rationale: "See, folks, it comes and goes, so it's a cycle!"

Economic raids and busts become "market adjustments." Public blackmail and plundering through bailouts become "necessary rescue packages." Giveaways to corporations under the guise of public works and creating employment become "stimulus." The chief responsibility of economists is to name things in accordance with government and corporate interests. The function of the public is to acquire debt and maintain "consumer confidence." When the public staggers to its feet again and manages to carry more debt, and buy more poker chips on credit to play again, it's called a recovery. They are back in the game.

Dealer, hit me with two more cards. I feel lucky.

To anyone who is paying attention, things look doomed. Fortunately for American capitalism, nobody is paying attention. They never have. Even given the unemployment numbers, foreclosures, and bankruptcies, most Americans are still not feeling enough pain yet to demand change. Not that they will. Demand change, I mean. We haven't the slightest idea of any other options, outside those provided by the corporate-managed state. So in a chorus well-schooled by the media, the public demands "reform," of the present system — the pathogenic system based on exploitation of the many by the few, the one presently eating our society from the inside out. How do you reform that?

We are clueless, and the state sees to it that we stay that way. Take the price of gas, about which Americans are obsessive. In one way or another, petroleum is the subject of much news coverage, nearly as much as pissing matches between egomaniacs in Hollywood or Capitol Hill. So one might think that, by now, Americans would have a realistic grasp of the petroleum business and things like oil and gasoline prices.

Hah, think again! This is America, this is Strawberry Fields, where nothing is real and the skies are not cloudy all day. We're stewed in a consumer hallucination called the American Dream, and riding a digital virtual-money economy that nobody can even prove exists.

If we decide to believe that debt is indeed wealth, we damned-sure know where to go looking for the wealth. Globally, 40 percent of it is in the paws of the wealthiest 1 percent. Nearly all of that 1 percent are connected to the largest and richest corporations. Just before the economy blew out, these elites held slightly less than $80 trillion worth of assets. After the blowout/bailout, their combined investment wealth was estimated at a little over $83 trillion. To give some idea of what this means, this is worth four years of the gross output of all the human beings on earth. It is only logical that these elites say the only way to revive the economy—which, to them, consists entirely of the money economy—is to continue to borrow money from them.

However, the unasked question still hangs in the air: Does the money economy even exist anymore? Is it still there? (Was it ever?) Or are we all blindly going through the motions because:

> (a) We do not understand that, for all practical historical purposes, it's over;
> (b) We do not know how to do anything else, so we keep dancing with the corpse of the hyper-capitalist economy;
> (c) The right calamity has not come down the pike to knock us loose from the spell of the dance; or
> (d) We're so friggin' brain dead, commodities engorged, and internally colonized by capitalist industrialism that nobody cares, and therefore it no longer matters.

This is multiple choice, and it counts ten points toward survival, come the collapse.

If there is no economy left, what the hell are we all participating in? A mirage? The zombie ball? The short answer is: Because the economy is a belief system, you are participating in whatever you believe you are. Personally, I believe we are participating in a modern extension of the feudal system, with bankers as the new feudal barons, and credit demographics as their turf. But then, I drink and take drugs. Whatever it is, the money economy is the only game in town until the collapse, after which chickens and firewood may become the national currency. The Masai use cattle, don't they?

At the same time, even dumb people are starting to feel an undefined fear in their bones. When I was back in the States last month, an old high-school chum, a sluggard who seldom has a forward thought beyond the next beer and Lotto scratch-ticket, confided in me, "Joey, I can't shake the feeling that something big and awful is going to happen. And by awful, I mean awful."

"Happen to what?"

"Money, work, our country. Shit, I dunno."

"Probably all three," I opined. "Plus the environment."

"Cheerful fuck, ain't ya?"

"That's what they pay me for, Bubba."

Some in the herd are starting to feel a big chill in the air, the first winds of the approaching storm. Yes, something is happening, and you don't know what it is, dooooo yew, Mistah Jones?

However, the most adept economists and other court sorcerers are going along as if nothing too unusual is happening—calling it a recession or, more recently, a double-dip recession (don't you love these turd-balls, making it sound as harmless as an ice-cream cone—gimme a double dip, please!), or even a depression. But no matter what it is, they smugly assure us, there is nothing happening that the world has never seen before. Including the insider scams that ignited the catastrophe. It's just a matter of size. Extent.

OK, it's a matter of scale. Like the Gulf oil spill. We've seen spills before, just not this big. But over the next couple of years, as the poison crud circulates the world's oceans, the Deep Horizon spill will prove to be a global game-changer, whether economists and court wizards acknowledge it or don't. Anything of global scale, whether it is in finance, energy, foreign aid, world health, or war contracting, is accompanied by unimaginable complexity. That makes it perfect cover for criminal activity. Particularly finance, where you are always close to the money.

Jim Kunstler, never at a loss to describe a ludicrous situation, sums up the paper economy's engineering of our collapse nicely:

> Wall Street—in particular the biggest "banks"—packaged up and sold enough swindles to unwind 2500 years of western civilization. You simply cannot imagine the amount of bad financial paper out there right now in every vault and portfolio on the planet ... the people fabricating things like synthetic collateralized debt obligations (CDOs) had no idea what the fuck they were doing—besides deliberately creating documents that nobody would ever understand, that would never be unraveled by teams of law clerks ... and were guaranteed to place in jeopardy every operation of the world economy above the barter level.

Phew!

So, for $5,000 and an all-expenses-paid trip to Rio: What does a good capitalist do after having stolen all there is to steal from the living, and then stolen the nation's future wealth from the unborn through debt, both public and private?

Tick tock, tick tock. The wheel spins.

Blaaaaaamp!

"Your answer, please."

"A good capitalist would 'invest' his haul in some other racket, some other scam in the money economy."

"Vanna, a pie in the kisser for this guy, please."

The problem with the answer is that the economy is now toxed out. Radioactive. Crawling with paper vermin, especially toxic derivatives — about $1.4 quadrillion worth (even as we are still trying to get used to hearing the term "trillions"), according to the Bank of National Settlements. That is $190,000 for every human being on the planet. There is not now, and never will be, enough wealth to cover that puppy — because there is not enough natural world under the puppy to create it. Not the way that capitalism creates wealth.

Defenders of capitalism who say it can and must be saved must also admit that there is not enough money left to work with, to invest. There is only debt. Oh, yeah, we forgot: debt is wealth to a banker. Well then, all we gotta do is collect $190,000 per head from people in Sudan and Haiti and the rest of the planet.

Naw, that's too hard. Elite capital's best bet is a good old-fashioned money raid on the serfs; create another bubble that will buy enough time before it pops to make the-already rich a few billion richer. To that end, the G-8 is blowing one last bounder out there in hyperspace, where the economy is alleged to be surviving. Naturally, they are doing it in order to "save the world economy." The tough part is figuring out what to base the next bubble on.

May I suggest Soylent Green?

From the outset, capitalism was always about the theft of the people's sustenance. It was bound to lead to the ultimate theft, the final looting of the source of their sustenance—nature. Now that capitalism has eaten its own seed corn, the show is just about over, with the nastiest scenes yet to play out around water, carbon energy (or anything that expends energy), soil, and oxygen. For the near future, however, it will continue to play out around money.

As the economy slowly implodes, money will become more volatile stuff than it already is. The value and availability of money is sure to fluctuate wildly. Most people don't have the luxury of escaping the money economy, so they will be held hostage and milked hard again by the same people who just drained them in the bailouts. As usual, the government will be right there to see that everybody plays by the rules. Those who have always benefited by capitalism's rules will benefit more. That cadre of "money professionals" that holds captive the nation's money supply, and runs things according to the rules of money, can never lose money. It writes the rules. And rewrites them when it suits the money elite's interests: Capitalism, the Christian God, democracy, the Constitution.

It's all one ball of wax, one set of rules, in the American national psyche. Thus, the money masters behind the curtain will write The New Rules, the new tablets of supreme law, and call them Reform. There will be rejoicing that "the will of the people" has once again moved upon the land, and that democracy's scripture has once again been delivered by the unseen hand of God.

24

Algorithms and Red Wine

[October 25, 2010]

Ferrara, Italy

I'm sitting in a trendy wine bar, one of those that brings out food to match your particular choice of wine, mystified by the table setting. What was that tiny baby spoon for? Cappuccino, surely, at some point, but why no big spoon to go with the knife and fork? The things a redneck American does not know grow exponentially in Bella Italia, starting with the restaurants—not to mention several civilizations beneath one's feet. Being in a house that has been continuously occupied for over 1,000 years—resisting the temptation to piss in the hotel-room bidet, that sort of thing.

One thing the Italians can never be accused of is being a culture given to vinyl-sided sameness, fast-food franchises. Another thing is lack of a good educational system, given that Italy's is among the very best in the world. So here I am sitting with some college kids trying to hang onto my end of a discussion of evolutionary consciousness, and whether Italy can withstand the cultural leveling of globalism.

"And, Mr. Bageent, what do you think of Pierre Teilhard de Chardin's concept of the hive mind and the noosphere? Can monolithism and totalitarianism possibly be resisted in the cybernetic age?"

Huh?

"*Il regno mondiale dei computer*, global computerization. Do all those disassociated shards of human input constitute an overarching hive intelligence? Or are they the emergence of further evolutionary structures?"

"Ahem, uh, well, Timothy Leary once convinced me that they are," I said. "But after the drugs wore off, I was not so certain. And now I'm certain again that he was right. But with a far more chilling outcome than he or Chardin could have ever predicted."

Which was pretty good for pulling it out of my ass.

In any case, it seems that, 40 years in retrospect, the human hive enjoys monolithism and totalism far more than anyone would have ever guessed back in the Sixties. Most of industrial humanity, as it turns out, is, or would be, quite happy to come home from a hard day in the mines and settle down to Facebook or Twitter or hive-broadcast "news" and passive entertainments, distributed by unseen "corporate entities." I dunno, I think I liked dope and live music and sex better. But as all three diminish in my life with age, I've learned to settle for *The Larry King Show* and/or a lot less at times.

On the other hand, this whole business of the new hive-cybernetic connectivity could be just a swarm of data bits with no particular significance, in and of themselves, other than the magical-thinking belief that they do. Which ain't no small thing, given that what we agree upon as reality is achieved by social consensus. Hell, to some people, Beelzebub still stalks the earth. To others, America is a free republic, not a company town. We all have our hallucinations.

One thing for sure. Most people in the (over) developed world think that the connectivity and speed of the algorithms behind the cyberhive are worth it. Even teachers teach to a standardized test so their students will conform to an algorithm—and if that ain't a hive mind, I don't know what is.

Besides, if the worship of algorithms is not worth it, it does not matter. Whether we are like the Tanzanians in the 2004 documentary film *Darwin's Nightmare*, or some Stanford professor writing economic algorithms, the people who control all our lives in the globalized economic world believe that algorithms are critically important.

For example, bankers and investment houses believe that intelligent algorithms (Big Al) can calculate the human risk involved in making loans. That an algorithm can predict whether a 35-year-old lawn-sprinkler installer in Tuscaloosa will be able to steadily make $2,300 monthly payments on his $220,000 twice-refinanced "snout-house" (so-named because of the four-car garage sticking out the front) for 30 years. Most of us would be more than happy to make that prediction for them, and with far greater accuracy, for a fraction of what they paid the pinhead to write the algorithm.

In the pre-digital hive era, there were limits to what the organic human brain, and therefore the mind, plus past experience, could calculate and then evaluate. At some point, one was forced to recognize the limits of a financial proposition or investment. Familiarity with the actual basis of an investment was necessary. (Hmmm. Lawn sprinklers, huh? And yer paying on a new Dodge Ram, too?") But there was no stopping such things as computer-assisted hedge funds, and the techno nerds' faith that you could remove the human risks through complex algorithmic structures. So mythical financial instruments such as derivatives, and layers of bets on derivatives, and bets on those bets, bloomed out there in the "virtual economy," sending out algorithmic spores that spawned even stranger financial flora. The whole of it could not be understood by any single human participant. Even the individual parts were understood only by their specific designers. As in, "Just trust me on this, Marv. This instrument even creates its own collateral" (which many of them did). Information, of course, is not reality, not even close to the juicy anecdotal stuff of which our daily lives are made. In essence, investment is reduced to an algorithmic Google search for debt, which is wealth to a banker, and then mathematically rationalizing that debt as wealth for the rest of us.

Life is lived anecdotally, not algorithmically. And anecdotal evidence is not allowed in the new digital corpocracy. As one poster on Democratic Underground put it:

> Anecdotal now has this enforced meaning such that no one is supposed to believe what they experience, what they see, hear, taste, smell, etc. The Powers That Be have basically extinguished the notion of inductive reasoning. Everything has to be replicated in a laboratory and since 90 percent of all the labs in this nation are operated by Corporate Sponsored monies, not much truth comes out of them.

The trouble with the algorithmic age is that life is not a finite sequence of steps that define and contain the algorithmic concepts used. Even when created with the best of intentions (and we can all agree by now that there were few good intentions at Goldman Sachs when they were creating and bundling these mutant investments), they cannot account for our uninsured sprinkler-installer getting cancer, or divorcing the other half of the household income—or for the end of America's residential-construction orgy.

The digital folly is never-ending. The knock-on effect just keeps rolling. The latest is the rising scandal of millions of illegal foreclosures created by MERS (Mortgage Electronic Registration Systems), which enabled the big financial firms to securitize and swap mortgages at super-high speed. But not to worry: Nancy Pelosi and Christopher Dodd are on the case, and there is sure to be a congressional committee appointed. Whoopee! Have one on me.

Meanwhile, we have our social-networking software to better weave us into the hive. "Social-networking software"—now there's a term that should scare the piss out of anyone with an IQ over 40. It is the database as hive reality. Facebook, online banking, shopping, porn, years of one's life playing electronic games or whatever, online dating, and reducing romance and companionship to fit the software. Or 4,000 Facebook "friends"—data on 4,000 Americans voluntarily collected for Facebook corporation. The concept of "friends" is cheapened, rendered meaningless as it passes through a database. In fact, all human experience is cheapened by that process. Information is not reality.

As my second wife, who was a mathematician, can tell you, I know as much about algebra as a flatworm. So I turn to experts when I write this stuff—or sometimes just make it up as I go. But even a dumb person can ask questions. And one of my questions as I sit here background-Googling the subject is this: Does a search engine really know what I want, or am I dumbing down to fit its hive algorithms? Probably the latter.

Anyway, allegedly, the hive does many things better than paid experts do. Wikipedia is an example of this assertion. Most web content is generated by hive inhabitants for free, profiting the new elite cybernetic ownership class, which is to say some corporation or other. This also means that content becomes worthless—that the efforts of skilled and devoted journalists, artists, and others become valueless, unsellable, just more info-shards in the hive. Only advertising has value in the cyberhive. In a nation whose social realism has been represented by advertising for three-quarters of a century, that was to be expected.

Of course, the real global economic problem is seven billion people in increasing competition for ever-scarcer vital resources. But capitalism loves competition, as long as (a) it is the people's capital involved, and (b) it is not the capitalists doing the competing. Either way, we're talking money here and what most people consider to be "economics." Economics equals money. Right?

But the actual world revolves around meeting our genuine needs, which may or may not involve money. In the big picture, money is just one small, much-abused abstract tool. Money has been abused from the beginning—probably about fifteen minutes after the first shekel was minted—but now the abuse has reached such levels that the entire notion of money is collapsing in on itself. Our concept of money needs to be re-evaluated and probably abandoned in the distant future.

The waiter comes with something on a plate I can actually—by pure luck—identify. Octopus gnocchi. The conversation rolls on. "What do you believe allowed such abuse and calamity?" I ask.

An intense young woman leans across the table, all black hair and red lips, making an old man moan and sigh inwardly.

"Fossil fuels, of course," she says. "An unnatural supply of energy. But once that is gone, we're going to have to go back to a whole different way of doing everything. Everything."

"Spot on," I agree. At that moment she could have gotten me to agree that the earth is flat.

But the truth is that each gallon of fossil fuel contains the energy of 40 man-hours. And that has played hell with the ecology of human work, thanks mostly to the money economy. For instance, a simple loaf of bread, starting with the fossil fuels used to grow the wheat, and to transport, mill, and bake it, and to create the packaging materials and packaging, and to advertise and distribute it, uses the energy of two men working for two weeks. Yet this waste and vast inefficiency is invisible to us because we see it only in terms of money, jobs, and commerce. Cheap oil allowed industrial humans to increasingly live on environmental credit for over a century. Now the bill is due, and no amount of money can pay it. The calorie, pure heat expenditure as energy, is the only currency in which Mother Nature trades. Period.

Despite the fact that America produced thinkers on the subject of living simply such as Thoreau, modern hydrocarbon-based civilization has driven expectations of material goods and convenience, and the transactions surrounding those expectations, through the stratosphere. Money has abstracted the notion of work to the point where, I dare say, there are not 100,000 people in America who truly understand that, although there are at least a few million trying to understand and liberate themselves.

I'm gonna take a wild shot here, and say that understanding and liberation come through self-discipline and self-denial, and that it's nearly impossible for Americans to practice self-discipline. They cannot imagine why self-discipline, and a more ascetic life—becoming less dependent on the faceless machinery of algorithm-driven virtual money—is necessarily liberating.

If there can be a solution at this late stage, and most thinking people seriously doubt there can be a "solution" in the way we have always thought of such things, it begins with powering down the economy. That, and population reduction, which nobody wants to discuss in actionable terms. Worse yet, there is no state-sanctioned, organized entry-level for people who want to power down from the horrific machinery of money. There are too many financial, military, corporate, and governmental forces that don't want to see us power down (because it would spell their death), but would rather we power up even more. That's called "a recovery."

When viewed from outside the virtual-money economy, and from the standpoint of the planet's caloric economy, probably half of all American and European jobs are not only unnecessary, but also terribly destructive, either directly or indirectly. Yet what nation or economic state acknowledges the need for a transition away from jobs that aren't necessary? None, because such an economy could not support the war machines or the transactional financial industries that dominate our needs' hierarchy for the benefit of the few — such as lending us money we have already earned, and stuffing us with corn syrup. And I won't even go into the strong possibility that everybody does not need to be employed at all times for the world to keep on turning.

One of the Italian students, Mariarosa, asks, "Is it true that so many Americans are struggling and suffering right now?"

"No," I reply. "Not in the real sense. If they are suffering, most of them are suffering from commodities withdrawal. What they really are is people oppressed by metastasized capitalism. Which is its own form of suffering, I guess. They are squeezed hard for profit every moment of their waking lives. They've got families and dare not make a move, even if they knew how."

Everyone nods in agreement.

"It's coming to Italy, too," says one young man. Again, all nod in agreement.

Yet, despite Berlusconi, despite the rightist takeover in progress in Italy—which I am guessing will be successful, because I've seen it all before in America through globalization—so many are still able to ask the right questions. They seem able to filter what they need, and what is best for the majority, from what they want. But looking at the overall country is like watching the Reagan era unfold again before your very eyes. Only faster. All of these kids probably own an iPod or a cell phone—the only difference being that they do not let them interrupt a good meal.

The third bottle of wine arrives, and the topic turns to global competition, and the E.U.'s charges that "Italy is not competitive enough." A student named Cristiano sits directly across from me, sporting one of those fashionable three-day beards. (I tried that once—people just asked me, "How long have you been depressed, Joe?) Cristiano offers the comment that cooperation would get us all a lot farther than competition. Applause from everybody on that one. I raise my glass in salute. I've raised a few too many glasses in salute in my life, but what the hell.

Societies such as Italy, Greece, and many others are viewed by global capitalism as inferior economies. This is especially true for agrarian societies, where different rates of exchange and economies of scale are set for them by capitalists. Global capitalists never want to see regional food security, energy security, or any other kind of security, for that matter.

And I look at the faces of these young men and women, who are among the brightest, best-educated, and common-good-oriented that the world has to offer. A taxi's headlights flash through the window of the darkened wine bar. Each face is illuminated for a moment, and then golden dimness again prevails. And I am saddened.

I do not expect that the world they have inherited will show them one ounce of mercy. But it is heartening to see clear, competent minds drawing the right conclusions.

And I ask myself, what chance does America's far less informed and purposefully misled public stand against all this?

One shudders.

25

America: Y Ur Peeps B So Dum?

[December 7, 2010]

If you hang out much with thinking people, conversation eventually turns to the serious political and cultural questions of our times. Such as: How can the Americans remain so consistently brain-fucked? Much of the world, including plenty of Americans, asks that question as they watch U.S. culture go down like a thrashing mastodon giving itself up to some Pleistocene tar pit.

One explanation might be the effect of 40 years of deep-fried industrial chicken pulp and 44-ounce Big Gulp soft drinks. Another might be pop culture, which is not culture at all, of course, but marketing. Or we could blame it on digital autism: Ever watched commuter monkeys on the subway poking at digital devices, stroking their touch screens for hours on end, their wrinkled Neolithic brows jutting out above their squinting red eyes?

But a more reasonable explanation is that (a) we don't even know we are doing it, and (b) we cling to institutions dedicated to making sure we never find out.

As William Edwards Deming famously demonstrated, no system — including the American social system — can understand itself and why it does what it does. Not knowing shit about why your society behaves the way it does makes for a pretty nasty case of existential unease. So we create institutions whose function is to pretend to know, which makes everyone feel better. Unfortunately, it also makes the savviest among us — those elites who run the institutions — very rich, or safe from the vicissitudes that buffet the rest of us.

Directly or indirectly, they understand that the real function of American social institutions is to justify, rationalize, and hide the true purpose of cultural behavior from the lumpenproletariat, and to shape that behavior to the benefit of the institution's members. "Hey, they're a lump. Whaddya expect us to do?"

Doubting readers may consider America's health institutions, the insurance corporations, hospital chains, physicians' lobbies. Between them, they have established a perfectly legal right to clip you and me for thousands of dollars at their own discretion. That we so rabidly defend their right to gouge us, given all the information available in the digital age, mystifies the world.

Two hundred years ago, everyone would have thought that the sheer volume of available facts in the digital information age would produce informed Americans. Founders of the republic, steeped in the Enlightenment as they were, and believers in an informed citizenry being vital to freedom and democracy, would have been delirious with joy at the prospect. Imagine Jefferson and Franklin high on Google.

The fatal assumption was that Americans would choose to

think and learn, instead of cherry picking the blogs and TV channels to reinforce their particular branded choice of cultural ignorance—consumer, scientific, or political, but especially political. Tom and Ben could never have guessed we would chase prepackaged spectacles, junk science, and titillating rumor such as death panels, Obama as a socialist Muslim, and Biblical proof that Adam and Eve rode dinosaurs around Eden. In a nation that equates democracy with everyman's right to an opinion, no matter how ridiculous, this was probably inevitable. After all, dumb people choose dumb stuff. That's why they are called dumb.

But throw in 60 years of television's mind-puddling effects, and you end up with 24 million Americans watching Bristol Palin thrashing around on *Dancing with the Stars*, then watch her being interviewed with all seriousness on the networks as major news. The inescapable conclusion of half of heartland America is that her mama must certainly be presidential material, even if Bristol cannot dance. It ain't a pretty picture out there in Chattanooga and Keokuk.

The other half, the liberal half, concludes that Bristol's bad dancing is part of her spawn-of-the-Devil mama's plan to take over the country, and make millions in the process, not to mention make Tina Fey and Jon Stewart richer than they already are. That's a tall order for a squirrel-brained woman who recently asked a black president to "refutiate" the NAACP (though I kinda like refutiate, myself). Cultural stupidity accounts for virtually every aspect of Sarah Palin, both as a person and a political icon. Which, come to think of it, may be a pretty good reason not to "misunderestimate" her. After all, we're still talking about her in both political camps. And the woman OWNS *The Huffington Post*, fer Christsake. Not to mention a franchise on cultural ignorance.

Cultural stupidity might not be so bad, were it not self-reproducing and viral, and prone to place stupid people in charge. All of us have, at some point, looked at a boss and asked ourselves how such a numb-nuts could end up in charge of the joint.

In my own field, the book biz, the top hucksters in sales and marketing, car salesman with degrees, are put in charge of publishing the national literature. Similarly, ex-Pentagon generals segue from killing brown babies in Iraq into university presidents and CEOs. Conversely, business leaders such as Donald Rumsfeld, who fancy themselves as battlefield commanders and imagine their employees as troops to be "deployed," find themselves happily farting behind Pentagon desks. On the strength of having mistaken Sun Tzu's *The Art of War* as a business text, they get selected by equally delusional national leaders to make actual war on behalf of the rest of us.

But the most widespread damage is done at more mundane operational levels of the American Empire, by clones of the over-promoted asshole in the corner office where you work. At least one study has demonstrated that random selection for corporate promotions offset the effect significantly. Research again confirms what is common knowledge around every workplace water-cooler in the country.

Cultural ignorance of one sort or another is sustained and nurtured in all societies to some degree, because the majority gains material benefit from maintaining it. Americans, for example—especially the middle-class Babbitry—reap huge on-the-ground benefits from cultural ignorance generated by American hyper-capitalism in the form of junk affluence.

Purposeful ignorance allows us to enjoy cheaper commodities produced through slave labor, both foreign and, increasingly, domestic, and yet to "thank God for his bounty" in the nation's churches without a trace of guilt or irony. It allows the strong-arm theft of weaker nations' resources and goods, to say nothing of the destructiveness of late-stage capitalism — exhausting every planetary resource that sustains human life.

The American defense, on those rare occasions when one is offered, runs roughly, "Well, you commie bastard, I ain't never seen a sweatshop, and I got no Asian kids chained in the basement. So I've got what the guvment calls plausible deniability. Go fuck yerself!"

Uh, don't look now, but the banksters own your ass, your country has become a work gulag/police state, and most of the world hates you.

Such a thriving American intellectual climate enables capitalist elites to withhold and ration vital resources like health care simply by auctioning it off to the richest. Americans fail to grasp this because the most important fact (that a helluva lot of folks can't afford to bid, and therefore get to die early) never gets equal play with capitalist political propaganda — to wit, that if we give free medical attention to low-income cleft-palate babies, a wave of Leninism will seize the nation. That is cultural ignorance. We breathe the stuff every day of our lives.

But when Americans too poor to buy health care nevertheless vote to retain the corporate auction-process, that is cultural stupidity.

(Let us now pause to clutch our hair in our fists and scream AAAAAAGGGGGHHHHHH!)

Like the old song says, "Them that don't know don't know they don't know." I venture to say that even if they did, they would not know why. Primary truths elude us because of the junk affluence and propaganda. We get buried under a deluge of commodities that suggest we are all rich, or at least richer than most of the world. A mountain range of cheap shoes, cars, iPods, ridiculous amounts of available foodstuffs, and the entire spectacle of engorgement defines and is enforced as "quality of life" under materialistic-commodities capitalism. The goods we have in our clutches trump the philosophical, or even the most practical, considerations: "I may die early eating unidentified beef byproducts soaked in waste chemicals, but I'll die owning a 65-inch HDTV and a new five-speed automatic Dodge Durango with a 5.7 L Hemi V-8 under the hood!"

Even the threat of toasting planetary life is not enough to shake Americans loose from this disconnect. As Guy R. McPherson, professor emeritus of natural resources and ecology & evolutionary biology points out, "79.6 percent of respondents to a *Scientific American* poll are unwilling to forgo even a single penny to forestall the risk of catastrophic climate change." *Scientific American* readers undoubtedly are better informed than the general populace. And yet they won't pay a thing to avoid the extinction of our species. Kinda makes you warm and fuzzy all over, doesn't it?

Let us pray the next generation is a tad sharper.

The "American Lifestyle," increasingly suspect as it is these days, is heavily soldiered and policed in the name of keeping us self-defined lotus-eaters safe and secure from a jealous outside world. Which, according to cultural consensus, is a world that is at this very moment stuffing its under-drawers with explosives, and buying plane tickets to Moline. Cultural ignorance dictates that the best way to stop foreign terrorists from flying into the country is by humiliating American citizens flying out of the country. Go ahead, grope me, X-ray my dick, and for God's sake don't let anyone bring a large bottle of shampoo on board. In an obedient, authority-worshipping police state, physical insult and surveillance are proof of safety.

It's profitable, too, and not just for scanner manufacturers. The brouhaha over body scanners and crotch-groping provide the media with titillating fuel for ratings, thereby driving up TV advertising rates, which is passed on in the price of the products we buy. So we pay to be insulted, to have the hell scared out of us, and to unknowingly have our behavior shaped. Under American-style capitalism, this Mobius strip of cultural ignorance is called a win-win situation for everybody.

This also conveniently distracts us from the everyday human insult we practice on one another, as a result of state-manufactured cultural misinformation—fear. Ten years of orange alerts and post-9/11 fear-mongering have led us to draw some paradoxical cultural conclusions.

Let us briefly career off into one of these paradoxes. For instance, the belief that we can taser our way to domestic security and tranquility. Yes, it's an ugly business, but tasing the citizenry must be done. And besides, in these days of high unemployment, it's a paycheck for somebody—usually, the guy who sat behind us in grade school happily eating chalk.

With taser-packing police officers in thousands of schools, even grade schools (a weird-enough cultural statement to begin with), the resulting deaths of and injuries to school kids have personal-injury lawyers shouting Eureka, needless to say, and contemplating new recreational sail-craft moored at Martha's Vineyard. Such are the rewards of righteous works through cultural ignorance.

In any case, the chance at a juicy lawsuit is accepted as a satisfactory offset to any screaming and writhing in our school hallways. What are 50,000 volts and a little nerve damage compared to a shot at paying off the credit cards, upgrading the family ride, and maybe remodeling the kitchen, too?

But we gotta stick to the subject of cultural ignorance here, mainly because I wrote the title first and am determined to maintain some illusion of a theme, or at least bullshit the reader into thinking that I have.

Soooo ...

It can be safely said that cultural ignorance consists of the rational, sensible questions that never get asked. But it also includes the weird ones that are. For instance, one of the questions asked regarding tasering school kids is: What is the allowable weight range of a child to be tasered (Taser manufacturers say it is 60 pounds.) Somehow, by this geezer's prehistoric reasoning, that sounds like the wrong question, not to mention one that by its nature leads us away from the cultural truth.

The truth is that we live in a society which sanctions the semi-electrocution of its own children on the grounds that it is not fatal, and therefore not true electrocution. It springs from the same streak of cultural cruelty that deems semi-drowning by water-boarding not to be torture because it is seldom fatal.

This is not to be uncharitable to American communities willing to pony up tax money for school tasers. They've amply demonstrated their affectionate commitment to their children by bringing creationism and pizza-for-breakfast into the schools. But there remains the question, "What kind of community comes up with the idea of tasering its own children?"

It is the job of our combined institutions to manage cultural information so as to deny the harmful aspects of the rackets that they protect through legislation and promote through research. That's why research shows that cell-phone microwaves cause long-term memory loss in rats, but do not harm people. Evidently, we are of different, more bullet-proof mammalian material.

Our hyper-capitalist system, through command of our research, media, and political institutions, expands upon and disseminates only that information which generates money and transactions. It avoids, neglects, or spins the hell out of information that does not. And if none of those work, the info is exiled to some corner of cyberspace such as the *Daily Kos*, where it cannot change the status quo, yet can be ballyhooed as proof of our national freedom of expression. Here come the rotten eggs from the Internet liberals.

Cyberspace by its nature feels very big from the inside, and its affinity groups, seeing themselves in the aggregate and in mutual self-reference, imagine that their role is bigger and more effective than it is. From within the highly directed, technologically administered, marketed-to, and propagandized rat cage called America, this is all but impossible to comprehend. Especially when the corporate-owned media tells us it is.

Take the recent world-shaking WikiLeak's "revelations" of Washington's petty misery and drivel, which are just more extensive details about what we all already knew. Come on, now, is it a revelation that Karzai and his entire government is a nest of fraudulent, double-crossing thieves? Or that the U.S. is duplicitous? Or that Angela Merkel is dull? The main revelation in the WikiLeaks affair was the U.S. government's response—which was to bring the U.S.'s freedom-of-speech policy firmly in line with China's. Millions of us in cyber ghettoes saw it coming, but our alarm warnings were shouted inside a cyberspace-vacuum bell jar.

Bear in mind that I am writing this from outside the U.S. borders and media environment, where people watch the WikiLeaks story unfold more in amusement than anything else.

The WikiLeaks affair is surely seismic to those whose asses ride on the elite diplomatic intrigues. But in the big picture, it will not change the way the top lizards in global politics, money, and war have done business since the feudal age—which is to say, with arrogant disregard for the rest of us. Theirs is an ancient system of human dominance that only shifts names and methodologies over the centuries. Two years from now, little will have changed in the old, old story of the powerful few over the powerless many. In this overarching drama, Obama, Hillary, and Julian Assange are passing players. Watching the sweaty, fetid machinations of our overlords with such passionate involvement only keeps us from seeing the big picture—that they are the players and we are the pawns.

Still, I for one am in favor of giving Assange the Médaille militaire, the Nobel Prize, 15 virgins in paradise, and a billion bucks in cash as a reward for his courage in doing damned-well the only significant thing that can be done at this time—momentarily fucking up government control of information. But "potentially stimulating a new age of U.S. government transparency" (according to the BBC), it ain't.

Which brings us to back to the question of cultural ignorance. For ten points, why was Julian Assange forced to do what the world press was supposed to be doing in the first place?

Bulletin: PayPal has caved to government pressure to pull WikiLeak's PayPal account for contributions. However, the feds generously let PayPal keep its porn and prostitution clients.

It is a form of cultural ignorance to believe that at some point or other in the past, we were more in charge and that our government was somehow more transparent. Societies declining into obsolescence understandably resist looking forward, and hang onto their past mythologies. Consequently, both liberals and conservatives in America feed on myths of political action that died in Vietnam. The results are ludicrous. Tea Partiers attempt to emulate the 1960s protest gatherings by staging rallies sponsored by the richest beneficiaries of the status quo.

For the average TP participant, the goal, near as I can tell, is to "start a new American Revolution," by wearing foodstuffs, screaming, threatening, and voting for nitwits. Media pundits proclaim the Tea Party "a historic populist movement."

Neither a populist nor authentic movement, the Tea Party may yet prove historic, however, by seriously fucking things up more than they already are. Spun entirely from manufactured spectacle (and thus void of cohesive political philosophy or internal logic), the Tea Party lurches across the political landscape, bellowing at the cameras and collecting the victims of cultural ignorance in a sort of medieval idiots' crusade. But to the American public, seeing the Tea Party on television is proof enough of its relevancy and significance. After all, stuff doesn't get on TV unless it's important.

Progressives also fancy a revolution, one in which they participate through Internet petitions and media events such as the risk-free Jon Stewart Rally to Restore Sanity, where no one risked even missing an episode of *Tremaine*. Seeing people like themselves on television was proof that they were fighting the good fight. The Stewart rally was nonetheless culturally historic; we will never see a larger public display of post-modern irony congratulating itself.

In the historical view, cultural ignorance is more than the absence of knowledge. It is also the result of long-term cultural and political struggle. Since the industrial revolution, the struggle has been between capital and workers. Capital won in America, and spread its successful tactics worldwide. Now we watch global capitalism wreck the world, and attempt to stay ahead of that wreckage while clutching its profits. A subservient world kneels before it, praying that planet-destroying jobs will fall their way. Will unrestrained global capitalism, with all the power and momentum on its side, and motivated purely by the machine-like harvesting of profits, reduce the faceless masses in its path to slavery? Does a duck shit in a pond?

Meanwhile, here we are, American riders on the short bus, barreling into the Grand Canyon. With typical American gunpoint optimism, we've convinced ourselves that we're in an airplane. A few smarter kids in the back whisper about hijacking the bus and turning it around, but the security cop riding shotgun just strokes his taser and smiles. Not that yours truly has the ass to take on the security surveillance-state. Hell, no. I jumped out the window when the bus shot past Mexico.

Republican honcho Mitch O'Connell says that what America needs is for Republicans to finish beating the snot out of Obama, and to strengthen the already rich by eliminating taxes for them and shifting the burden onto us. Obama says that America needs to find bipartisan cooperation with the party of ruthlessness. Elton John says that America needs more compassion. (Thanks, we never noticed.)

What America really needs is a wall-to-wall people's insurrection, preferably based on force and fear of force—the only thing that oligarchs understand. And even then, the odds are not good. The oligarchs have all the legal power, police, jails and prisons, surveillance and firepower. Not to mention a docile populace.

Shy of open insurrection, a nationwide refusal to pay income taxes would certainly shake things up. But broader America is happy in the sense that they know happiness as an undisturbed regimen of toil, stress, and commodity consumption. Despite the way it looks in the news, most Americans remain untouched by foreclosure, bankruptcy, and unemployment. So risking loss of their work-buy-sleep cycle in an insurrection looks to be sheer lunacy to them. Like cows, they are kept comfortable, in the pure animal sense, to be milked for profit. Animal comfort

AMERICA: Y UR PEEPS B SO DUM?   297

kills all thoughts of revolution. Hell, half of mankind would be thrilled with the average American's present material situation.

And besides, revolutionary history does not exist for Americans. The 20th century's successful revolutions in Russia, Germany, Mexico, China, and Cuba are wired into our minds as history's evil failures, because all but one were Marxist. (The only successful non-Marxist revolution of the 20th century was Fidel Castro's in Cuba.)

So if we are talking about change through revolt, we're necessarily talking about deconditioning, because the thing we fear already has a life deep in our own consciousness. Deconditioning ourselves from our state of cultural ignorance is at the heart of any insurrectionary politics.

Deconditioning also involves risk and suffering. But it is transformative, freeing the self from helplessness and fear. It unleashes the fifth freedom, the right to an autonomous consciousness. That makes deconditioning about as individual and personal an act as is possible. Maybe it is the only genuine individual act.

Once unencumbered by self-induced and manufactured cultural ignorance, it becomes clear that politics worldwide is entirely about money, power, and national mythology, with or without some degree of human rights. America still has all of the above, to one degree or another. Yet, for all practical purposes, such as advancing the freedom and the well-being of its own people, the American republic has collapsed.

Of course, there is still money to be made by the already rich. So the million-or-so people who own the country and the government use their control to convince us that there is no collapse—just economic and political problems that need to be solved. Naturally, they are willing to do that for us. Consequently, the economy is discussed in political terms, because the government is the only body with the power to legislate, and therefore to render the will of the owning class into law.

But politics and money are never going to fill what is essentially a public vacuum that is moral, philosophical, and spiritual. (The latter was instantly recognized by fundamentalist Christians, disfigured by cultural ignorance as they may be.) Not many ordinary Americans talk about this vacuum. The required spiritual and philosophical language has been successfully purged by newspeak, popular culture, a human regimentation-process masquerading as a national educational system, and the ruthlessness of everyday competition, which leaves no time to contemplate anything.

Still, the void, the meaninglessness of ordinary work and the emptiness of daily life, scares thinking citizens shitless, with its many unspeakables, spy-cams, security-state pronouncements, citizens being economically disappeared, and general back-of-the-mind unease. Capitalism's faceless machinery has colonized our very souls. If the political was not personal to begin with, it's personal now.

Some Americans believe we can collectively triumph over the monolith we presently fear and worship. Others believe that the best we can do is to find the personal strength to endure and go forward on lonely inner plains of the self.

Doing either will take inner moral, spiritual, and intellectual liberation. It all depends on where you choose to fight your battle. Or if you even choose to fight it. But one thing is certain. The only way out is in.